# SUSU ECONOMICS

# THE HISTORY OF PAN-AFRICAN (BLACK) TRADE, COMMERCE, MONEY AND WEALTH

# SUSU ECONOMICS

## THE HISTORY OF PAN-AFRICAN (BLACK) TRADE, COMMERCE, MONEY AND WEALTH

By

**Paul Alfred Barton**

ISBN: 1-58721-454-7

1stBooks – rev. 4/18/00

# ABOUT THE BOOK

The book, *Susu Economics: The History of Pan-African (Black) Trade, Commerce, Money and Wealth* is one of the most thorough and exciting books which deals with the development of culture and civilization in ancient and prehistoric Africa, and how trade and commerce contributed to the migrations of Africans worldwide and the establishment of cultures and civilizations from the Sahara to India and China, around the globe to ancient Olmec Mexico.

This massive trade network contributed to building the wealth and influence of many ancient African kingdoms and empires such as ancient Egypt, Nubia-Kush, Wagadu-Ghana, Nok, Punt, Zimbabwe and many others. African wealth and influence also spread to parts of Europe when Africans settled parts of Ireland and England as well as Iberia, hundreds of years before Christ. The book examines the trade goods used and commodities traded for thousands of years.

# TABLE OF CONTENTS

# CHAPTER ONE

# TRADE AND COMMERCE AFTER 200,000 B.C.

The very first traders on earth were Black Africans. The practice of engaging in trade begun when people recognized the value of whatever they possessed and wanted something of comparable value in return. The very first humans on the planet, Africans may have engaged in hunting and gathering. These methods of gaining subsistence led to the tracking of wild game from one region to the other. Eventually, the prehistoric Africans spread out to the entire world, including the Americas and Australia. Trade routes and networks became fully developed in Africa before there were migrations outside of the continent, moreover, during the period of African development into the homosapien stage, Europe and the North was covered with ice and experiencing the Ice Age.

According to Cheikh Antah Diop [1991, p. 18], Europe was less attractive to large movements of people during the Ice Age, compared to Africa of 200,000 to 10,000 B.C. Still, during short recesses in the cold and bitter climate, African migrants did make their way to parts of Europe, Asia and even the Americas. In most cases the temperature and climatic conditions during such recesses in the cold weather when large herds of animals moved from one area to another in search of good grass, was such that groups of hunters or family bands were able to travel.

While Europe and much of the Northern Hemisphere suffered from the Ice Ages, Africa benefited from it. Much of Africa may have been covered with forests, grasslands, rivers and lakes. Traveling within the continent may have brought about the hardiness of Africans as well as their ingenuity, which led to the invention of boats before any other humans had developed out of the African homosapien type. In fact, between 40, 000 B.C., when the Black African Grimaldi Man migrated to Europe and eventually replaced the Neanderthal to about 10,000 B.C., much of the northern half of Africa including vast areas of the Sahara was covered by a vast, inland sea.

1

According to Wayne Chandler in African Presence in Early Asia [1995,p. 376],

'The findings of the UNESCO International Scientific Committee states that ca. 20,000 B.C.E., large lakes, streams, rivers, and swamps. The various cultures and people which inhabited this area used these waterways as a mode of travel and cultural ex- change, and became known as the 'Aquatic civilization.

This civilization, which once lived around the perimeter of the Inland Sea, then inhabited an area which spread across the continent, from the Atlantic coast to the Nile Basin. Numerous archaeological sites have been unearthed in the Saharan highlands and the southern fringe of the desert from the upper Niger, through the Chad Basin, to the middle Nile, and south as far as the East African Rift Valley. These aquatic people of West and East Africa varied in their physical type but skeletal remains indicate that they were most certainly a Negroid people, harmoniously living and trading with one another. Evidence shows that they were master ship builders and traveled the lakes and rivers from one part of the continent to the other. This civilization thrived for several millennia until adverse climate began to dehydrate and reduce the aquatic size and productivity of the region.'(1)

Chandler's description of the prehistoric Sahara clearly shows a region where various types of cultural activity was taking place while the northern regions were still covered with thick layers of ice and snow. If the Sahara was well watered between 20,000 B.C. to 10,000 B.C., it is very likely that conditions between 200,000 B.C. to 100,000 B.C. may have been such that wild game were plentiful, migrations were easier for both human and beasts, and the climate in Africa much milder particularly in the northern regions.

The development of Blacks in Africa during the period of 200,000 B.C. to 100,000 B.C. took on a very different route

2

compared to the Neanderthal types who resided in Europe at least 80,000 years ago. It has been discovered that Africans invented sophisticated tools of stone and bone earlier than 100,000 years ago. They were the very first to create tools of such sophistication at such an early period in human technological development. An article in the San Francisco Chronicle [April 28, 1995, p. A 21] by David Perlman clarify this fascinating find.

According to Perlman, scientists who once believed that the first sophisticated tools were made by homosapiens in Europe about 14,000 years ago have concluded that sophisticated tool making behavior must have come out of Africa. Perlman's article states,

'The discoverers say the spear-like tools they have unearthed are far, far older, fashioned during the Middle Stone Age by African peoples who lived 100,000 years or more ago and speared huge fish near Zaire's Lake Rutanzige, known in the colonial days as Lake Albert.' Perlman expresses the view of archeologist Alison S. Brooks of George Washington University. 'This shows that humans in Africa had invented sophisticated technologies long before their European counterparts, who have long been credited with initiating modern culture.'(2)

The tools, weapons, houses, clothing, social and family life, jewelry and adornments and many aspects or early civilization and culture had already taken root and had developed to suit the environment in Africa, while the Neanderthal in Europe was struggling to survive in the harsh environment. In Africa, the hot climate helped in some cases and hindered in others, particularly the hot, dense forests regions where diseases and insets made settlement and living impossible for some such as the taller, robust Africans, while bearable for some such as the Pygmies. The inaccessibility of the forest areas made the savannas and sparse woodlands more attractive to the taller, more robust Negritid types. These areas also held the greater percentage of

3

the African population. During the period of 30,000 to 15,000 B.C., the foundation for developed and settled cultures and civilizations in parts of Africa were being laid. At the same time, trade may have improved tremendously and may have spread over a very wide area which included lands far from the African continent. Between 50,000 B.C., to 10,000 B.C. new races appeared particularly in Asia, Europe and the Americas, while the original African Negritic Homosapien remained distinct and in his original form due to the lack of need to adapt to a climate where his dark skin complexion and Negritic racial features needed suit the environment. The new groups included the Caucasoid who changed from the Black Grimaldi to the Cro-Magnon, and the Mongoloid who may have been a crossbreed race which came about due to the mixing of Africans and Cro-Magnon types. These groups remained in the harsh, cold northern climates. According to J.A. Rogers in his book Sex and Race; Volume One [1957, p.56], the European stock may also bea mixture of ancient Africans and Neanderthals, who mixed about 50,000 years ago. (3) However, new findings clearly prove that the present population of humans do not have any genetic relationship to the Neanderthal but direct descendents of Africans.

Africans who migrated out of the continent and settled in climates similar to the hot African climates remained distinct. For example, the Australoids, the Melanesians, the various Black peoples of Asia and pre-Columbian America retained their Negroid features, changing little in physical appearance. As for the Mongoloids, many were migrating and following the Pygmoids and Negroids to the Americas where they inter-mingled to crate some of the many very different 'Indian' tribes found throughout the Americas today. In fact, some of these tribes, such as the Eskimoes look similar in appearance to the Chinese and Japanese, while others such as the Garifuna, Black Californian, Jamassee, Ouachita and ancient Olmecs, look identical to Black people from West Africa and the Nile/Sudan region.

In the northern hemisphere, life was quite harsh and those who lived there spent much of their time partaking in activities

4

necessary for their survival, such as hunting, fishing and storing plant foods and roots. During the long, cold winters, many of the inhabitants of Ice Age Europe and parts of Asia took shelter in caves where they also struggled to stay alive and to keep themselves protected. Some of their struggles involved live and death confrontations with the cave-bear, a ferocious and huge wild bear who lived in the very same caves and caverns coveted by the Neanderthals and later, the Cro-Magnon people.

During this same period and for thousands of years before, Africa and the warm zones of the earth were inhabited by large numbers of Negroids who developed what was to become human civilization. In places such as the Sahara, the East African Lakes Region, the Congo River Basin, the Nile Corridor and Southern Africa saw the rapid development and the establishment of a variety of cultures more advanced than any which existed at anytime before. Cheikh Antah Diop explains in Civilization or Barbarism [1991, p. 14], that these very Africans, in the form of the Grimaldi Man, established the first industries and cultures in Europe during the European Upper Paleolithic Period known as the Aurignacian Industry. Diop explains further that the older Combe-Cpelle Man's Lower Perigordian Industry was also created by Black African migrants to Europe before the arrival of the Grimaldi Man. Around 100,000 B.C. sophisticated stone and bone tools were being crafted in Zaire, and possibly various parts of Central Africa, thus it is proper to conclude that a wide area of Africa was undergoing advanced culture at a very early period in human history when Europe, Asia or the Americas was not yet settled by the more advanced African Homo sapiens. Diop strengthens his position. He states:

'The Grimaldi Negroids have left their numerous traces all over Europe and Asia, from the Iberian Peninsula to Lake Baykal in Siberia, passing through France, Austria, the Crimea, and the Basin of Don, etc. In these two regions, the late Soviet Profess-or Mikhail Gerasimov, a scholar of rare objectivity, identified the Negroid type from skulls found in the Middle Mousterian Period. Marcellin Boule and Henri-Victor

Vallois insist on the fact that the localizing layers of the Grimaldians are always in direct contact with those of the Mousterian period in which the last Neanderthal lived; in other words, there is no other variety of Homo sapiens that precedes the Grimaldi Negroid in Europe or in Asia,' [Diop, 1991, p. 15]. (5)

In retrospect, it is accurate to say that the Negroid Grimaldi existed in Europe in the Homosapien or modern human form before any other type and therefore brought about the existence of the so-called Cro-Magnon Man due to genetic mutation, which in turn brought about albinism or fair complexion. Thus, about 20,000 years to 30,000 years ago [Diop, C.A., 1995, p. 15], the Cro-magnon, who scientists regard as the prototype for the Caucasian race appeared in Southern Europe. Their closest relatives today would be the Basques of Southern France who occupy the very same region where it is believed that they evolved from the Cro-Magnon Man.

During the period of 40,000 years Before the Present to 10,000 years B.P., trade and commerce as well as migrations from Africa to all parts of the world increased. Although the Ice Age in the Northern Hemisphere continued during this period, the warm intervals which occurred during such occurrence helped migrants travel northwards. Trade also increased during this period among Africans and between Africans and those of other regions. By this period, it is certain that some form of iron ore was being mined in Swaziland in Southern Africa, for use as body paint. The product red ocre [which is still used by some tribes for decoration], may have been first used in that region before it was traded to any other people. At such an early period in human history and possibly earlier, red ochre was not produced in many places, thus its value became known far and wide when those most likely to use it, the Africans from Central and Southern Africa, migrated to the northern regions with this commodity and other types of goods.

The ability of people to travel without much difficulty became possible with the invention of primitive, yet workable watercraft, the use of animals such as the dog, and possibly beasts of burden such as the buffalo. The horse may have not been tamed by 40,000 B.C., however, the many paintings of horses shown in ancient caves in France, Southern Europe, the Sahara and as far south as South Africa, indicates that the first Homosapien Africans regarded the cow, horse and buffalo as important.

During their migrations throughout the world, the Africans may have engaged in the exchange of goods among themselves and between them-selves and their kinsmen who had gone before them but had already settled wherever they were encountered. During the prehistoric period, African Homosapiens occupied a very extensive area of the world. Their very ancient remains have been found as far north as Siberia and as far south as Tasmania, where aboriginal Negroid Blacks still exist. These ancient Africans were spread in an east-west direction from Africa to the Americas and from East Africa to Hawaii. From about 40,000 B.C. to about 3500 B.C., Blacks dominated large areas of Europe, Asia, the Americas, the South Pacific, and a number of other places including Japan, Indonesia [where they are being exterminated by the Malays, which the Black world must put a stop to immediately], the Mediterranean, and the Indian Ocean region, including India, Sri-Lanka, and the vicinity. There are also similarities in the tools, weapons, and articles used for everyday tasks by races as distinct in outward appearance as the Mongoloid is to the Nubas of Sudan.

The Africans who remained on the continent, spread out to every part of it. At that time [40,000 B.C. to 20,000 B.C.], the present-day barriers which prevent easy, overland travel in Africa such as the massive deserts of the Sahara, did not exist as they do today. There were waterways throughout the Sahara; grasslands, lakes, forests and meadows were all part of a productive ecosystem suitable for human and animal occupation, exploration and travel. Most of all, the Sahara and parts of West and East Africa consisted of a massive Inland Sea. According to Wayne Chandler in the book, African Presence In Early Asia, [edt. by Ivan Van Sertima, 1995, pp. 376-377],

7

'The findings of the UNESCO International Scientific Committee states that ca. 20,000 B.C.E., most of West to East Africa was an inland sea which began to recede and drain leaving by, 10,000 B.C.E., large lakes, streams, rivers, and swamps. The various cultures and people which inhabited this area used these waterways as a mode of travel and cultural exchange, and became known as the 'Aquatic Civilization.'

'These aquatic people of West and East Africa varied in their physical type but skeletal remains recovered indicate that they were most certainly Negroid people, harmoniously living and trading with one another. Evidence shows that they were ship builders and traveled the lakes and rivers from one part of the continent to the other. This civilization thrived for several millennia until adverse climate began to dehydrate and reduce the aquatic size and productivity of the region. I believe it was at this point in history, ca. 5000-4000 B.C.E., that extensive migrations took place out of Africa into West Asia carrying with it the vestiges of West African cultures as seen with the Ifa.' (6)

Among the methods of travel used by the ancient Africans were boats made of logs or reed. Reed boats were common along the Nile and many of the rivers which crisscrossed the Sahara, while log boats, rafts and canoes dugout from felled trees, were used along rivers such as the Congo River and the Niger. These types of craft contributed to the development and spread of riverine trade to areas far away from the immediate area they settled to lands far away.

The development of culture during the period of 40,000 B.C. to 20,000 B.C., was not limited to Northern, Western and Eastern Africa, exclusively. The area around south of Central Africa, Central Africa and Southern Africa, were all areas of developing cultures. West Africa was another center of culture during the period already mentioned. These regions were the primary contributors to what became Egyptian and Nubian culture and civilization between 15,000 B.C., to the present.

8

Most of the goods, raw materials, people, plants, animals, and ideas came to Egypt from Kush, and from what was called 'Yam' or 'The Land of the Gods.' Yam was much of Central Africa and beyond. From there, a variety of products were traded such as animal skins, meat, weapons of flint and bone, tools, wood, fruits, nuts, medicines, animals, precious stones, skins of animals, and a wide variety of pro-ducts.

Many types of goods may have been transported over the large and expansive waterways which were part of the ancient drainage system of Africa. Rivers were frequented and preferred as a means of moving a greater amount of goods, as well as travelling from one place to the other. Apart from the log canoe and reed boats, boats of animal skins and tree bark may have also been common.

These boats appear to have had the capability to make ocean journeys, across the seas, or in relay fashion, by hugging the shores of the land and sailing or rowing from one point to the other. Boats and canoes were small, however there is much evidence in existence that small boats can and have crossed the oceans. Many adventurers have crossed large oceans such as the Atlantic and the pacific in everything from kayaks to canoes. The original wanders of the Pacific Ocean, the Black Melanesians who started their ancient migrations out of East Africa more than ten thousand years ago, sailed as far as Hawaii in out-rigger canoes with sails. The Polynesians also participated in this feat later on in history. During the Paleolithic Era [40,000 B.C. to 20,000 B.C.], Africans took the initiative and crossed wide bodies of water and oceans, using canoes sailing boats, paddled boats as well as rafts. It is even possible that such journeys begun as early as 100,000 B.C., considering that the Aboriginals may have crossed over to Australia by boat as early as 60,000 B.C., and the Black Negritic Tasmanians and others may have crossed even earlier.

So, even if there was no land bridge between Alaska and Siberia, or between South-East Asia and Australia, it may have been quite possible for Africans to journey to both the Americas and Australia without having to travel on land in either case, while crossing the places where the hypothetical 'land bridges' are supposed to have been. Moreover, these areas may have had the very same type of channel which exists in both these areas today, with strings of islands close together. There is no reason why the Grimaldi Negroids, the ancient ancestors of today's Aboriginals, or the earliest African migrants to Australia, would have been incapable of rowing from one point to the other. After all, the Africans of 100,000 B.C. had been developing more advanced technology about the very same period the great migrations begun, furthermore, many stone-age peoples who exist today such as some Australian Aboriginals, American Indians of South America, some Papuans and New Guineans and many others in parts of the Philippines are among the best carvers of canoes and boats. These vessels are not only very seaworthy, but in many cases perform better than the ships of more modern peoples.

The use of the boat to travel over long distances helped spread the practice of bartering and exchanging commodities and goods. Not everyone will accept the idea that Africans had boats capable of ocean travel between 40,000 to 20,000 years ago, still UNESCO's work in the Sahara has already proven that indeed, Africans used sailing ships around this period. Furthermore, considering the vast (7) age of Homo Sapiens [150,000 years according to Diop, C.A., 1991, p.23], it is possible that journeys along waterways occurred in the Congo Basin about the same period the Africans begun developing sophisticated tools and weapons, [about 100,000 years ago, according to Pearlman, San Francisco Chronicle, April 28, 1995.

African people settled in the South Pacific and Australia more than 40,000 years ago and about as early as 100,000 years ago. It is interesting to note that the time period given for the migrations of particular groups of Black Aborigines is about 40,000 to 60,000 years B.C. This is the time period usually given for the migration of the Grimaldi Negroid Man from Africa to Europe and Asia. Is it possible that the Australian Aborigines are one wave of the Black Grimaldi Man who migrated towards the East, while the prehistoric ancestors of the Tasmanians and other Pacific and other Negritic types found in parts of North-East Australia are remnants of a much earlier group of Africans? Due to current data based on mitochondrial DNA, it is accepted that all humans today descended from Africans who existed about 100,000 years ago and are therefore of monogenetic origin. Thus, it is unlikely that either the Negroid-Australoid Australian Aboriginal or the Melanesian Negritic originated in their present regions, but rather on the continent of Africa.

The bartering of goods between African Homo sapiens and groups who were established in the areas they migrated may have occurred. Trade may have been the catalyst which caused the ancient Africans to move eastward and in all directions. By the time the ancestors of the Australian Aborigines arrived in Australia, there may have been groups of Negroids similar to those who existed in Africa during that period [60,000 to 40,000 B.C.] and even to this very day. At the present time, the distribution of the Australian aboriginals compared to the present location of the descendents of the Tasmanians on the Island of Tasmania, clearly show a pattern of migration, whereby, the Tasmanians who are of a pure Negritic type of shorter stature, were pushed southward by a pure Negritic-Australoid Aborigine type who were taller. However, a mystery remains. The Tasmanians seem to live mostly on the Island of Tasmania. Unless Tasmania broke off from Australia while the Tasmanians occupied the part that broke off, they may have crossed the Bass Straits and paddled about 150 miles to the northern coast of the island of Tasmania in canoes, boats or on rafts.

Many of the great cultural contributions to the development and further existence of humans began before the migrations of Africans out of Africa. Watercraft was most likely among the most important inventions used by the ancient Africans to move from one area to the other. It does not take too much scientific knowledge to build good, seaworthy boats or rafts that are capable of traveling long distances. The presence of dugout canoes, rafts, reed boats and other types of watercraft among Black populations throughout the world, with very similar designs comes from the possibility that they were first invented in Africa and carried or sailed to their present locations. It should be no surprise to find dugout canoes in West Africa sewn

11

with rope, or fired in the same way as those found in Australia, the South Pacific, or Southern Japan. The similarities between reed boats of Lake Titicaca and Lake Chad and the Nile River today are good examples of the spread or transmission of ideas from Africa in prehistoric times.

There are two main types of watercraft that may have been used by the Africans of 40,000 B.C. to 10,000 B.C. These types were rafts constructed of logs or bamboo, shaped rafts and sewn-plank and dugout boats. When the sea and coastal routes taken by the early African voyagers is examined. It is found that there is a heavier concentration of both rafts and sewn-plank boats in the areas they migrated to, such as the South Pacific, Australia, SouthEast Asia and the Mediterranean basin. A heavy concentration of these of watercraft are found along the east and along the west coasts of Africa, on its rivers and around the Lake Regions of East Africa and other parts of Africa. They are found in all parts of the world where the climate was comfortable enough for the migrating Africans to live and survive without difficulties such as cold climate and ice, including the tropical and sub-tropical regions of the Americas.

Sewn plank boats begin from the West-Central and NorthWest parts of Africa and go eastward all the way to the Pacific Ocean. They are found as far north as Sakalin Island in the northeast part of Asia, to the SouthEast Pacific, about 5,000 miles east of New Zealand. The path followed by these particular types of boats show a migratory pattern similar to that taken by the Grimaldi Negroids about 60,000 to 40,000 years ago, after they left Africa. What is noticed is that rafts go as far north as Southern Japan, an area where Polynesians, a Negroid people with Mongoloid and pure Negroid types settled as recently as a few hundred years ago. In fact, the Negroid-Polynesian geographic race still exists in parts of Southern Japan and may have settled the entire island chain long before the arrival of the Mongoloids.

The ancient occupation of Japan by Blacks is a fact of history that has already been proven. The very first inhabitants of Japan were most likely Blacks. Furthermore, the evidence clearly shows that they were indeed Blacks who may have originally migrated from Africa. According to an article by James E. Brunson, Runoko Rashidi and Wallace Magsby, Jr., [African Presence in Early Asia, ed. Ivan Van Sertima, 1995, pp. 316-317], 'Meaningful indications of an African presence in ancient Japan have been unearthed from the most remote ages of the Japanese past. To begin with and as a significant example, a 15th February 1986 report carried by the Associated Press chronicled that;

> 'The oldest Stone Age hut in Japan has been unearthed near Osaka. Archeologists date the hut to about 22,000 years ago and say it resembles the dugouts of African Bushmen, according to Wazuo Hirose of Osaka Prefectural Board of Education's cultural division.
> 'Other homes, almost as old, have been found before, but this discovery is significant because the shape is cleaner, better preserved' and is similar to the Africans' dugouts.' ['African-Like Stone Age Hut is Unearthed in Japan,' Associated Press, 15 Feb. 1986]. (8)

What this evidence clearly indicates is that there was a Black presence in pre-historic Japan which continues to exist to this very day, not only in some of the racial characteristics of some Japanese, but in the very Japanese language itself. This African connection had to have been made due to travel across Asia from Africa, via India and across the Sea of Japan to the Japanese Islands. One has to conclude that these prehistoric Africans [about 22,000 B.C.] crossed to Japan on boats. In fact, a people with much Negroid admixture and related to the Polynesians do exist in Southern Japan today.

Rafts are not found in great numbers north of Southern Japan where the Negroids may not have used rafts to a large extent, or where the Ainu, a race usually called 'Caucasian,' but look closer to Negroid-Australoids, may have existed in large numbers as a more mixed racial type in the northern islands of Japan, and may have had a culture different from the Blacks.

13

The truth may be however, that the Ainu did not exist as a fair skinned race, and that the northern half of Japan was probably covered with ice.

Rafts are not found in great numbers north of Southern Japan where Negroids inhabited in ancient times, nor are they found north of Southern California. California had its own indigenous Black population who existed as a separate tribal group [apart from the African-Americans and Afro-Mexicans], who existed in the entire region for thousands of years before the Spanish and Mexican invasion of California. These Blacks still exist and are in fact part of the current African-American population of California. Others were absorbed in the Mexican/Chicano population, whose extremely dark complexion is based on African as well as Black Californian ancestry.

Many of the Black Californians existed during the era of Spanish colonization of California. These aboriginal Black people were fought with over their lands in California by the Spanish Californios, the Mexicans and finally, U.S. troops and settlers. It is of interest to note that when the first Europeans arrived along the coast of California, they claimed to have seen Black women bathing on the beaches. They were also told by the American Indians that Blacks with curly hair had been sailing from California to lands beyond the Pacific Ocean, and were returning to California with goods.

Knowledge of the presence of Blacks in California before the Spanish invasion of the region, may have come to them from the Black Moors of West Africa, probably the Mende/Mandinka speakers, who had thousands of years of travel between West Africa and the Americas. In fact, a romantic novel written about 1510 called, 'La Sergas de Espladian,' by Garcia Ordonez de Montalvo, mentions the 'Island of California.' This so-called Island was inhabited by Black Amazons, who possessed much gold and wealth. According to Delililah Leontinum Beasley, in her book, The Negro Trailblazers of California, [Bancroft Library, Berkeley, Calif., pub. L.A. Calif., 1919, pp. 17-18], the text by Ordonez de Montalvo contains the following information;

14

'Know ye that on the right hand of the Indies there is an island called California, very near the Terrestrial Paradise which is peopled with black women with any men among them, because they were accustomed to live after the fashion of the Amazons. They were of strong and hardy bodies, or ardent courage and of great force. The island was the strongest in the world from its steep rocks and great cliffs. Their arms were all of gold and so were the caparisons of the wild beasts which they rode after having tamed them, for in all the island there is no metal but gold.'(9)

As fictitious as this story may sound, the facts sound uncannily close to the fiction. First of all, California's Black warriors may have grown their hair long and tied them up in bundles or let them hang on their backs as the photograph of a Black Californian warrior in J.A. Rogers' book, (10) Africa's Gift to America [Rogers' Publishing Co., St Petersburg, Fl., 1967] clearly displays. Any Spanish ship surveying the area from afar [or Black Moorish ship, before Columbus] would mistake these warriors for women, after all, during the period [perhaps 400 B.C. to 1492 A.D.], long hair was not connected with men, but with women.

Secondly, California's pre-Columbian Black population existed and existed as a distinct tribal group as recently as the 1800's. These Blacks, the true owners of all of the state of California and much of the South Western United States were at war with the Spanish, Mexican and U.S. troops and settlers as recently as the 1880's. They became part of the Black population of California and exist today as African-Americans.

These Blacks may have participated in a network of trade which included the Pacific Ocean, the Gulf of Mexico and the Caribbean, and the Atlantic Ocean as far as the coast of West Africa. The mention of their going back and forth across the Pacific by the American Indians to the first Spanish explorers is evidence that they were people who traded and traveled far and wide.

There was also large concentrations [and still may be] of sewn-planked boats around the Iberian Peninsula, another landmass inhabited by Blacks in the very early prehistoric period. In fact, the very first Africans of a type which existed about 400,000 years ago called Homo antecessor, after a recent discovery in Spain by Spanish scientists [Discovery Magazine, December, (11) 1997], entered the Iberian Peninsula at least that long ago. These Africans however may have been Neanderthals on one hand or Homo sapiens on the other. These discoveries simply show that Africans crossed over into Europe at various periods. Although the technology for ship and boat building may not have existed as early as 300,000 B.C., there is no evidence they did not cross using the most rudimentary methods of transportation. After all, these were people capable of thinking and making tools and weapons. Tying some logs together and making a large raft to cross the straits of Gibraltar was possible. Later on in history, about 60,000 years ago, there is no doubt that African migrants were making boats and crossing from S.E. Asia to Australia.

These early migrations had to have been inspired by the need for trade and commercial activities, hunting and searching for food sources with other human types who existed throughout the region. During this period of pre-history, no other races existed, thus, they had most likely not crossed from Siberia to Alaska across the Bering Straits, or across the sea from China to Japan. The watercraft used by the ancient Africans were not found in the far north of either Europe, Asia, or the Americas. However, the American Indians of the area from Southern California to the mid southern part of Chile, had the same types of rafts as those found around Africa, the South Pacific and Australia.

The ancient Africans of the period about 60,000 to 10,000 B.C. were not merely curious to find out what lay beyond their immediate regions in the Indian Ocean, the Pacific, or across the Atlantic to the Americas. As trade increased by land, they were interested in going further from their immediate regions, to greater distances in order to take advantages of new opportunities and to settle permanently. Goods such as red ochre, which was produced only in parts of Southern Africa, may

16

have been very valuable as a commodity for people who had used it in the past and wanted to be supplied with more of the same.

Trading, bartering and the buying and selling of goods occurred between the Gramaldi Negroids and those they met along the way on their migrations throughout Africa and to Europe, Asia, Australia and the Americas. Among the goods traded may have been coconuts, yams, plantains, bananas, sweet potatoes, cassava, mangoes, cotton, dogs and other animals, meat, stone, bone and flint weapons, tools and precious stones. The diffusion of fruits and vegetables by the Africans as they journeyed to all directions of the tropical and temperate regions of the earth occurred. The above mentioned food products may have been used in trade as well as to supplement the feeding of those who took part in the migrations, similarly to how the Melanesians and Polynesians of a few thousand years ago, supplemented their travels by stocking their ships to last for many months. The food products carried by the prehistoric Africans on their long migratory journeys such as the banana and cassava, were unable to grow and flourish in the temperate zones of the earth, but in the tropics, they flourished.

Many tropical fruits and vegetables, such as the breadfruit, which originally came from the Pacific Islands, or bananas, have been credited to the European for their dissemination throughout the tropics. Yet, coconuts corn, plantains, yams, and crops such as peanuts are not only tropical crops, but some of these crops were already in some of the places and lands where it is claimed that they were introduced by Europeans. One example is the peanut which grew abundantly in the Andes region of South America [Muslim Journal] during the 800's A.D. At the same period, the peanut was also in Africa being used by the Yoruba and other African nationalities. Rubber is another product that the Africans used in trade. It was in widespread use during the Ghana Empire 400 A.D. to 1200 A.D., yet, rubber was also widespread in Mexico long before the time of Columbus. Corn [maize], a grain found in various parts of the Americas is also made reference to in the Old Testament. Corn was grown in Africa for hundreds of years before Columbus stumbled upon it in the New World, according to some scholars who have studied the distribution of corn [They Came Before Columbus, I. Van Sertima(12), 1977]. Columbus may have been told that Africans in the Cape Verde region of West Africa brought the corn from the Americas due to their lucrative trans-Atlantic trade with the Native Americans, which had been ongoing for hundreds of years. The transportation of corn from California to the South Pacific, the to East Africa by Africans or the Black Californians who have existed in California for thousands of years is very possible. In fact, the first Spanish explorers to California were told by the American Indians that Black men with curly hair lived in California and made constant trips across the Pacific with goods and returned to California with more products.

The coconut is another fruit that Africans may have brought back and forth from one part of the tropics to the other, for it is found in every part of the tropical Southern Hemisphere where it is able to grow. Although coconuts may have been brought to the Americas by the first European explorers, they may have not been the first to people to introduce it in the areas where they are found today, or in other parts of the tropical belt. Coconuts have the ability to stay afloat on water for many months and they may have spread across and around the Southern Hemisphere on their own with the help of ocean currents. On the other hand, humans were also responsible for the spread of the coconut and coconut plant, as well as its planting and harvesting.

The ancient Black African mariners and sailors who left their lands along the coasts of East Africa and perhaps the Nile/Sahara region, took a wide variety of crops on their journeys. They planted these crops throughout Asia and the South Pacific as well as the Indian Ocean. The Polynesians also helped in spreading the coconut and other plants such as the cassava, taro and sweet potato throughout parts of the South Pacific. These Polynesians, who consist of a major group in the Pacific Islands, along with the Melanesians are a mixed race who appear to have been originally Negritic like the Melanesians and their brothers on the African continent.

The similarities in the cultures of the Black people of the present day South Pacific, Australia, India, Africa, the Americas, and the entire tropical belt is striking and is due primarily to diffusion in early prehistoric times. There are many cultural habits and activities of great similarity practiced in Africa, yet they have also been practiced by these Diaspora Africans. One example is the use of the hollow, log drums used to send messages. This drum is common in Africa and is used to send tonal messages that can be understood by those who speak the languages imitated on the drums. The same type, style and size of drums are also used in New Guinea and parts of Melanesia and the South Pacific, where Blacks inhabit.

Another cultural similarity practiced by the two branches of the Negritic race, the African and the Melanesian [actually they are one branch who split up tens of thousands of years ago], is dental beautification or mutilation. The practice of filing the incisors was common throughout much of tropical Africa to the extent that pre columbian remains of an African discovered at Hull Bay in the Virgin Islands, was dated to about 1250 A.D. The remains were of Blacks who entered the region before the landing of Columbus on the Bahamas, by about 242 years. That's quite recent considering that Blacks passed through the region during the Olmec period, as early as 1800 B.C., and perhaps as far back as prehistory, about 30,000 to 60,000 B.C., when many anthropologists agree, that a people with the group b blood-type [found in Africans and Pacific Negroids] entered the Americas from Africa, after crossing the Atlantic. This very possibility gives a student chills just considering that this may have indeed occurred.

Writers and historians such as R.A. Jairazbhoy [1974], Ivan Van Sertima(13), Wayne B. Chandler [1992, p. 241], and LeGrand Clegg [1992], point out in their various works that Africans have been part of Asia since pre historic times. Furthermore, they were the very first people in existence in that region. They created Asia's earliest civilizations such as the Indus Valley Harrapa and Mohejodaro, established Xia and Shang China's Dynasties were both Black, and established a number of kingdoms and civilizations from India to the Philippines and South Pacific.

During the prehistoric Nubian civilization of TaSeti, the world's very first civilization [perhaps as early as 8,000 B.C. according to New archeological findings in Nubia this year, 1997], there may have been frequent trade and travel between the Pacific and Africa. The Nubians of the Dynastic period, the Khemites [Egyptians], the Abbysians, the Swahili, the Puntites, Black Sabeans of South Arabia, and other Black civilizations carried out trade and commerce with the farthest reaches of Asia.

One of the issues raised by some anthropologists, particularly over the past year [1994 to 1995], has been the blood type differences between some Blacks of Asia and the Blacks of Africa. This so-called difference may seem significant to some; however, these differences are irrelevant since they are not unusual in other racial groups. In fact, blood groups can vary in the same distinct race. The predominance of blood-type b in the Blacks of Asia and some of the South Pacific Polynesians and Africans clearly show a connection between Blacks in general and their migration to South America as early as 30,000 to 60,000 years ago. Further more, a separation of prehistoric Africans about that period and earlier could very well contribute to minor changes and variations in the original blood type. Mixing with other peoples over the past tens of thousands of years can also bring about some changes. Yet, it is fascinating that the Blacks of Asia are very similar in outward appearance to those of Africa. The minor mixing which occurred thus causing an infusion of non Black blood types into the Melanesians is more apparent in the large number of obviously mixed races who are a mixture of Black and Mongoloid who exist in Asia today. The Polynesians, Pilipinos, Japanese, Southern Chinese, and a number of other subgroups are mixed.

The reason for the outward racial similarities between the Blacks of New Guinea, the South Pacific, Melanesia, and parts of Asia who are of the Negritic stock, may have to do with the similarities in the conditions which brought about the evolution of Blacks in Africa to the Homosapien stage about 150,000 years ago. These conditions were and still are, being in the equatorial regions where the heat is sometimes above 115 degrees Fahrenheit, being constantly exposed to the sun and having no

20

other racial groups where racial miscegenation would occur, thus blending out the original characteristics, [Goran Burenhult, 1994, Aborigines, pp. 77-97; Melanesians, 99-122]. (14)

In retrospect, trade, the hunting and tracking of animals, migrations by boat or rafts and the search for new and fruitful lands were responsible for the migrations of Africans out of Africa to the other regions of the world. By 40,000 B.C., the Africans were more technically advanced than the Homo Erectus [in fact, the Homosapien African had invented sophisticated tools as early as 100,000 B.C., according to Perlman, [San Francisco Chronicle, April 28, 1995]. There is no doubt that if these Africans were making sophisticated weapons and tools by 100,000 B.C. in Congo, they could have advanced to a greater level by 40,000 B.C., when the Grimaldi Negroid began his occupation of Europe. He could have displaced the Neanderthal and brought about the existence of more modern humans who are all related today, to Africans.

# CHAPTER TWO

# TRADE, PASTORALISM AND COMMERCE

One of the early industries developed by Africans during the Paleolithic through the Mesolithic Ages (circa 40,000 B.C. to 10,000 B.C.) was the domestication and tending of animals such as the dog, cattle and perhaps buffalo. Pastoralism may have developed out of the tracking and following of animals during periods of hunting as the animals moved along the wide savannas and plains of Africa, Europe, Asia, the Americas and most of the regions inhabited by the Homosapien Grimaldi Negroids, the first fully human type to exist. Some of the earliest cave paintings in Europe, Africa and Asia show cattle similar to the long horned type, such as the famous Watusi cattle, found in parts of Africa today. Savannah animals such as the warthog, lions, buffalo and some of the animals found today in Africa were also among the ancient animals which roamed the plains of Europe and Asia not covered by sheets of ice.

The domestication of animals by the pastoralists helped to bring trade and commerce to higher levels. It made a ready and reliable supply of meat, skins and milk available for people who lived in small settlements away from a steady supply of meat. For example, it may have been difficult finding a steady supply of meat in some areas of the extensive savanna. This reality increased the importance of the pastoralists, who moved from one area to the other, had a steady supply of meat and milk, and was able to trade with the more sedentary savannah dwellers. Moreover, the consumption of milk and the introduction of other dairy products into the diet of the savannah dweller, opened the way for extensive trade between the pastoralists and the settlements of preagricultural people.

It is possible that most of the lactase negative peoples of Africa, Asia and Europe as well as peoples who were non pastoralists or had no use for cattle or livestock, such as a large percentage of Africans, some East Indians of pure Kushitic stock (unmixed with the descendants of the invading Eurobarbarians from the north), East Asians, American Indians, Australian Blacks and some Southern Europeans were the people who lived in settled, sedentary communities, had no contact with cattle keepers. On the other hand, people such as the Fulanis, Northern and Central Europeans and Arabs not only kept cattle or other livestock, but they also followed a nomadic way of life. Consequently, all of the great civilizations on earth were began by settled, sedentary peoples who were originally of the Black racial type.

Among the areas most suitable for pastoralism was the Sahara region. During the Upper Paleolithic to the Mesolithic Age and as recently as around 4000 B.C. to 3000 B.C., the Sahara was well watered. There were forests in some areas and in others, there existed extensive grasslands suitable for grazing cattle and other livestock. In fact, rock drawings going back to a period before 7000 B.C. were discovered in the Tassili area of the Sahara. These drawings clearly show Black Africans tending cattle, fishing with nets, hunting and performing other tasks connected to a settled way of life.

In many parts of Africa, Asia and Europe, paintings of similar themes produced by people who were similar in physical characteristics to the so called Bushmen and other Africans have been studied for their remarkable similarities with one another, as well as their similarities in their ages. Some of these paintings are much older than the period during which the so-called Cro-Magnon Man (C.A. Diop, 1991, p. 44) changed from Black to Caucasian due to the necessity to adapt to the cold and temperate climate. That period is between 30,000 to 20,000 years ago.

These paintings were created by the Negroid Grimaldi Man, who also left female representations of the Negritic type throughout Africa, Asia and Europe, in stone and other materials. These small statuettes are sometimes called "Venuses" or "Mother Goddess" representations by some anthropologists, scientists and writers. Most of those found, as shown in some of the pictures of Cheikh Antah Diop's book, Civilization or Barbarism, (p. 46-49, (1) 1991). They represent the Negritic racial type, from the representation of curly/kinky hair to the portrayal of steatophygia. Among the most remarkable is the so

24

called "Venus of Willendorf," an example of Aurignacian Perigordian art, carved during the Paleolithic Era (40,000 to 30,000 B.C. according to Diop (1991, p.47).

The first Africans of the Homosapien form to migrate to Europe and Asia may have been pastoralists and traders who either followed herds of animals toward the north or migrated in order to find new lands and to conduct trade and commerce, or new sources of raw materials. These first anatomically modern humans existed between 200,000 to 100,000 years ago, however during a period of perhaps 60,000 to 40,000 years ago, they migrated into Asia, Europe, Australia and the Americas. Their migrations brought about a cultural renaissance on a worldwide scale due to their spread of art, industry and advanced culture to these continents from Africa, where the spread had been occurring for more than one hundred thousand years previously.

On the continent of Africa, what appears to have occurred is that the early pastoralists and hunters remained in the areas where food was abundant, while others migrated and spread throughout the continent. That possibility may be one of the reasons why some types of Africans such as the Pygmy (Cwa) and Kong-San people are found in specific areas of the continent, while the taller, robust agriculturists are found in every part of it. In very ancient times, these agriculturists may have originally been migrating pastoralists, hunters and traders.

The early pastoralists and those people who lived in settled communities were the first people to take an interest in astronomy. The ancient Africans learned to read the stars and developed astronomy due to their exposure to the heavens and the wide open spaces during the night, while tending their animals or waiting in the open for prey. They also became expert at predicting changes in the weather and the coming of drought, floods and other natural disasters by studying the positions of the stars, clouds or other natural phenomena in relation to the rest of the year. In fact, the earliest evidence of astronomical observation on an advanced scale on earth occurred in the savannas or grasslands which once existed in the Sahara, Khem (Egypt), West Africa, parts of Europe and parts of the Americas and Australia. In fact, the oldest astronomical observatory so far known was discovered in the country of Sudan (1997). This observatory is older than 7,000 years B.C. and larger than Stonehenge of England.

# CHAPTER THREE

# THE BEGINNINGS OF AGRICULTURE AND PATTERNS OF TRADE AND COMMERCE

Agriculture developed out of the pastoral African culture. This development included those who first begun to follow the sedentary culture, such as the prehistoric Africans who lived in the Sahara, the Nile region, West Africa, the Great Lakes of Africa, the Middle East, Asia and Europe. The early development of agriculture may have begun due to the keeping of animals in one particular area, for many months, until the grass or grazing areas settled by the animal herds and their keepers became exhausted, or the climate changed. During such periods of grazing, when herdsmen and their families remained sedentary and did not move their cattle, they mixed the practice of agriculture and the gathering of fruits and plants as their means of keeping a steady supply of food. This type of mixing of pre agricultural habits and pastoralism is still practiced all over Africa by people such as the Fulani, Masai, Bantu cattle keepers such as the Zulu and others.

Organized agriculture first began in Africa sometime before 10,000 years B.C. In fact, as recently as the period between 1991 and 1993, scientists discovered grains of sorghum or millet that had been planted and harvested in the nation of Sudan. These grains were dated to be more than 10,000 years old. These were also the earliest grains domesticated on earth. Apparently, these grains and many others were being used by Africans for food as well as items of trade. Based on current methods used today to store grains in Africa, these grains may have also been stored in large, clay storage bins built above the ground in order to keep out rodents, pests and water.

Due to the early beginnings of agriculture in Africa, a revolution in trade, commerce and civilization occurred. Between 20,000 B.C. to 5,000 B.C., Africans laid the foundations for the first high civilizations on earth in the regions

27

where agriculture was first established. These areas were Sudan, the Upper Nile, the Sahara and West Africa. Evidence such as the discovery of an 8,000 year old abacus from the Congo (J.A. Rogers, (1) Africa's Gift to America), or the recent discovery of stone and bone tools of high sophistication along the banks of the Congo River (Jet Magazine, April, 1995; David Perlman, San Francisco Chronicle, April 28, 1995). (2) These tools and weapons were between 75,000 to 100,000 years old. The discovery of these tools indicate that long before organized agriculture was being practiced, Africans had invented and used sophisticated tools which were used for a variety of purposes including horticulture, hunting and fishing. Tools such as the adze, sickle, digging stick and hoe may have also been invented during this period in order to make working much easier. The availability of domesticated animals such as the ox and buffalo gave way to the use of the plough and draft animals in parts of the Sahara as well as the Nile Corridor (Modern Ethiopia, Sudan, Egypt, parts of East Africa).

A wide network of trade and commerce developed because of the practice of storing surplus grains and other commodities and crops. The early agriculturists traded these items in exchange for meat and dairy products from the pastoralists, meat, hides, ivory, plants and forest products from the hunter gatherers, and plants, food crops and forest products from the agriculturists and forest dwellers. At least three regions were engaged in this trade between 40,000 B.C. to 5,000 B.C. These areas were Africa, parts of Europe (South and Central) and Southern and Western Asia. The Sahara was a hub of activity during this period, as the Tasili cave paintings seen by Henri Lhote the explorer clearly shows.

During the Upper Paleolithic and Mesolithic Ages (approximately 40,000 B.C. to 10,000 B.C.), the Sahara was covered with large lakes in some areas. In others, fertile topsoil which contributed to rich, lush forests and grasslands covered much of the area. There were rivers which flowed freely, lakes, swamps, animals of all sorts, villages, towns and other settlements. It is highly possible that the very first towns and cities built anywhere on earth were built in the present location of the Central Sahara, particularly to the South Western Sahara in the region of Mauritania. These cities and towns were built long before Jerico an ancient city in the Levant (around Isreal) which was built by Black Canaanites about 6000 B.C. These early African towns and cities were part of a network of trade and commerce. Ancient rivers, roads, paths and chariot highways helped to make traveling from one area to the next with trade goods. Current research has revealed that as early as 15,000 years ago, a Black empire existed in the region known today as Mauritania. An article from Mobetter News (OMNI U, P.O. Box 1447, South Holland, IL. 60473, Vol. VIII, No.3, January 1998), explains how the African flag, with its red, black and green colors was first planted all over Africa by Emperor Tirus Afrik, Emperor of the Zingh Empire which existed in the region of Mauritania, West Africa, over 15,000 (3) years ago. This revelation clearly points to the presence of African civilization in the region of West Africa's portion of the Sahara, during a period when the entire region was well watered, fertile and prosperous.

The Eastern and North Eastern portion of Africa was similar in climate and fertility to West Africa. This area was also covered with fertile, well watered lands, lakes, rivers, forests and grasslands. Much of the Nile Delta was quite different from what it was to become later, a fertile region. In the very early period, the entire region of northern Egypt from Inebhedj (Memphis) to the shores of the Delta, may have been covered with water and swampland, or the sea may have been in this area. The Nile River nourished the area by pouring tons of silt and mud into it during the rainy seasons. As Africans from the South and Central regions (the sources of the Nile) migrated downriver, networks of trade and commerce were established and prospered. The Africans who left the Great Lakes region of Africa, the Southern Part of Sudan and the Central part of Africa (Yam) to settle Khemet (Egypt) and the lands downriver of the Nile, conducted trade and commerce with their brothers and sisters who remained in the upperlands or the southern regions of Africa.

This ancient trade network may be among the reasons why Khemites (ancient Black Egyptians) such as Snefru (2600 B.C.), Sahure (2500 B.C.), Hennu (2000 B.C.), Hatshepsut (1493 B.C.) and Nekau (600 B.C.), sent their ships to Punt (perhaps the entire region of Africa south of Sudan as well as other regions such as the Americas where BLACKS EXISTED AND BUILT CIVILIZATIONS) or sent expeditions to Yam (Central Africa). They regarded these lands (in Africa) as their place of origins and called them, "The Land of the Gods," according to (4) Ian Cameron (National Geographic, pp.10-11, 1987). These visits occurred at a much later period in history compared the the very early ages when Blacks, the only humans in existence, migrated from Central Africa and Eastern Africa to people the entire continent and the world. The earliest migrations from the source of human beginnings (Eastern, Central and Southern Africa) to the rest of the world occurred between 200,000 to 100,000 B.C., according to current research.

The bartering of goods was the rule during the era when the Grimaldi Negroids (who were the ancestors of modern Europeans) and Blacks like themselves throughout Africa, began spreading to all regions of the earth. These migrations occurred between 60,000 B.C. to 20,000 B.C. and afterwards. Between 20,000 B.C. to about 5,000 B.C., the same patterns of trade, commerced and bartering continued among the Africans of the Nile Corridor, West Africa, Western and Central Africa, South Asia, West Asia, East Asia, the South Pacific, Europe Australia and the Americas. In fact, new discoveries of civilizations which existed before 10,000 B.C., or mythical civilizations such as Atlantis, Mu and others may have been founded by these early Africans. Moreover, the mention from biblical sources of civilizations which existed before the Great Flood, would most logically have been African or Black civilizations. This conclusion can be made because Caucasoids or Mongoloids had not fully developed into distinct races, nor had they developed any great civilizations during that period. On the other hand, Blacks had developed advanced cultures and civilizations as early as 20,000 B.C. (the aquatic civilizations of the prehistoric, wet Sahara and Eastern as well as Western Africa), and were

30

creating sophisticated tools weapons and other rudiments of early civilization in Zaire (Congo) as early as 100,000 B.C. to 75, 000 B.C. (see Perlman, San Francisco Chronicle, April, 1995). (5)

A wide variety of products were traded during the prehistoric period. These included animals both as pets and or as food, such as monkeys, apes, birds and fowl, deer, wild boar and others. Plants, food crops, precious stones, precious metals such as gold, woods such as ebony, stone tools, copper, red ochre and perhaps iron ore, animal skins and a variety of manufactured products and handicrafts were sold or bartered by the Africans of the South to those down river of the Nile.

The earliest forms of agriculture, the horticultural phase may have been practiced in the western half of Africa north of the Equator, from the Mediterranean Sea to the Congo River and from the west of the Nile Basin to the Atlantic ocean. Two types of agriculture may have been practiced in that region. One was suitable for the more sparsely populated-forested areas of the Sahara, while the other was more suitable for the heavily forested regions. The first may have included a mixture of pastoralism and early horticulture and proto agricultural practices, while the other was more suitable for the forested areas and included similar practices but with hunting and gathering to supplement the food intake.

Much of the agricultural activities taking place in the Sahara covered by grasslands and sparse vegetation was done by pastoralists, according to M. Posansky ("Introduction to the Later Prehistory of sub Saharan Africa," p. 298, General History of Africa, UNESCO, Paris, France; 1990) (6). They were not as settled as the more sedentary populations of those regions of the Sahara where the soil and topography made it possible to practice agriculture on a more permanent basis. The more permanent farmers occupied an area from the mid Sahara to the Congo River. The practice of slash and burn agriculture in which the trees were chopped down, burned and the ashes used to nourish the soil, may have been practiced.

After the harvest, the farmers would have let the places where they planted to remain fallow for a number of years before they begun planting again. During this period of waiting, they cleared another area. This practice is responsible for the deforestation of much of the Sahara and West Africa today. The need to find wood to produce charcoal in order to smelt iron ore, beginning from the Late Stone Age (about 8000 years ago), till the present time is another reason for this tragedy.

Hunting was widespread in the area between the mid Sahara to the Congo River, yet it is very likely that the relationship between the two groups of Negroids who inhabited the region then, was the same as it is today. Most agriculture was practiced by the taller, more robust Negritic types and the Annoid (Blacks who were medium to tall stature and occupied the Nile Valley and parts of East Africa between 20,000 B.C. to 3000 B.C.; known as Anu). The Pygmies and Kong San (Bushman, who were spread throughout Africa at the time) were engaged in hunting and garthering as well as some forms of agriculture or horticulture, and pastoralism.

There was trade and commerce between these groups in ancient times, as there is today. In today's transactions between the Pygmies, Kong San and the Bantu or Nilotic types, the Pygmies or Kong San who live in the forests or bushlands exchange their meat, animal skins and medicinal plants from their areas for the metal weapons, cloth and utencils from peoples such as the Bantu. The Pygmies and other hunter gartherer peoples may also have lived among the Bantus in prehistoric times. According to Jared Diamond (Discover Magazine, Feb. 1994, pp. 74-75), these hunter gartherer peoples still transact with the Bantus and Nilotic farmers.(8)

In areas such as the edges of the forests, where the savannah Blacks and the Pygmies met, trade and bartering was quite common. The flourishing trade which developed among the three types of Black peoples; the tall Negritics, the Pygmies or Kwa and the Kong San (Bushmanoid), which developed in the northern, western, eastern, central and southern parts of prehistoric Africa, helped to develop a culture of trade and dependency among them. Cultures developed on the fringes of the forests and Savannah lands and groups became more organized. One such groups, the Ishongo people of the Congo,

32

developed a sophisticated form of mathematics and used an abacus about 8,000 B.C., a time when cultural changes were taking place among African populations worldwide.

The population of African Negritics (Blacks), Pygmoids and Kong San Negroids were not as unequal as they are today. Moreover, both the Pygmies and the Kong-San occupied much wider areas of Africa than they do at the present time. There were more areas covered with forests about 8,000 B.C., and peoples such as the Kong-San were not restricted only to Southern Africa and parts of East Africa. They spread as far north as the Horn of Africa (L.S. (2) Stavrianos, 1983, p. 232) and the Red Sea, where they were surrounded by other Black populations of the more robust and taller types. However, because the Kong-San and Pygmies (Kwa) were hunter-gatherers, while the Bantu and Nilotes were agriculturists who occupied large areas of land, the Bantu (Niger Kongo) language family, and that of the Nilotes (Kushitic-Khemetic language family), remained settled, developed advanced cultures and were able to sustain large families and strong political, social and economic units which regarded family as very important to their economy and survival.

Some of the Kong-San people may have led more settled life during the period of Egyptian and Kushite as well as Puntite (Somalian, East African) and West African civilizations. Drawings and bas reliefs on Egyptian and Kushite temples show Negritic types similar to the Kong-San people of Southern Africa, with racial features such as the epicantus fold, kinky hair and yellowish brown to dark brown complexions. The reliefs show the Kong-San being held as captives by the Egyptians during a period which portrayed a battle. This evidence which also shows the type of clothing, weapons and armor worn by the Kong-San people brings about the possibility that the Kong-San were advanced in culture during the time when this battle occurred, a period between 2600 B.C. to 1000 B.C., when journies were taken by the Khemites to East and Southern Africa for trade and commercial reasons.

The Kong-San people or a Black African racial group similar in features to them may have inhabited a region from the tip of

Southern Africa all the way north into northern Europe, during prehistoric times. In fact, statuettes of them found throughout Europe and labeled "Venuses," resemble the Bushmanoid type presently living in Southern Africa. According to some anthropologists, the Kong-San are genetically the closest to West Africans and other Negritic Blacks of Africa, then to people who live in parts of Arabia and the Middle East (where Blacks were the original inhabitants and where a considerable pure and mixed mixed Black type still dominates certain regions, ("The Peopling of Ancient Egypt and the Deciphering of the Meroitic Script," p. 39, General History of (3) Africa, G. Mokhtar and J. Curry, 1990). Since the Kong-San are another branch of the Black race and since they were among the ancient peoples who migrated from Africa during the Upper Paleolithic period (40,000 B.C. to 10,000 B.C.), then they had been in the Middle East thousands of years before the Semites came into being out of a mixture of Negritics and Caucasoids about 3,000 years Before Christ.

The more robust and taller Negritic peoples, the ancestors of all Black Africans, Africans of the Americas, Europe, Asia, India and the South Pacific today, remained agriculturists and horticulturists, while the Kong-San and Kwa (Pygmies), continued with their hunter-gartherer way of life. The Black farmers inhabited the Sahara, Nile Corridor, the Sudan, the Upper Nile region, West Africa, the Ethiopian Highlands and the Great Lakes region of East Africa. The short, reddish brown skinned Pygmoids inhabited the forest areas and the short, yellowish-brown to dark brown Kong-San who are racially Negroid with features similar to that of Mongoloids, remained in the eastern and southern parts of Africa. Together, these three groups of Black Africans created a wide network of trade throughout Africa, South-West Asia and southern Europe. (The term "Black African," is not being used to differentiate between Africans who where white or of other races, since other races came to reside on African soil during the late phases of the prehistoric era).

Agriculture and pastoralism spread from Africa to South-West Asia and the rest of the world, soon after they were established in Africa as methods of industry, commerce and earning a living. A study of the pattern of the spread of agriculture shows that from the Sudan (in the nation of Sudan), in the Upper Nile Valley, to Egypt, agriculture spread to West Asia, then the rest of the world. These areas included the Middle East, the Indus Valley of India, China, Europe, South-East Asia, the Americas and Australia and the South Pacific, where horticulture is still practiced today, by the Blacks who are the original inhabitants of the region and continue to live there. One of the grains which was taken along during the migrations of Africans to all four corners of the earth was sorghum. It is found from West and Central Africa to China. Millet, wheat, barley and other crops, including cotten in later years, may have spread from the Sahara and Central Africa, where they were domesticated by prehistoric Africans.

The earliest periods for the cultivation of grains in other parts of the world is much more recent compared to the period when grains were first domesticated harvested and cultivated in Africa. This lapse in time periods show what may have been the amount of time it took for the same people (Africans) to spread the art throughout the world where they ventured, or to spread the grains through trade and commerce. In South-West Asia (Isreal, Jordan, Syria, Arabia, Turkey, ect., ), which is closest to Africa compared to other regions, the first grains were harvested between 7,000 to 9000 years B.C. In Europe the time period was about 6000 years B.C., East Asia it was about 5,000 B.C., in India about 3500 B.C. (of course it had to be much earlier, back to 7000 B.C., when Kushitic types began the first civilizations in the area). Maize was being planted and harvested in the Americas about 7,000 B.C. In South America, the cultivation and harvesting of grains is given at about 3500 B.C.

The Mongoloid racial type is a more recent racial development, compared to the Negroid type. In fact, their presence on the world scene occurred between 7,000 B.C. to 10,000 B.C. According to Cheikh Antah Diop, (1991, p. 52), the vast majority of the inhabitants of East Asia were Negroids. He comments:

"When we move to Asia, the old Asia of the Orientalists, what strikes, contrary to all expectations, is the extremely recent appearance of Homo sapiens sapiens. The carbon-14 analysis done by the Chinese themselves helped establish that Ziyang Man-estimated by scholars to be 100,000 years old-dates from 7500 + 130 B.P., or 5500 B.C. Likewise, the man of the Upper Cave of Choukoutien, whom specialists thought equally to be 100,000 years old, dates from 18,000 + 420 B.P. or 16,915 B.C." (Archeologia, no. 123, Oct. 1978, p. 14). (4)

According to Diop, of the two skulls, one resembled a Negroid from Melanesia, while the other looked like an ancient example of an Eskimo (Aleut) skull. These two races may have combined to create the Chinese people, in the same way that the Japanese people evolved into their present racial type about three to four thousand years ago. The Japanese people are a mixed race composed of the the Ainu (possibly descendants of the Black Negroid Anu of prehistoric Egypt), Black Pygmy, Mongoloid from Korea, Polynesian and Asiatic Negroid. In fact, many Ainu, particularly those with less of the Mongoloid strain resemble fair-skinned Australian Aboriginals. In any case, it would seem that the transfer of Northern African grain crops to China was the work of people who looked like Africans, and did in fact migrate out of Africa at various periods between 100,000 B.C. to 2000 B.C. The so-called Melanesian skull found in the cave may have been that of a pre-Mongolid migrant who came from Africa or people of the African Negritic race who had lived in China just after the first Homo sapien Africans left the continent about 150,000 years ago. Moreover, the present Mongoloid Asiatic racial type may very well be a mixture of the ancient Australoid-Negroid type once found throughout East Asia (where they still exist in an area from India to Australia), Negroids from Africa and Melanesian Negroids.

It is believed that wheat, barley, oats and other "temperate" types of grains grown in the cooler climates were first harvested in the region of Mesopotamia. That belief may be the reason why the region of Mesopotamia is called, "The Fertile Crescent." What is not told is that the earliest inhabitants of Mesopotamia were Negroids of the Kushite branch who are still found in vast numbers in Sudan and the rest of East Africa, the Nile Valley, parts of West Africa, Southern Arabia, the Gulf States, India and Ethiopia. Furthermore, the highlands of Ethiopia and parts of Kenya in East Africa, along with Southern Africa are the cradles of humanity. The most ancient remains of humans were found in these areas. Ethiopia is also one of the cradles of civilization. In Kenya, Ethiopia and Southern Africa, temperate grains are grown due to the climate in parts of these nations that are suitable for the cultivation of grain. The Atlas Mountains region of North-West Africa as well as much of the northern part of Africa suitable for growing crops have grown grain. In fact, Egypt was the breadbasket of the ancient world for thousands of years. In all these regions, Blacks existed when no other races were in existence. The cultivation of grains in these regions, particularly southern and central Sudan has been occuring since before 10,000 B.C.

Along with grains, fruits may have also been spread from one area to the other and were among the first plants and trees that the prehistoric Africans domesticated and used in organized agriculture. Having been pastoralists, the prehistoric Africans may have discovered the value of agriculture by throwing away seeds of fruits and vegetables they had collected while they moved their livestock. Hunters may have noticed the value of tending fruit and other edible plants in the same manner. While waiting for herds, they may have dined on fruits and vegetables. The discarded seeds grew while they were waiting for animals to migrate. Consequently, they discovered that seeds sprouted into plants, which became trees and bore edible fruit. These were then plucked and consumed. This observation led to organized agriculture.

# CHAPTER FOUR

# THE BEGINNING OF SETTLED LIVING DUE TO AGRICULTURE

In the last chapter, the transformation of Africans from pastoral activities to agriculture and how the need to find and create accessible food sources led to the tending of fruits, vegetables and crops was thoroughly examined. The need to remain close to their livestock brought about the need to build temporary settlements and to depend on plants and fruits until the grazing lands were exhausted. During these periods, discarded fruits and other edible foods and plants as well as their seeds, had the time necessary to grow and produce fruits before the next moving of the animals. While the fruit trees grew, they survived on what was available as well as meat and milk.

The earliest Africans developed pastoralism from following herds of animals such as the wild ox, buffalo, wildebeast and other animals, during their migrations from one end of the African Savannah to the other. While these animals migrated, some may have been stalked, tracked, trapped and captured, while others were felled with javlins given force by the atlatl. It also occurred that some of these animals were captured, corralled and tamed for future use and as supplies of meat, milk and skins. Their horns were used as tools and their bones as weapons and tools. As these animals increased in number and produced offspring, the early Africans may have kept them instead of following their herds from place to place. They discovered it was much easier keeping the animals in one place, rather than following them around.

Early agriculture developed out of pastoralism, for it seems more logical that the ancient pastoralists would have had the time, land and need to grow crops while they waited for their cattle to graze, before moving them at the end of particular seasons, or when the grazing area became exhaused. This process would have taken many months, enough time for certain edible fruits and plants to grow and be harvested. The ancient pastoralists also found out that pastoralism and agriculture could go hand in hand as some of the ancient pastoralists of the Sahara found out.

While this social and economic change was occurring, the need for permanent settlements also increased. Thus, instead of building tents and temporary settlements, they built small villages and permanent settlements, while their livestock grazed in the fields outside of their homes. As the years went by, organized villages sprung up all over the landscape with animal corrals for livestock, and with fields and meadows teaming with cattle, oxen, sheep and other animals.

The very first villages were probably built by families who owned livestock such as sheep, goats, cattle and oxen. They practiced an early form of agriculture and felt satisfied with having fruits and vegetables as well as sources of meat while their plants grew. The need for nomadic existence diminished as villages and other types of permanent settlements became the norm.

The early villages were built in a variety of tapographical areas. For example, apart from the flat grasslands were cattle was kept, riverbanks where fish was easier to catch and areas where the soil was fertile such as valleys contributed to the expansion of settlements. Rivers made travel from village to village much easier by boat, than walking with heavy loads. These factors contributed to the expansion of trade and commerce along rivers such as the Nile, the Congo River, and the now dried-out rivers of the pre-historic Sahara. The fertile region of the great freshwater lakes of East- Central Africa and the Niger River Basin, were also areas where villages and very ancient settlements first began.

The establishment of small villages and settlements near strategic areas helped in the expansion of trade for many families. For example, those who had easy access to the rivers were not only able to use it for moving from one place to the other, but they were able to use it as a source of water, fish, drinking water and primarily as a source of irrigation where needed. In many ways, the river helped settlements on the banks grow and expand due its ability to be used as a highway and its other versatile uses.

Africans improved their trading practices soon after they begun building premanent settlements. The need to trade and exchange goods increased since there was a surplus of commodities due to the planting or raising and production of more than had been attempted previously. As the need to conduct more trade became of crucial importance, a level of sophistication came into being during the conduction of trade. New methods of exchange, new ways to set prices and better products were furnished.

Some people were not as good at hoarding and trading their surplus goods to others, therefore, they depended on a specific class of people to supply them with goods. The early Africans saw the need to create new products to sell to those who wanted them but were unable to gain access, or were engaged in other types of activity which took away much of their time. An example would have been those people who moved from place to place with their cattle, and who spent less of their time producing weapons, cloth, sandals and other goods. They would have had to depend on craftsmen and women who were more settled and had the time to produce what they wanted for the times spent moving their cattle or livestock to areas away from the village or settlement.

The steady flow of goods between various peoples and settlements occurred. Unilie the past when trade was broken down into trading between regions wuch as the forests, the savannah and other areas, settlements and villages became the main receipients of the practice of trade. This cycle of trade brought about the steady flow of goods and increased commercial activities throughout Africa and other parts of the world.

The evolution from small settlements to villages, the keeping of cattle nearer to settlements, the practice of horticulture then early agriculture and the use of rivers for travel and the movement of goods and products helped bring the lifestyle of hunting, garthering and the tending of livestock to a lower level of importance for a number of people. Settled life and early

41

agriculture became more important because the early Africans and humans in general were able to produce more goods in one area through farming, exchanging food crops for the products of the pastoralists and using excess products as a means of exchange.

The availability of food in plenty, cattle, livestock, water sources and other necessities essential to living without stress were easier to acquire. The population of the agriculturists increased while that of the hunter-garthers and pastoralists remained stagnant, or grew at a much slower rate. The families of the hunters and gartherers and those engaged in the tending of animals had to be kept small due to the constant mobility of their families and their hunting and herding parties.

The village dwellers preferred large families (and they still do today, which is good, for large families ensure survival), so that there would be a sufficient number of males to do the hunting, fishing, tending of flocks, clearing trees, and defending the settlement. Females were needed in large amounts for the raising of families, planting and tending crops and in some cases, handling the trading and selling. As the division of labor became more valuable to villages and families, Africans realized that large, well managed families not only contributed to the wealth of families, the also helped to ensure the survival of the future generations incase diseases cut the amount in families. Large families also helped to increase the wealth by increasing the families' ability to produce more. Thus, the earliest family businesses were the invention of the earliest African agriculturists.

The increase in the population of the taller, more robust agricultural Negroid Africans over the shorter Pygmoid and Kong-San Negroids helped the agriculturists dominate most of the continent, improve their culture and survive. The notion that too many people is bad for African or Black nations while not for others, such as those of Europe or East Asia, where overpopulation is a much bigger problem than in Africa, is a very biased notion based on racist attitudes. The idea that Africans should control their populations is one of the great tricks used against the Pan-African people, who are being systematically exterminated in Southern Sudan by Arabs and Arab wanna-bes and in Indonesia by the Malay invaders of these Islands.

The history of Africa will show that the more people there are to defend the nation, plant the crops, do the industrial work, and contribute to the economy, the more powerful and long-lasting the society will be. Why is it that nations such as England, France, Germany (where they are calling for an increase in the already 80,000,000 German population), Russia, Spain, Japan, Singapore (where incentives for the wealthy and middle class to produce more children was proposed about five years ago) and other wealthy and white nations not encouraged to control their own populations? These nations realize that having large populations give them the feeling of being looked upon as big, powerful and important.

The African population worldwide should be increased and no attempt should be made to decrease it. However, it should be well managed not by reductions in population, but by having Blacks settle lands that were stolen from Blacks such as Australia and other colonized lands where Blacks were the original and aboriginal owners. That of course would include much of the Southern U.S., all of North Africa, much of the Middle East and even areas around the Caspian Sea in Russia, South East Asia, South and Central America and other regions. Blacks should also spread out in places such as Botswana, Namibia and other areas.

The increase in the population of the early African farmers and agriculturists during the Mesolithic Age, contributed to a new way of life. Village life led to large families but it also opened the way for people to spend more time doing other things, such as making better tools and weapons (something that recent archeological evidence shows may have occurred about 75,000 to 100,000 years ago in Zaire), cooking utensils, pottery, nets, hooks for fishing, houses and clothing.

Africans spent their spare time on activities such as carving wood, ivory, bone and stone, and inventing useful things such as musical instruments. During the Mesolithic Age, the opportunity to develop better laws, religion, the arts, the sciences, mathematics and culture was taken and applied. That is a fact, for there is evidence which shows that as early as 17,000 B.C., advanced culture was developing in the Nile Corridor. By 20,000 B.C., Africans in the Sahara, which included wide expanses of water were building ships and boats for fishing and for traveling. The Ishongo had been using mathematics by 8,000 B.C. The discovery of the Ishongo Abacus used for keeping mathematical records was discovered. It was used to calculate the number of animals caught or trapped by the user. (J.A. Rogers, Africa's Gift to America).(5)

The improvement of customs which improved commerce, such as counting, calculating, bargaining and the importance of setting and keeping appointments, and using time and space, occurred during the movement to settled living. Laws and taboos were in many cases established before that period, however others were added and the ancient ones were changed due to the new environments which needed the laws to adapt. For example, whereas the pastoralists may have demanded smaller families due to their constant movements, being childless was looked upon as being unblessed.

## The Early Beginnings of Susu

One of the earliest forms of economic practice which grew out of storing food on a collective basis and having the right and opportunity to use what was stored in the collective pot was susu. It was also used as a method of holding goods so that more useful and valuable purchases would be made when necessary. The need to buy oxen to plough fields, or a canoe to make trips on the rivers may have required more than the usual commodities used in bartering such as some food crops, grain or clothing. The need to save or to form a collective pot or pots and to pool resources together was quite essential to the acquiring of more valuable merchandise.

Susu developed in West Africa as an economic system and was brought to the Americas by Africans during the slave trade (as is recorded, but Africans were in the Americas long before the slave trade and may have used susu during that period). The basic rule of susu is that people who contribute to a pot on a regular, fixed and even basis, must have access to the pot at a fixed, agreed upon period of time, for example, if there are five people, each would get all what is in the pot every five months, depending on his place on the list as first, second, third, ect...

If ten people each add $100.00 dollars to the pot every month, there will be $1,000.00 in the pot every month end. If a member of the pool needs $1000.00 and he or she is first on the list to receive the money, he or she will get it, but must continue to add $100.00 every month until the other nine people in the pool each receives money ten months ago, would have the opportunity to receive more.

In ancient times, long before the invention of money cattle and other commodities were used in susu. The use of cattle in the conducting of of trade and in the measurement of wealth is quite ancient. The value of cattle may have been realized about the time when they were first domesticated about 10,000 years or more ago. There were instances when a man wanted to purchase goods but did not have enough of his own commodities to exchange for what was of a higher value. He and his trusted friends or relatives form a pool and would combine their resources so that each person, including the one who wanted to purchase the goods would be able to use the collected resources at a specific time. He would continue to the pot of grain, food crops, tools, utencils or whatever he had, until it was his or her time to use what was collected. That would have occurred after all those before him had their turn and his turn had finally arrived.

Other examples would be the use of the susu pool for very valuable commodities. If a pool of ten men wanted to exchange ten cows for ten canoes, and non of them had enough to get the canoes, each would contribute a cow and would get what they needed. If one man wanted to start a fishing fleet of ten, then he along with ten others in the ten-man pool would add resources collectively each month, so that he and the others in the pool would get commodities worth the value of ten cows before closing the susu, or starting a new rate of collection.

# CHAPTER FIVE

# THE STRENGTHENING OF THE FAMILY STRUCTURE

The settling of villages along river routes, savannas, valleys and foothills, brought about the first village to village road networks. These villages were not simple settlements but larger clusters of villages, with more dwellings, better built houses and larger buildings. Early road networks which linked these large clusters of houses also developed. At first, they were mere foot tracks, but later they developed into important arteries which connected the various groups of settlements. These early roads and foot tracks made it easier for people to trade with each other.

Unlike in the past, when whole families were moved from one area to the other, in search for food or to graze their livestock, the villagers returned to their homes after performing their tasks. They had no need to migrate with their herds due to the exhaustion of the grass. In some cases, the use of the land was acquired on a rotation system, whereby, it was left unfarmed for a few years while bush grew without hindrance. After a few years, the land was cleared, bush burned and the ashes used to fertilize the soil. That same land was sometimes for grazing, particularly if the people using it preferred to have their animals use it, instead of letting it overgrow with bush. In these cases, after the animals had exhausted the thick grass, the land would be used for farming. Due to the neccessity to remain in one place, the family structure became stronger than before.

Many aspects of African life developed because of inter communal and intervillage connections. These connections grew out of the need to trade and barter goods, and the need to create family ties and connections. Men found it better to take wives from villages and settlements far from their own, in order to have access to the other areas, as well as to prevent the possibility of marrying someone who could be related to them. This soon caused the coming together of villages and the develop ment of clans and large political and family units. The first steps towards nation-building began at that early stage. The bringing of women from other settlements or areas was also important since much of the agricultural work performed in early Africa, as is still the case today [particularly light work such as tending, planting, ect...] was done by women, while the men performed the heavy work such as felling trees, building dams and irrigation systems, heaving plowing, and so on.

Women may have been involved in agriculture the Mesolithic Age or since the very beginning of agriculture between 10,000 to 15,000 years ago. During this era, men were still very much engaged in agriculture, however, they also engaged in hunting, trading, fishing, partaking in war when necessary, doing construction and a variety of tasks. While they were occupied in these activities, some which were far from their home areas, the women remained in the homes in order to take care of the children and sometimes, older relatives. Their presence around the household and in areas where their gardens and plots were nearby, gave them the opportunity to plant, tend and harvest crops. These tasks were sometimes done while these women had small children. It is not impossible to imagine 59 that about 10,000 years ago, an African woman was out tending her family plot or field, while her baby was wrapped on her back.

While it was the duty of the man to cut the trees, clear the bushes, and plough the field to prepare it for planting, it was the woman's task to plant the seedlings, then the crops and help them grow and prosper. It is easy to see how the prehistoric African woman with her maternal skills already being applied to her children, would apply such skills to the crops and plants of the family plot. Such valuable roles played by the ancient [and modern] African woman to the economy of her household added to her value in the eyes of the family she originally came from, as well as the one she married into.

The removal of the woman or girl from her family due to marriage in another family was a loss to the girl's family, therefore, the man had to make a compensation to the family or some sort of dowry, for the loss of their daughter. Yet, this removal was also part of the accepted practice of preventing the marriage of families who are related by blood. Cheikh Antah Diop examines this custom in Civilization or Barbarism; An Authentic Anthropology [1991, pp. 116-117].

'The passage from clan to monolingual tribe, i.e., to ethnic group, to nationality, is a consequence of clan exogamy; bio-logical and material reasons, the nature of which is still being discussed by specialists, very early led archaic society to practice the prohibition of incest, which marked the starting point of civilization. Clan endogamy being prohibited, several neigh-boring clans contracted marriage ties that with time became bonds of kinship by alliance. All these clans that occupied the same territory ended up speaking the same language even if their idioms were originally different. The number of clans that can garther together to form a more or less powerful tribe does not follow any rule and depends , at the most, on the fertility and extent of the land occupied by the group. Thus was born nationality. The individual would bear the clanic name, especially after detribalization. (1)

Children born to families were cherished and kept. The practice of infanticide and the discarding of 'unwanted' children [a practice that many of today's misguided and tricked believe is a matter of one individual's right, while contributing to the extermination of Black people], was not tolerated, neither was the lifestyle hospitable to the mentality that children were a burden. In fact, lots of children was regarded as a blessing. The practice and acceptability of infanticide as normal and the fanatical hatred for children and the aged was more common among the wandering nomads and barbarians of later history [6,000 B.C. to 400 A.D.], who ravaged Eurasia and were stopped in Africa, when the Hyksos [who were also among this group], were expelled from Black Egypt. These nomads, wandering tribes and barbarians regarded lots of children, the weak and (2) aged to be a burden and a hinderance, [Diop, 1991, p.p.112-113].

These barbarians begun with the Cimmurians and ended with the Germanic Goths, Vandals, and so on.

Prehistoric African families made homes for all children, including those who were not related to them by blood. No extra children were regarded as a burden, but as a source of wealth and extra help in societies where agriculture was becoming king. Children helped the ancient agriculturists to maintain, tend and help contribute to the labor force needed to build family industries such as farming, animal husbandry, keeping livestock, fishing and trading. Large families had the amount of personnel needed to expand the various types of economies they were engaged in. Most importantly, Africans put much value on human life and existence, therefore, the abandoning of children, abortion or methods of disposing of children was avoided.

Families who could not support themselves or their children were helped by others or by the extended family or the economic safety network established by the village or family clan. Susu was one of these economic systems. Land was communal and owned by the whole village, tribe or extended family clan. Communal ownership of land may have developed due to the need to prevent destitution among members of the group and to make available a place where members of a tribe could grow crops for their families. This system helped to prevent destitution and poverty. As long as individuals were willing and able to work, there was a place to apply such work in the raising or crops, or the keeping of borrowed cattle or animals. Sharing was widespread among close families, just as trading between villages and settlements was common.

The general attitude of the ancient African agriculturists was one of liging in a peaceful and harmonious manner with themselves and their neighbors. That is not to say that Africans during the Mesolithic Age allowed aggression to go unchallenged. In fact, they were strong people who had invented numerous weapons and martial arts. There was a warrior mentality, yet, it was restricted to those who were specifically trained for the purpose of defense.

In general, the ancient Africans were quite peaceful and spent more of their time developing their economies, crafts, and

50

industries, rather than going on raids against their neighbors, as compared to the Indo-Europeans of later ages, and some historical Africans, particularly during the slave trade. Such civility on the part of the prehistoric Africans made the Africans vulnurable to invasions thousands of years later [particularly around 1700 B.C. with the Hyksos], when warrior types and wandering, barbaric nomads from Eurasia, the Arab Peninisula and Europe invaded the African continent.

In later years [since about 1700 B.C. with the battles against the invading Asiatics], Africans such as the Khemites [ancient Black Egyptians] and Kushites developed formidable armies which stopped, or crushed foreign invasions. The crushing defeat of the Arabs by Kalydo-sos during the mid-600's A.D. [Chancellor Williams, 1975], the defeat (3) of the Assyrians by Pianke [700's B.C.], and countless other examples should be in inspiration to those fighting to eliminate the last vestiges of alien occupation of the great Nubian and Kushite civilizations remnants who are today fighting for the return of their lands in Sudan today. They should take a lesson from the ancient ancestors, that a strong defense, offense and determination is neccessary in order to eliminate the last vestiges of alien occupation of what most of the world's Blacks regard as the Holy Lands, and the lands of the origins of humanity which begun as Black Africans, as well as the true cradle of all civilization.

### Religion and Science

The development of trade and commerce, the establishment of permanent settlements, and the turn to agriculture contributed to the further development of various social, cultural and scientific practices and discoveries. Among these practices were more organized forms of religious practice. These religious practices were connected to the worship of the sun and of nature. These mighty forces of the universe were not mere elements. Both nature, in the form of the rain, hurricane, earthquakes, life, and the rivers, and the sun's ability to create and brighten up the darkness, helped create the air of mystry that the ancient Africans held in regards to the sun and nature.

They regarded the sun to be the ultimate manifestation and representative of what was a much greater universal power. To the ancient Africans, the sun was not only the representative of a supreme being, it was to them the proof that such force existed and that the sun was merely a representative of that force. They regarded the sun as the father whose rays penetrated the earth mother and brought forth life unto the earth. Anything that resulted because of the sun's power and the nourishment of the earth was considered sacred or living, whether they were small plants, large trees, animals, rocks, forces of nature, or carved represen tations of Gods. Everything had a force within it.

One of the most significant observations made by the prehistoric Africans was that light rays and heat coming from the sun had a direct on them. It kept their skins dark or black and helped protect them from being scorched or harmed by its deadly rays. Out of this reality, the belief that they were the 'Chosen' or protected among all people spread among them. Perhaps these Africans who encountered the first prototype of the Caucasian race of southern Europe also noticed that they were unable to resist the scorching sun, as the Africans were. In fact, this observation continued into Khemite-Kushite history, down to the present day. Thus from the very early beginnings of Nile Valley civilization as well as overall African civilization in general the phrases, 'Chosen People of the Sun,' 'Men of Men,' 'autochonous,' 'Original People,' have been used by Africans and others to describe Black Africans. Even in nations far from Africa, such as China, Japan, India, the Phillipines, Mexico, parts of Europe and parts of the Americas as well as Australia, the Blacks have always been regarded as the aboriginal peoples, even when the population has decreased or has unfortunately been absorbed into the invading population.

The early form of sun and nature worship developed as the malenias went by. These became the religion of the Khemites, Kushites, Puntites and many ancient African civilizations as well as those influenced by Africans such as the Olmecs of Ancient Mexico, the Black Xia and Shang Dynasties of Ancient China and a number of others. Some of this sun and nature worship exists today in West Africa, South America, the Caribbean, the United States, Africa and a number of other places. The emphasis today is primarily on ancestor worship, shamanism, and forms of metaphysic spiritualism such as Voodoo, Shango, Macumba and others. In these religions, the emphasis of the worshippers has always been immediate results and the application of mental sciences. The symbolic aspects have merely been added as props. Thus many people, particular Western influenced people, have been fooled into believing that these highly scientific religions are forms of witchcraft. The practicioners of African religions today may not worship the sun directly, however, candles may be used as a symbol of the sun.

Science and scientific principles developed out of the study of religion and religious rituals, sometimes mislabled, 'magic.' From the beginning of African history and culture, Africans realized that changes that could not be explained by mere spiritual forces occurred when particular forces and effects were combined to create a facinating result. For example, they noticed that their prolonged exposure to the sun kept their skins dark, and to them, that was a blessing directly from the sun and from God. Still, in the case of plants and the way in which they grew, or how fire was created, how stones were smoothed by rubbing them against each other, they realized that more than mere magic or devine intervention were at hand.

Through trial and error, and through observation, they kept in mind that 'magic' could be made by mixing certain elements and expecting results. Observations such as the above, created the interest in science. This interest had always been with the Africans as early as one million years ago, when fire was first discovered in Southern Africa. However, during the Mesolithic Era, a renaissance in science occurred which led to the great scientific accomplishments of ancient Kush and Khem.

The spread of more organized religious concepts spread quickly due to the networks of trade that became improved due to the establishment of villages and other clusters of settlements. Ideas on the nature of humans, the source of life and the heavenly bodies, the worship of ancestors and other religious concepts travelled with traders from one region to the next. This process was intensified during the periods of religious revivalism from 4,000 B.C. to the Middle Ages.

The earliest form of religious practice not dealing with natural phenomena or the worship of the sun was the worship of ancestors. It seemed logical that becuse of the foundness of people for their family [in most cases], those elderly ones who passed on or who had a positive effect on the living, would have been adored, remembered and even worshipped.

Those who first studied the stars, sun and other natural pheno- mena contributed to the establishment of a body of priests and shamans. These men and women regarded religion and science [magic] to be inseparable. They experimented, studied and helped create formulas and scientific concepts. They believed that scientific results received from expirments, or from natural phenomena such as lightening, was proof of the existence of a supreme being who was in control of all that occurred and existed.

In retrospect, although religion had always been part of the conciousness of prehistoric Africans long before the Upper Paleolithic Era [40,000 B.C.], the ability to remain in one place due to agriculture, and to spend more time observing, helped to improve and develop new religious concepts during the Mesolithic age. In the case of science, it can be said that the Homo erectus, or whoever existed in Southern Africa about 1,000,000 years ago, contributed to the greatest scientific discovery ever made, he or she invented the making of fire.

This discovery contributed to the migrations of Africans to Europe, Asia and the Americas at a time in history when the rest of the world was not inhabited by other races, or the mutated offspring of the original Black Homo sapien who existed from about 150,000 years B.C. Had fire not become part of the discoveries of the very first humanoid Africans, they may have not survived in Europe when the Homo Erectus, an early species of the humnanoid groups migrated from Africa to the rest of the world about 800,000 to 1,000,000 years ago. Finally, the combination of fire in many of the religious practices of ancient and modern times would not have occurred.

# The Beginning of Organized Industry

The growth of villages into larger areas of settlement, more productive economic units and areas of arts and crafts production occurred between 15,000 B.C. to about 6,000 B.C. Of course, recent discoveries [such as the discovery of sophisticated tools of stone and bone in Congo, formerly Zaire, near Ishongo] show that there was a rapid development as early as 100,000 years ago, in Central Africa. Unlike in the past when the primary occupations were made up of agriculturists, hunter-gartherers, a few keepers of livestock and fisher-folk, the period mentioned, which included the Mesolithic Age, was a period of rapid change and technological development. Africans created systems of specialized craftsmanship where products were made for the use of the community as well as for trading.

The manufacturing of tools, clothing, leather products, sandals, weapons of stone and flint, jewelry and personal decorations, combs, spear heads, needles and many other necessities expanded as the demand for these products increased. Most of the craftsmen and women were engaged in specialized production of goods and had little time to make products they were not proficient in producing. The goods and services of others was therefore greatly needed. Thus, the man who made san- dals but did not produce cloth, went to the producer of cloth to get his supplies so that his wife, or someone specialized in the making of cloth would produce his garments.

Africans began to organize themselves into groups which specialized in particular types of industries, in order to serve the needs of the many who were creating other types of products. These early groups evolved into the African trade guilds which became one of the core systems of African vocational education and training. The guilds functioned as the suppliers of manufactured products, as well as the keepers of trade secrets, methods of creation, control of the value and price of products, the training of apprenticeships and all functions which dealt with trade, commerce and manufacturering.

One of the primary functions and objectives of the guilds was making sure that craftsmen were well trained and goods were of the highest quality. Such early interest in quality of craftsman and production, contributed to the importance and the power of the guilds. Organized commerce emerged out of the long years of interaction between people who belonged to guilds and both producers and consumers of goods. Due to their great value, the guild system became numerous in some areas but not in others. They also became the primary system of clubs, or other social organizations.

Most industries and crafts or trades had guilds which looked after the interests of their members. Among the type of guilds which existed were guilds for canoe and boat builders, weavers, stone carvers tool makers, fishermen and many others. These early organizations helped make the African continent and its people the world's most organized traders, merchants and business people at a very early age. By the early Mesolithic age, [15,000 to 10,000 B.C., the foundations for the more organized trading practices of the Khemites [Egyptians], Kushites [Sudan], Mesopotamia, Punt-Negau [Somalia to South Africa], and a number of ancient African civilizations and cultures were well established in the Nile Corridor and the Sahara.

Some of the early, unwritten rules concerning the proper management of trade goods, surplus and resources may have been organized in a manner similar to the way they are managed today among villagers throughout Africa;

[1] Families made sure that members contributed to the village grain silo or storage bins.

[2] Family members and their contributions helped keep the village and family groups strong.

[3] Goods were to be manufactured with the highest quality. craftsmen and women regarded their products to be a reflection of their own character and their inner being.

[4]    Customers were to be found among the trustworthy, with whom trade could be carried out. All necessary steps were to be taken to keep them satisfied.

[5] Susu was practiced by putting together resources, labor and time, to build homes, acquire cattle or help those who needed assistance to make their farms productive.

The philosophy which drove the early traders included the principle that markets had to be established or found in all possible regions. With the movement in watercraft and boats as early as about 60,000 B.C., [when the Australian Aboriginals are said to have sailed over to Australia from South East Asia in boats, rather than crossing a landbridge by foot], the desire to gain goods and commercial partners became more of a reality. Boats, porters, draft animals and other means of transportation moved goods to a wide range of territory. Goods were transported by reed boat, log raft or canoe both downriver [northward] and up river [southward] along the Nile. Some crossed the Mediterranean Sea to Southern Europe and South-west Asia. This analysis can be made because there is no doubt, that the tall, Negritic Black who lived in the then fertile Sahara and the area which now includes Egypt, Sudan, Ethiopia, West Africa, and parts of East Africa, was more concentrated in these areas and began advanced cultures there before they migrated to all parts of the world.

In retrospect, the strengthening of family ties, the expansion of villages and the improvement of trade practices all contributed to the improvement of the lives of the prehistoric Africans. Due to this stability, religion, science and other cultural activities improved. Most importantly, because of the change from pastoral activities to sedentary living and industries connected to agriculture, the first concepts of organized labor and education were put into use in the form of trade guilds.

# CHAPTER SIX

# THE PRE-SOLAR CALENDAR AGE: 15000 B.C. TO 4241 B.C.

The official date given for the first time the Khemite [Egyptian] solar calendar was used is 4241 B.C. [James Breasted, 1909].(1) Between 10,000 B.C. to 4241 B.C., many significant changes took place. Among these developments was the early beginnings of classical African civilizations particularly Nubia-Kush [about 8,000 years B.C.], the Black aquatic civilizaions of the Sahara [10,000 B.C. to about 5,000 B.C., UNESCO has done some important work on them, but much is left to be done], Egypt [5,000 B.C.], Punt [5,000 B.C.], West Africa's proto civilization from which the Nok Culture was a continuation [3,000 B.C.], and others spread out in South Arabia, Mesopotamia, India and parts of the Far East and the Americas. The continued of the material aspects of African civilization improved at a level greater than ever before [as far as archeological findings indicate at present].

During the 10,000 year period between 15,000 to 4241 B.C., the western part of the Sahara experienced a wet phase which contributed to the continuous growth of vegetation. The eastern part of the Sahara may have experienced the same type of climate during the period mentioned, furthermore, as already mentioned in previous chapters, the region included large lakes, rivers, a massive inland sea, and a drainage system. Trade and commerce was widespread throughout these areas. Towns, cities of stone and hardened mud brick, and villages were scattered over the region. There were important waterways, roads and highways on which people, animals, chariots and draft animals travelled from place to place. Goods flowed from various directions, into the southern part of the Sahara towards the Nile Valley, and from the south towards the north.

Many aspects of civilization found in ancient Egypt, such as mumification, naturalistic paintings, boatmaking, building in stone, the making of weapons of metal, and improvements in the quality of plastic arts were first began in the Sahara. This period of cultural, economic, and material improvements [15,000 B.C. to 4241 B.C.] ended due to the gradual change in climate brought about by the end of the Ice Age in Europe. The amount of rain necessary to support such a large region was becoming more and more insufficient. According to A. Abu Bakr, in General History of Africa [1981, p. 62], 'The decrease in rain caused the nomadic peoples of Saharan Africa to immigrate to the Nile Valley in search of a permanent water supply. The first actual settlement of the Nile Valley may thus have begun in early Neolithic times [about -7000].' (2)

Other historians and archeologists push the period of settlement in the Nile Valley to about as early as 17,000 B.C. According to C.A. Diop, 'The Paleolithic industry has been attested to in the Nile Valley. It therefore appears that this valley was necessarily populated solely by Blacks from the origin of humanity up to the appearance of the other races [20,000 to 15,000 years ago].'[Diop, 1981, p. 17].(3) Thus, there ppears to have been a wide overlap in the time periods between which the Sahara and the Nile Valley were major centers of culture.

The lives of the early agriculturists, pastoralists and occupiers of the Nile Valley and the Sahara may have been similar to the lives of many Africans who presently follow the pastoral and agricultural economies in the regions south of the Sahara today. Yet, current cultural habits may have developed long before the Neolithic Age [7,000 B.C.], and certainly about the period between the Mesolithic [10,000 and earlier] to the Neolithic [7000 years ago] Ages.

Apart from the cultural developments which occurred in the Sahara and the Nile Valley, one of the most important developments was the improvements made in agriculture from basic horticulture, using impliments such as the digging stick, to basic agriculture using the hoe and tilling the soil by hand, to more advanced agriculture where the plough and more advanced farming tools were used extensively. Farms were also better organized then before and a wider variety of crops were planted. New methods of irrigation developed as the water supply

60

became crucial to the maintainance of large fields and farms after 7,000 B.C.

The population of the Sahara and the Nile Corridor may have experienced a greater increase due to the improvements in the production of food. As the population increased, the inhabitants of both regions may have noticed that new methods of planting and harvesting were necessary in order to reduce the possibility of the land going to waste. More efficient methods of fertilizing as well as crop rotation were applied. Some of these methods of cultivation were used later on in Egypt and Nubia-Kush [Nubia-Kush as early as 8,000 B.C., Egypt as early as 5,000 B.C. by the Negroid Badarian Culture], originated in the Sahara and based on the fact that UNESCO scientists now agree that there was an African 'aquatic civilization,' which existed between 20,000 B.C. to about 10,000 B.C. and as recently as 5,000 B.C., when the Sahara begun to dry up.

J. Yoyotte [1991, p. 79] describes Egypt's ability to grow productive crops as being fueled by, 'A system of flood basins, which controlled and distributed the flood water and silt inside earth embankments, endured until the modern triumph of year-round irrigation: there is evidence that it existed as early as the Middle Kingdom, and in all probability it had taken shape even earlier.'(4) These same conditions and types of environments could have been created in the Sahara before it dried up. Such would have been an environment which would have contributed to the growth and development of cultures and the improvement in life.

The Sahara and for that matter most of Africa entered a renaissance which may have begun before the Neolithic age. In fact, if we are to consider the making of more advanced stone and bone tools in Congo [formerly Zaire found by scientists in April, 1995] to be the beginning of a renaissance, and the very first, then that renaissance begun about 100,000 years ago. However, the period under discussion [10,000 B.C., to about 5,000 B.C., experienced a significant improvement in the material culture of the region.

There was a marked improvement in the creation of everyday necessities such as tools. These were polished to a smooth finish compared to the crude manner they had been made in ages past. Metals such as copper, tin, iron ore, and small amounts of precious metals may have been used for weapons and ornaments long before the actual Age of Metals began.

Pottery making developed in places where grasses for basket making were unavailable or in short supply. Clay and mud were found to serve a function similar to woven baskets, therefore the use of clay became common in the making of utencils and pottery. Materials such as stone, alabaster and glass wereused in the making of pottery, in the ancient cultures of the Sahara before the great migrations began.

The expansion of settlements in the Sahara, the Nile Valley, West Africa, East and Central Africa, and Southern Africa also contributed to the building of better houses and small to medium sized towns. By about 10,000 B.C. to 4241 B.C., improvements in the style, size and materials used in the construction of homes and dwellings improved. In a few years [centuries], after the peak of the Megalithic revolution in the Sahara, some of the greatest monuments ever built were constructed in Nubia-Kush and Egypt. The first Khemite architect know to have taken the building in stone to a higher level [according to what is now known, although there may have been great architects as early as 10,000 B.C. or earlier], was Imhotep who was not only an architect but a physician, administrator, author and priest. He lived during the Third Dynasty about 2686 to2613 B.C. The ability to build massive monuments out of evenly cut stone was began by Imhotep, a pure African who also designed the Step Pyramid for Pharaoh Zoser, according to Runoko Rashidi in the book Egypt Revisited, [1989, p. 106; ed. Ivan Van Sertima].(5)

One of the most important cultural contributions which originated from the prehistoric African settlements of the Sahara was the production of cotton and the making of cloth. Henri Lhote's observation of drawings done in prehistoric times during his exploration of Tassili in the Sahara, included what was the figure of a human wearing cotton clothing. This painting was among many found at Tassilli whose origins extend into the prehistoric period, when the sahara was still fertile and had lakes, rivers and forests. Michael Bradley points out in his book, The

Black Discovery of America, (1981, p.137), that, "Old world cotton cultivation was originally in the Sahara, and refugees from increasing drought brought knowledge of cotton cultivation with them to their adopted havens." Thus, the reasons mentioned by Bradley for the spread of cotton out of the Sahara, may have been the same reasons why it may have found its way to the Nile Corridor and as far away as the Southern States of the U.S., where Ivan Van Sertima states in his book, They Came Before Columbus (Random House, 1976). (6)

Weaving may have also developed in the Sahara before the Africans took their techniques to the Nile Corridor (Nubia-Kush, then Egypt, respectively). As already stated, Henry Lhote realized through his work at Tassili, that ancient Africans who resided in the Sahara during the Mesolithic age may have worn cotton cloth as clothing. The importance of cotton in the making of cloth may have been brought about due to the scarcity of animals with skins suitable for clothing in the Sahara, the refusal of herders and pastoralists to kill their animals and use the skins for clothing, or the inability to meet the demand.

## The Improvement in Political Organization

Political organization improved during the period under study (10,000 B.C. to 4241 B.C.). Hereditary chiefs were common and were usually descendents of the first settlers of a region, according to Chancellor Williams, in his book, Destruction of Black Civilization: Great Issues of a Race, From 4500 B.C. to 2000. The eldest patriach was (7) usually chosen as the leader based on his ability. They led villages, towns and were highly regarded within their communities.

Each such organization became more efficient than the systems used in the past, such as those better suited for the nomadic and pastoralists lifestyles. The merging of religious and political ideas became part of the usual way of discussing whatever issues were of importance, to those who listened. Rituals and systems of belief were still based on the worship of the sun, nature, a supreme being and the ancestors. The priestly class developed and became as important as the hereditary chiefs, although in many cases the priests and chiefs were the same.

The expansion of small villages into towns occurred as villages became trade centers and various types of people from areas far and wide made these trading places more important. Traders from all parts of the region, and from all regions converged on these early centers all over the Sahara and the rest of Africa by boat, canoe, on foot, by draft animals and possibly even horses. The need to travel to far-away places to trade in rare goods increased. Trade networks as a result became crucial and essential to the growth of villages, towns and cities which played a direct role as stopovers on the way to the source of the goods, or as the actual source of the goods and merchandise being sought.

The movement of people from their home areas of origin to other areas helped create a feeling of being and belonging to a greater world. The four core areas of African civilization became urbanized as their populations increased. These four areas included, the Sahara (which is still being studied), the Nile Corridor [(Nubia-Kush, Khemet (Egypt)] the Niger Basin, and Congo-Ishongo area, the original centers of Nile Valley civilization and of world culture in general. These four areas developed similar types of settled living, such as large clusters of villages built of mud, sticks and straw in the wetter regions of Central Africa, and of stone, mud brick and firehardened mudbrick in the dryer parts of the Nile Corridor and West Africa. Wood was used where there were plenty of trees, particularly in the Upper Nile, while brick and stone became widespread in parts of the Sahara, West Africa and the Nile Corridor, by 5000 B.C.

# CHAPTER SEVEN

# THE SAHARA

The earliest form of trade to develop in the Sahara before it dried up and became desert about 3,000 B.C., was bartering or the exchanging of one product for the other of comparable value. The earliest inhabitants of the Sahara were Black Negroid hunter-gartherers similar in physic to the Bushman and tall robust Negroid type now found throughout Africa, the Americas, South Asia, Europe, Melanesia and the South Pacific, as well as Europe and Australia. Archeologists have found their remains in very ancient deposits in all these lands and regions. They lived from as far north as Siberia and far south as Tasmania and possibly New Zeland. From east to west, they were and are still found from the Americas in the West to Hawaii in the east. Thus, at one time, Blacks occupied the entire planet, and they were the only people in existence in the Homo sapien form until about 30,000 to 20,000 years ago, when the Cromagnon, the prototype for the white race came into being due to mutation suffered by the Black Grimaldi Man, who changed to today's Europoid, in order to adapt to the cold climate of Europe.

With the development of pastoralism and agriculture, trade in agricultural as well as pastoralist goods grew steadily, as both types of industries increased. Goods were manufactured specifically for export. Dried meat, animal skins, birds, precious stones were among the materials exported. Manufactured goods (handicrafts) included leather products, stone, bone and flint knives, weapons and tools, pottery and jewelry. Trade between Africa, South West Asia and Southern Europe, all regions with heavy Black populations during the period, was constant. During that period (15,000 B.C. to 4241 B.C.), there was no massive invasion by Asiatics and Europeans in Northern Africa, nor in parts of Southern Europe and S.W. Asia, although a few may have trickled into these areas and were not an immediate threat to the Black who lived there.

Blacks inabited large parts of Europe, such as the Basque region of Spain. They were not only the original inhabitants of Southern Europe, the Far East, South East Asia, Australia, S.W. Asia, the Medi terranean and even Siberia, some anthropologists point to the habitation of the Americas more than 20,000 years ago. Frank C. Hibben describes these ancient Blacks and their range of occupation:

"During the last of the Pleistocene period, there were several distinct kinds of people in eastern Asia. Two of these were the Asiatic Negro and the Asiatic Negrito or Pygmy. Some of the indigenous population of the Philippine Islands were dark-pigmented people of very short stature. Certain tribes of the Philippine Islands today exhibit these same characteristics in face, head, and body. They are very similar to the Pygmies of Central Africa and may be related to them. Similarly, in southern and southeastern Asia, there lived in ancient times, dark-pigmented Negroids. Some of these Asiatic Negroes were the original inhabitants of India and South east Asia. Some of the very earliest of these dark-skinned Asiatics made their way across the ocean straits to Australia.

The Australian Aborigines are often called "blacks," by modern Australians of European descent. The Australian blacks have beetle-brows, low, broad noses, generally Negroid faces, and their pigmentation is Negro. The present population of New Guinea is also of Negroid strain. New Guinea and the islands surrounding it are often called, "Melanesia," because of the dark-pigmented inhabitants."(1)

We know that Asiatic Negroes and Negritoes moved into these areas a very long time ago. There is also evidence that some of them moved northward, along the coast of East Asia. Some anthropologists believe that Asiatic Negroes (Blacks) or Asiatic Pygmies may have been the original inhabitants of North

America," (F.C. Hibben, 1945, p. 172, Thomas Y. Crowell Company, New York).(1)

The economies of these ancient Blacks who spread to every continent suitable for habitation, changed slightly. Many remained hunter garthers, while others changed to agriculture and settling down. Those who had been agriculturists and horticulturists in the Sahara, continued these forms of industry in the areas they settled, such as the South Pacific, Melanesia and Asia.

James Wellard brings attention to the type of culture and people who inhabited the Sahara before 4241 B.C.

"The Sahara was one of the well populated areas of the prehistoric world, as it has become the least populated within historicaltimes. It seems to have been inhabited, moreover by a race of men (Black people to the exact, according to Wayne Chandler, African Presence in Early Asia, ed. I.Van Sertima, 1995, pp. 376-377), whose domain extended from South Africa, for the rock paintings found in Spain, Eastern Spain, the Sahara Desert, and South Africa itself have striking similarities almost as though they belong to the same school. Thus, they all depict long-horned cattle in a similar style," (Wellard, The Great Sahara). (2)

The prehistoric Sahara was one of the regions where the Black African race developed culturally. It may become an archeologists paradise for that is where the ancient cities, towns, roads, palaces, castles, rivers, lakes, grave sites and possible ancient technologies that are part of the legends of many ancient and current African peoples may have begun. It should be no surprise if civilizations identical to that of ancient Egypt, Mesopotamia, ancient India or even Black Olmec Mexico, are buried beneath thousands of tons of sands which cover much of the Sahara. In fact, the ancient city of Kumbi Saleh of ancient Ghana, as well as many ancient cities and towns of ancient Nubia were covered or remain covered by desert sand today. We still are not certain about the history of human civilization before the Great Flood, yet we know that great civilizations existed, based on biblical information, particularly in Genesis; Chapter 6, verses 3-7. (3)

The similarities between cave paintings and other types of paintings and statuettes of Negroid peoples such as the Kong-San and other Blacks who lived in Europe before the white race appeared, are among the very significant pieces of information which points to the settlement of Blacks throughout Europe during the prehistoric era. This reality may be discomforting to the element in present-day Europe, who want to expell Africans from the continent. The fact is, these people are the secondary settlers of Europe, furthermore, many migrated from Central Asia, the Caucasius and Eastern Eurasia, while Western and Southern Europe were the homelands of Blacks, up to 3500 B.C.

Wellard observes that the region of Tassilinajjer has become a desolate place, where a few Tuareg tribesmen and their families inhabit. Long ago however, the place was fertile, there were many animal and they were hunted by the people who inhabited the area, as the large amount of cave drawings and paintings clearly show. The region was able to support life and was similar in its plant and animal life to the forrest and savannah lands of Central Africa and other parts of the continent to the south. According to wellard, the ancient inhabitants of the Sahara "hunted elephants, hippopotami, giraffes, buffalo, deer and wild cattle," (James Wellard, The Great Sahara). (4)

The ability to support such a varied amount of life means that there had to have had lakes and rivers in the area which are no longer in existence. This drying caused the drying of the region which was first experienced by the hunters who used lances with stone tips and throwing sticks (such as the boomerang) as their primary weapons. The first animals to leave were the elephants who exhausted their major source of food, the larger trees and plants.

After 3,500 B.C. or after the era called, "The Period of the Hunters," pastoralists took over the area where grass was plentiful. This is noticed in drawings which show cattle who appear quite healthy and produced milk. After 2,000 B.C., the dog, horse and wheel becomes more widespread in the Sahara and a number of nomadic peoples roamed over the vast region.

And so, the Sahara was like the Nile region, one of the original regions where African culture and civilization developed and florished. The other region which may have been even more ancient than the Sahara may have been Central Africa in the area near Ishongo, in the Congo, near the Great Lakes Region. The Nile Corridor, particularly Sudan was the original home of the invention of agriculture. The oldest evidence of planted and harvested grains was found there. West Africa was another original region of African culture. There, agriculture and a culture complex which influenced American culture earlier than 4,000 B.C., (the date given for the age of a Saharan cotton found in the Americas), related to the Mende-Mandinka culture of West Africa existed. In fact, the Mende culture and language goes back to 10,000 B.C. Most importantly, the blood group b, found among West Africans is predominant among the Native Americans of a region from Mexico to South America, where Black Native Americans such as the Ouachita, Yamassee (Guale), Garifuna (Black Carib), Black Californian and others existed since pre historic times. Current evidence show a predominance of blood type b among the Indians in the regions mentioned. Scientists point to a very ancient migration from Africa from across the Atlantic and the Pacific as early as 30,000 years ago.

The Sahara began turning to desert between 3,000 to 2,000 B.C. due to changes in the weather and climate Many of the inhabitants who existed there continued a series of migrations which may have begun as early as 20,000 to 30,000 B.C. Between 4,000 to 3,000 B.C. waves of migrants from the Sahara settled into parts of West Africa, and brought with them remnants of the prehistoric Black civilizations and cultres which originated in the Sahara. Thus, cultures such as the Nok culture which produced magnificent works of stone, terracotta, bronze and gold, were part of a widespread civilization which included parts of the southern Sahara and West Africa.

# CHAPTER EIGHT

# THE SUDAN REGION AND NILE VALLEY CORRIDOR

Between 15,000 B.C. to 4241 B.C., there was little distinction between the Sahara, the Sudan Region and the Nile Corridor compared to the rest of Africa. These areas resembled each other in that the vast deserts had not engulfed much of the region. The culture that became Khemet (Egypt) was spread from the Congo Basin to Kenya and the Ethiopian Highlands in the east, and from Liberia to Morocco in the west, from Morocco to Egypt along the northern coast of Africa, and from Egypt down to the Great Lakes region of Kenya, then to Somalia. This vast region of which the Sahara desert was to become part of, was the major cultural area of the Black Negroid African type who consist of the vast majority of the continent's people today, and who are related genetically and physically to the Tribals and Black Dalits of India, as well as the Blacks of Papua-New Guinea, Melanesia, the South Pacific, and parts of East Asia. In the area of Africa underscored, the languages culture and people of the rest of Africa first began to create and establish Homo sapien cultures, unlike the Homo Erectus, Old Stone Age cultures which existed as early as one million years ago in South Africa, Kenya and the Ethiopian Highlands.

The dominant language in the northern half of Africa was not the so-called Afro-Asiatic languages since Asiatics did not exist as a dominant cultural and language group in Northern Africa before 3,100 B.C., neither did they dominate any part of Africa before that period. The major language of the Sahara may have been the Niger-Congo, Nilo Saharan and Chadic languages, with the Niger-Congo being the most widely spoken. The fact that the Mende languages existed in parts of the Sahara and West Africa about 9,000 years ago is evidence of this Niger-Congo's language in the Sahara and not elsewhere.

The disasterous mixing of the races which completely wiped much of the pure Negritic African population from parts of North Africa and northern Egypt since the time of the Greek invasion (300's B.C., with the Ptolomies), had not occurred in the Sahara (and although that population has some mixed Berbers, Arabs and others, the majority population in the Sahara today is still Black African). Thus, the change of language from the African Mende, Nilo-Saharan and Chadic which still exist in the Sahara among the Blacks, seems to have come about with the invasions of North Africa by the Arabs and Berbers whose languages were introduced to the region and is spoken by their own people as well as the original Black inhabitants. The so-called Afro-Asiatic languages such as Berber and Arabic became widespread during the period of the 700's A.D. and afterwards. Many Africans also left the Sahara with their languages which they carried to parts of East, West and Central Africa. Goran Burenhult examines some of these languages in his book, Traditional Peoples of Today (1994, pp. 24-25; 'Nilo-Saharan Languages').(1)

It seems however, that the languages spoken by the Asiatic and Semites from South West Asia, may have originally been languages spoken by Black Africans and may have originated among the original Blacks of South West Asia who migrated out of Africa in Paleolithic times and afterwards. It is highly possible that since there are aboriginal Blacks in South West Asia today, as there has always been, and since they once dominated the area both in numbers and culturally, then their languages may have remained in the area. Thus, the so-called Afro-Asiatic languages may well have been African from the very beginning, with a later sprinkling of words from the Caucasian barbarians who invaded parts of Mesopotamia, Arabia, and the Middle East between 3,000 B.C. to 1000 B.C.

## The Sudan Region

The vast area called 'The Sudan' is not merely the nation of Sudan, but an enormous savannah and grassland area, just south of the Sahara Desert. The word 'Sudan' is Arabic and means,

'The Black Lands,' and refers to the vast number of Black Africans who lived in the region before the Arab invaders began ravaging the region and enslaving its population. The Sudan begins on the Atlantic shores and ends at the foothills of the Ethiopian Highlands, from a western to eastern route. This massive area was covered with vegetation during the period of 15,000 B.C. to 4241 B.C., yet it was one of the most traveled areas and consisted of vast networks of roads and foot trails, as well as wagon and chariot trails, which linked up a vast trade network of trade between the eastern parts of Africa with the western areas, and the north with the southern parts.

The Sudan region was at the crossroads of trade between these areas already mentioned. A wide variety of goods moved throughout this territory. Goods such as leapord skins and that of other animals, ivory, various types of plants, live animals, copper and many of the goods that had been traded earlier on in history, continued to move from one area to the other.

Before the Sudan was to become a region of high civilization, much of the area from Mauritania and Western Africa on the Atlantic coast, to the Ethiopian foothills, also contained rich, fertile grasslands where agriculturists and pastoralists allowed their farms, livestock and settlements to take root.

## The Nile Valley And Corridor

The Nile Valley and Nile Corridor consists of the lake region, where the Nile begins in East-Central Africa, stretching northward all the way to the Mediterranean Sea. Advanced civilization in this area begun between 15,000 B.C. and 8,000 B.C., specifically in Nubia, or as it was called, Ta-Seti, according to new information and archeological evidence, as well as some archeologists who suspect that Nubia was in existence thousands of years before Egypt, and gave Egypt its civilization, rather than the other way around.

Between 15,000 B.C. to 4,000 B.C., the entire Nile region had established itself as the original center of advanced civilization on earth. They built bigger temples, their cultural habits were more advanced, they charted the stars, invented writing, built cities of stone and baked clay bricks, and refined all aspects of civilization that had already been established thousands of years earlier. Thus, before the invention of the solar calendar and its re-establishment in 4241 B.C., the Nile Valley had undergone a great cultural change, as well as tremendous improvement in the material culture and artistic styles. These changes may have began before the Neolithic Age, which begun about 7,000 B.C. G. Hancock, makes reference to these cultural changes in his book, Fingerprint(2) of the Gods (1995, pp. 411-416)

In the year of 4241 B.C., the Khemites (ancient Black Egyptians) established the solar calendar in the great, sacred city of On (Heliopolis). From that date onward, dates were counted and the year was divided into twelve month intervals of thrity days each. Five days at the end of the twelf month was left for the worship of the major Gods. The introduction of the new calendar had a profound change in the Nile Valley the rest of Africa, and later on, the rest of the world. Today, this calendar is still in use.

The people of the Nile Valley improved on all the ancient arts and crafts, as well as on the social life, religion, sciences, mathematics, arts and crafts, manufacturing, and building. They also improved on weaving, pottery making, tool making, carving and so on. Buildings took on a new look, they were built bigger, more durable and with expert craftsmanship. Metals such as copper, tin and precious metals such as gold were experimented with and used extensively for onarments as well as armaments.

The worship of the sun and religion in general improved greatly. The belief in immortality spread and the methods of worship and rituals became more elaborate and complex. Ancestors were regarded as spiritual guides, as well as Gods. Massive temples, monuments and tombs were built in honor of them. The sun became the ultimate representative of the supreme God, and the belief that they the Khemites were the Chosen People of the Sun, because the sun had blessed them with its rays and made them black skinned, took on a higher level and much importance in their system of theology. In fact the Khemites (ancient Black Egyptians), called themselves 'Khmt' or 'The Black People,' they also called themselves, 'Hnmmmit,' or 'The Sunblessed,' in reference to their deep black skins.

The belief in immortality led to the building of massive monuments and tombs for the kings, who were considered to be Gods. Temples and other buildings were more important than the actual houses of the kings. Towns grew in size and were no longer small with narrow streets all over but were well planned, built with large streets lined with statues and trees. One of these early cities was No (called Thebes by the Greek invaders). It was the earliest center of Black culture, the most beautiful and largest city on earth before 4241 B.C. On was another of these great cities built before 4241 B.C. and it was in that city that the Sun God was worshipped to the highest degree and the solar calendar was first established. These prehistoric cities seems to have been built about the same period of time that Africans were on the last era of great civilization and building in the Sahara, before it turned to desert. George Hart, in his work Egyptian Myths brings attention to On (called Iunu by the ancient Egyptians).

Both No and On, as well as many other ancient cities along the Nile and in the Sahara and the Sudan, served as bases from which trade and trading activities were carried out between themselves and other parts of Africa and the world. It was the magnificence of these great cities that attracted Asiatic barbarians from SW Asia and other area, beginning about 3100 B.C., with the Asiatics, whom Narmer defeated. Ships were also undergoing a rapid change from straw to papyrus to longboats and ships made of sewn planks, and in some areas, dugouts made from trees. These ancient ships traded along the coast of the Mediterranean to the Greek Isles, the islands of Cyprus (called Khepra by the Egyptians), and Crete (called Keftiu by the ancient Egyptians). In the above areas they searched for or mined copper. The also traded with Canaan (Fenkhu), for cedar.

Khemite ships also went to present-day Somalia and further south for ebony, cedar, gold, ostrich feathers, perfumes, ivory and other products. During the period between 7,000 B.C. to

75

4241 B.C., Khemites were trading with nations that had not been as highly developed as they became later. Although the civilization of India's Black inhabitants, who originally came from Sudan and were of Black Cushitic stock, florished from as early as 6,000 B.C., it was later that they ventured into East Asia to introduce aspects of African civilization to China and the Far East.

Trade expeditions to the upper regions of the Nile, to the west and to other parts of Africa occurred. The Khemites became masters of the Mediterranean, the Ethiopian Sea (the Indian Ocean), and the Red Sea. They may have sailed across the Atlantic, and had sent expeditions to the North Atlantic, to Cronwall, England perhaps as early as the 3,000 years B.C. period. Evidence of early Khemitic and Phoenician travels and building in places like stonehenge in England, has made some wonder whether Africans had not visited the area in ancient times. Some of the rocks used to build stonehenge originated not in England or Europe, but in Africa and in many ways are similar to Mesolithic building techniques used by Africans in the Sahara as well as the Nile Corridor.

## The Invention of Writing

The development of writing had a profound effect on Khemitic life and appeared in Khem before 5,000 B.C., according to some historians and archeologists. The writing improved from simple pictures to more complex hieroglyphic ideograms during its development. Writing quickly propelled the Khemites into the first Information Age, which begun with the invention of writing by Africans more than seven thousand years ago. The art of writing contributed to many aspects of Khemetic life. Astronomy, letters, science, religion, philosophy, mathematics and so on. Due to the ability to write, and to record ideas on paper, improvements were made in the above mentioned areas. They were all given a major boost because of writing. Ideas and occurances became more important due to the ability to record complete ideas with characters and words. Still, some form of simple writing and numbers may have existed as early as 8,000 B.C., for the so-called Ishongo abacus, which was created about this period show knotches and strokes to represent numerals.

Hieroglyphics were the first form of organized writing known to have been first used by Africans, although, it is quite possible that there were forms of writing before the era of hieroglyphics. However, it was not the first form of communication used to represent human speech. The talking drums, or some form of drum may have been used to immitate speech thousands of years before hieroglyphics were invented. Writing in the form of symbols, the arrangement of beads in a particular manner and other methods of communication still used in Africa today, may have existed before the era of Hieroglyphic writing.

Writing may have overtaken drum signals in the sending of messages because records could be kept for later periods through the use of writing, whereas, they could not be kept in the same manner on the drums through tonal interpretations of human speech. There was no way to record them, and depended on the drummer knowing exactly what to transmit. Still, although some people may have known how to transmit messages on the drums due to having specialized training and skills, the hieroglyphic system of writing was not known by a large number of people. Issac Asimov states in his book, The Egyptians, "This system of writing was in the hands of the priests. Ordinary people could not read or write the complicated set of symbols any more than ordinary citizens today can make use of higher mathematics."

He continues, "Their system of writing remained very complicated, for instance with numerous symbols, some which represented individual words and some which represented parts words. The dwellers along the Nile, however, proud of their ancient civilization and tightly bound to their old ways did not accept an alphabet for nearly 2000 years."

Writing also developed in the south of Khem, where a twin civilization much older than Khemet (Egypt) was also undergoing a parallel development, yet at a higher level than that of Khem and whose development began at least three thousand years before Khem. This region was called Ethiopia by the

Greeks (not modern Ethiopia or Abbysinia, but the nation today called Sudan), Nubia by the Egyptians and Romans, and Kush by the Hebrews. According to Chancellor Williams in his book, The Destruction of Black Civilization, "The African system of writing was much better and quite different from that of the Khemetic (Egyptian), particularly during the latter part of their histories. It was simpler and had vowels, whereas the Egyptians had none. There were twenty-three characters or letters in the African alphabet-four vowel signs, sixteen consonants and two signs of the syllable. New concepts and new special words could be easily introduced by the old picture system. Clarity and easy reading was assured by measured space between words. There was developed a system of numerical symbols for mathe- matics. The African inscriptions on monuments and such records as those found in royal tombs are in a special category. General writing was done on tablets of wood or skins and prepared for that purpose. still, other artifacts were found such things as rocks, walls, vases and broken bits and pieces of earthenware."(3)

One of the greatest contributions of writing, after its use to events and important occurrances was its use in trade and keeping trade records, both verbal and numerical. It seems that before writing emerged, Africans had another system of record keeping such as etching notches on bone, stone or leather. The ancient abacus of Ishongo, Central Africa, is a typical example of a method of record keeping practiced about 8,000 years B.C. With the coming of writing, trade took on a new level of importance. Transactions were kept, dates, numerical amounts, values of goods, places where trade occurred, with whom trade was carried out and lots of other useful information related to trade and commerce.

Writing pushed Khemetic and Kushitic civilization further ahead, as the ability to use information beneficially became more important. Had the Khemites not invented writing or had they abandoned it, as some civilizations of the past have done, much less would have been known about them today. Having realized the value of writing, the Khemites and Kushites expressed it everywhere and not only on papyrus scrolls. They etched messages and events on their buildings, temples, obilisks and monuments. They spread the Khemetic script throughout the world, wherever they went or the script was copied from what they introduced and altered to suit the immitators. Although the Khemetic script began as a pictographic writing system, it later developed a phonetic style which made writing easier. However, they insisted on using the bulky hieroglyphic system as late as the Roman period, during the 200's to 300's A.D.

## Khemetic Religion And Trade

The religion of the Khemites was based on the worship of the sun God, Ra. Gods such as Amun, Montu, Osirus and others were also worshipped. The concept of one God was prominent among the Khemites, particularly during the reign of Akhenaton, who reformed the ancient religion. This concept was part of the ancient African religion, which recognized a supreme God, but whose power and influence was beyond the direct reach of mere mortals. Khemetic religion was the original religion from which the Jews, Christians and others patterned their own religions. Chancellor Williams states in Destruction of Black Civili zation (1976, Third World Press), that religion was among the most important aspects of Black life, and because of this they built many cities based on the worship of particular Gods and Goddesses. Cities such as No or Thebes, had the highest Gods and these cities were the most magnificient in their architecture, wealth and appearance.

To the ancient Africans, religion was a way of life, which they regarded as being real and the force behind their civilization. Out of religious practice grew the need for building on a grand scale in architecture, for the production of great art and the glorification of Gods.

The connection between religion and trade was present in a material sense. Although some of the material needed by the Khemites to carry out their religious ceremonies was available in Khem, others may have not been. Timber came from places such as Canaan or Phoenicia (called Fhenkhu by the Khemites), where the original Canaanites, who were as Black and Negritic as the

Egyptians as well as colonists from Egypt and who had a culture similar to the Egyptians lived. Ebony came from Kush, Punt or Central Africa. These woods were essential in the construction of temples, tombs, palaces, schools and houses. Asa G. Hilliard discusses these commodities in the book, Egypt Revisited (ed. by Ivan Van Sertima, pp. 215-218, 1993).(4)

The Khemites brought their religion to the places they visited on their trading ships. Lands such as Canaan or Phoenicia, where Blacks lived and followed a culture similar to that of Khem, are examples. In these kingdoms of old which now consist of Isreal, Syria, Jordan and Lebanon, many of the ancient Canaanite and Phoenician religious statuettes and naturalistic works of art portray Negroid features or Khemite religious symbols such as the sun disk, as well as clothing such as the Egyptian kilt and wigs.

The religion of the Khemites traveled with the Jews after they were freed from Khem (Egypt) by Pharaoh Merneptah between 1100 to 1200 B.C. The concept of one God and the practice of monophyism was first done on an advanced level by the Khemites and other Africans. This practice was later revived by Akhenaton. It was from the Khemites that the Jews learned this concept, furthermore during the time of the journey of the Jews to Canaan (later called Isreal, Lebanon, Syria, ect...), some of them returned to the old religion of Egyptian Gods. It was this practice which angered Moses, The Lawgiver.

As the Khemite ships sailed through the Mediterranean, they spread to other areas such as southern Spain and lands near the British Isles, including the British Isles, where they may have spread their religion or versions of it. There are some who have said that the Druid religion, though Celtic, may have some Egyptian influence. During the Khemite colonization of Greece before 2000 B.C. and long before there was anything called Greek civilization, the Khemites had already begun building, settling and developing the Greek peninsula and surrounding areas.

Other aspects of Khemetic culture were transferred from Egypt to Greece. This included aspects of language, architecture, art, religion and politics. Khemite Gods were given the features and names of the Greeks. In some cases, the Negroid Khemetic features were left intact. Gods such as Amun became Apolo, Isis became Athena and so on, as (5) Martin Bernal clearly points out in his book, Black Athena (1987). The concept of sun worship also left on Khemetic trading ships and in other ways. Some of this religion may have even entered the Americas, with the Black Olmec "Magicians," of ancient Mexico, during the Black Olmec Dynasties (1800 B.C. to 400 A.D.). The ancient Maya religion may have been influenced by the Black Olmecs. In fact, a Maya name for acolyte, "Ah Mens," sounds similar in sound to the name Amen or Amun, The Ram-Headed God.

## Trade Goods And Commerce

The Kushites may have been the very first mass manufacturers of goods on earth, followed by the Khemites. From what is now known about Nubian-Kushite civilization which flourished at least three thousand years before Egypt, then it is appropriate to say with confidence, that it was the Nubians (Kushites) who first began the mass production of goods and luxuries for sale to the rest of the world, including Egypt. In fact, an article carried in Time Magazine, September 15, 1997 written by Scott MacLeod, states, "French archeologists, for example have found exquisite ceramic figurines, bowls and funerary objects that date from at least 8,000 B.C. This strongly suggests to Hassan Hussein Idris, director of Sudan's National Board of Antiquities and Museums, that ancient Nubia might have been an important source of Egypt's civilization, as well as the other way around. (Time Magazine, September 15, 1997, p. 103).(6)

Although this chapter deals with Egypt, in ancient times, Egypt or Khemet, as the original Black inhabitants called their country, was part of the greater Nubian-Kushite Empire which included all Egypt, and parts of the Levant (Isreal, Jordan, Syria, ect...), as far north as Turkey. Chancellor Williams points out in The Destruction of Black Civilization, that this great empire broke up into Egypt and Nubia-Kush (Sudan), after Asiatic invaders infiltrated the region, despite their defeat about 3400 B.C. to 3100 B.C., by Aha-Mena and Narmer.

The Khemites applied the Nubian-Kushite process of manufacturing. They manufactured many of the luxuries that the Nubians also manufactured during the period of 8,000 B.C. to 4241 B.C. These goods were the products which were being manufactured as early as before the Neolithic Era. They ranged from pottery to weapons of copper, as well as furniture and foodstuffs. Khemite goods were loaded on ships and sold throughout the Mediterranean and other regions. The Khemite sphere of influence and trade included all the Mediterranean, India, the Far East, the interior of Africa as well as the coasts, Europe, Arabia, Central Asia, Western Europe and the Americas. The Khemites not only manufactured products from the raw materials of places such as Nubia-Kush, Punt, Fhenkhu (Phonecia or Canaan), Tarshish and others, they sold a wide variety of their own raw materials and products.

Khemite manufactured products were on a level similar to how Japanese products of today are said to be. They were of high quality and were dependable as far as their buyers and users were concerned. The customers admired Khemite products and immitated them. Products in the weapons category such as swords, maces and spears were highly valued. Kitchen utencils, furniture and jewelry were imported from Khem. The Khemite craftsman and woman put into their work the same type of energy that their descendents, today's Black people worldwide do put in, and should put into their carvings, paintings, craftwork, music, and other types of work. The ancient Khemites and Nubians believed that their work was an impression of themselves and their individual being. Each person's soul became part of his or her created work, in the same manner that today's African and African in the Americas and elsewhere, believes that "Soul," in music, walking or cooking is more than a physical task, but a highly spiritual task as well.

Barbara Sewell examines the Khemite craftsman and woman's methods of production and skill in her book entitled, Egypt Under the Pharaohs. "The earliest craft of all was that of the potter and the best pottery was made in predynastic times.

The polished red and black ware were modeled by hand before the invention of the potter's wheel in the Fourth Dynasty. The large body of craftsmen engaged on producting the utencils and luxuries which Egypt abounded are lost in oblivion as individuals, but are immortalized by the large amount of their handiwork which still survives to adorn museums. They are shown as potters, jewelers, carpenters and metal foundries.

Sewell presents examples of how these crafts were produced. "The manufacture of stone vessels of all shapes and sizes and fashioned from the hardest stones, reached a perfection and harmony in shape and finish during the first three dynasties that was never surpassed and seldom equalled in subsequent periods. The large ornate alabaster vessels which became fashionable during the 18th and 19th Dynasties and are exemplified by those found in Tutankhamun's tomb, show an exuberance of fantastic detail and ornamentation that can only be marveled at for the excitable taste and display. Less offensive are the ornate lamps made of alabaster and painted with colored designs which glazed brightly when lit from the inside."(7)

The Khemites (and Nubian-Kushites) worked gold to perfection. Silver was at one period more important than gold, particularly until the Middle Kingdom (about 2060 B.C. to 1780 B.C.). Much of this silver had to be imported from Greece and Canaan. It was one of the commodities that the Khemits retrieved in trade from across the Mediterranean. Gold came from Nubia-Kush and Punt. Khem was also famous for its wood products but had to import timber from Lebanon, Nubia-Kush or Punt.

Sewell explains that the carpenters of Khem were quite skilled in decorative carving on furniture and other everyday articles used in homes. Their furniture was made from trees grown in the region and a number of techniques applied in joinery today were used, such as nails of gold or other metal. They used a number of tools such as axes, saws, adzes, drills and chisels. They decorated furniture with sheets of gold and silver.

The description given attests to the high quality of Khemite goods. Such goods were in a state of development way back in prehistoric times when other peoples were still making and using less refined products. Such quality would have aroused the interest of other nations quickly as was indeed the case. This curiosity contributed to the importation of Khemite products in many places such as Canaan or Phoenicia, Isreal, Greece, the Far East, Babalonia, Central Asia, Inner Africa, Europe, and possibly the Americas. Current research and scientific findings have discovered that products from these areas including the Americas (in this case cocaine residue found in mummies) were imported from all thes regions to Egypt and most likely Nubia-Kush.

Sewell points out that Egypt had many resources except for timber which was important in the building of structures. Bronze, silver, lapis lazuli, spices, oils and other goods came from markets in other nations through trade or tribute. In return, the Khemites exported papyrus, leather, textiles, grain and dried fish, a bounty of the sea, some Egyptians regarded as being unclean. Gold was among their important export commodities. By 1580 B.C., articles were given value in gold, silver and copper, and some fixed weights were being used.

It seems that the hunger for gold by the nations to the north of Khemet was greater than Khem's need for it. This pervasive export of gold from Kush and Khem made the Khemites much wealthier than they already were. Gold was exchanged for goods of equal value whether it was timber from Fhenkhu (Canaan); silver from India, Greece, or Cronwall, England; copper from Cyprus (Khepra), Crete (Kheftiu), or Syria, or products such as amber from Armenia, Southern Russia and Central Asia.

The wealth of Khem garthered through trade, conquests and from their own nation, helped maintain and build the great cities such as No (Thebes), Hikuptah, On and others. Trade affected their wealth both directly and indirectly, for it is certain that some of the material used in the building of Khem's great cities came from other areas such as Canaan, Kush or Central Africa.

It seems that Khemite trade with the rest of Africa and the Mediterranean was a continuation of trade which began in Paleolithic times, such as the prehistoric trade in red ochre from Swaziland about 42,000 B.C.(mentioned by National Geographic), to other parts of Africa and the rest of the world inhabited by Homo sapiens, specifically those whose body type was able to make use of the red ocre. It has been shown that Africans or Black people, the first and original Homo sapiens, migrated out of Africa between 200,000 to 150,000 years ago. Since that time, they have migrated out of Africa to populate the entire planet in wave after wave to the Mediterranean's islands and northern regions, Europe, Asia, Australia and the Americas. Therefore, the exchange in products had gone on for tens of thousands of years, before the Khemites and Nubian-Kushites established the first great civilizations in the Nile Corridor. It had gone one as early as the inhabitants of the Sahara begun to take their ships and sale on the open inland sea which included parts of the Sahara, East and West Africa between 20,000 to 10,000 B.C.

Between 15,000 B.C. to 4241 B.C. (when the official Khemetic calendar was established in the city of On, Egypt), trade and commerce between and Khemites, Nubian-Kushites and other kingdoms in Africa and around the vincinity (the Mediterranean, Red Sea, India, Europe, the rest of Africa), was well established. The Nubian-Kushites and Egyptians may have traded with eath other before anyone else, since were the very first civilizations on earth with any strong organization or culture during the period mentioned above.

It was quite natural for the Nubian-Kushites and Khemites to trade with each other. In fact, this early trade was carried out within one large empire which consisted of a northern part and a southern part. Both the Nubian-Kushites and the Khemites were the same people, they were pure Black Africans, no different from Blacks who live in the southern part of Sudan, in Nigeria, or parts of North America today. Their cultures were identical since this culture which originated in Nubia, was one large and widespread culture. Moreover, the culture and race were spread from southern Turkey near Canaan all the way southward to the East African Great Lakes region, near Uganda. This massive area contained all the natural resources that the Khemites needed, including timber, which they had to import from Byblos, in Canaan as well.

With such a large and self sufficient land area, the Khemites and Nubian-Kushites made good use of what that land was able to produce, and unlike today, when the area is covered by desert, between 15,000 B.C. to 4241 B.C., much of the region was fertile, green and based on current data, it may have rained frequently, particularly when the Ice Age was coming to a close. The Kushites supplied timber, gold and other products to the less raw material rich, Khemites. The Khemites traded their cattle, alabaster products, turquois, grain and many other food products such as dates, to the ancient kingdoms of Africa such as Yam (somewhere in Central Africa), Punt (Somalia to South Africa), Ophir (India of the Black Indus Valley Civilization), Mesopotamia and West Africa, before they began such trade with their territories in the Mediterranean, Canaan and other places. Moreover, in very early times the civilizations that became Khemet was concentrated in the region of No and further south into Kush were the northern and southern parts of the Kushite-Khemite Empire.

The Khemites and Nubian-Kushites traded with two important parts of Africa and may have began such trade way back in the Paleolithic era. In fact, during the early centuries before the establishment of the solar calendar (4241 B.C.), migrations were taking place within the continent of Africa, and from Africa to other parts of the world. Among the places the ancient Egyptians and Nubians first traded with was a land in the interior of Africa called "Yam," and another called "Punt," or "Negau." Both areas were referred to as "God's Land." Yam was a region of dancing dwarves, thick forests and many natural resources. These same "dancing dwarves," were used by the Khemites as entertainers and court jesters. By what is already known, Pygmies were concentrated in Central Africa from the earliest times, as they still are today, as A. Abu Bkr states in History of Africa (ed. by G. Mokhtar, 1990, p. 68).(8)

Yam may have been to the South-west of Sudan, in Congo, or just to the west of the source of the Nile. If that was the case and it does appear to be, then not only would Pygmies have come from the area but also a wide variety of goods. If Yam was anywhere in Central Africa, and indeed it was, then the people were in many ways similar to the Khemites and Kushites. The Ishongo who established a culture earlier than 8,000 B.C. may have been an early source of sedentary culture on the shore of Lake Rutanzige, on the shores of Congo, on the mouth of the Semliki Valley. The inhabitants of Ishongo could have had trading relations with the Khemites and Nubian-Kushites from the earliest times.

As a trading partner, the land of Yam was a major source of all types of goods. Loepard skins, ivory, ebony and other types of wood, medicinal plants, animal skins, apes, baboons, metals, precious stones, food crops and other commodities were among the trade goods that was bought or bartered for from the area. The trade route had to have followed a route along the great rivers of Central and East Central Africa, to the western branches branches of the Nile and northward to Lake Rutanzige, Lake Victoria and Ishongo, an area close to where the Uturi Pygmies reside.

There seemed to have been few or no obstacles to travel in this area and between Nubia-Kush and Khemet to the north and down river. Boats traveling in relay fashion could have been carried on land beside cataracts and goods could have been transferred and allowed to continue sailing again. Goods left the area east of the Congo forests, down the Nile to the great cities of Meroe, Napata, Kerma, No(Thebes), Mempis to the Delta and throughout the Mediterranean region after they had been sorted out. The trade area covered a vast area much richer in natural resources than all of the other places the Khemites expected to barter goods with.

The Khemites also traded with Punt, where they exchanged their products for Puntite gold, exotic plants, mryyh, frankinscence, spices, ebony, wild animals and other exotic goods. The Puntites imported manufactured goods from the Khemites and Nubian-Kushites and most probably sold their own manufactured goods to the northerners in return. Goods such as grain and tools may have been exchanged for Puntite products. Barbara Sewell makes the point that commodities such as perfumes came from Punt, where Pharaohs had sent many expeditions over the centuries. Among the most important of the goods they took back to Khemet and Nubia-Kush was inscense which was used for rituals. The method of trade was by barter and luxuries not found in Khem such as certain valuable trees and plants from the south, were imported, replanted and used in Khemet.

The lands known as 'Punt,' by the Bibilical authors and 'Negau' by the Khemites may not have only included the modern nation of Somalia and the southern part of the Arabian peninsula, but the entire coast line and parts of the interior of East Africa, down to the southern part of Mozambique and Zimbabwe. When a careful study is made of the East African coast, it is found out that that one of the places famous for spice is the island of Zanzibar, off the coast of Tanzania. A magnificient tale about a shipwrecked sailor off the coast of East Africa quotes the ruler of Punt as saying to him, "You have no abundance of myrrh and every fine spice and incense. But I am the ruler of Punt, I've got the Myrrh in it, and the spice you said is plentiful on this island. It will happen that when you depart from this place, this island will never be seen again, for it will become water," (Cyrus Gordon, quotes The Shipwrecked Sailor).(9)

The island where spice is plentiful, brings to mind the isle of Zanzibar, unless there was such an island off the coast of the Red Sea, near Somalia. The history of the spice trade between Zanzibar and the rest of the ancient and modern world goes back to thousands of years before this tale was written. If Zanzibar was the place where the Khemites got their spices, then Punt would have had to include parts of East Africa south of Somalia as well.

How far to the south the Khemites traveled and what they traded in is historical knowledge. Pharaoh Hatshepsut's ships sailed southward on a journey to Punt, during her reign. The book, General history of Africa, Volume II, (edt. by G. Mokhtar and James Curry) carries this account. "In a room of a temple at Dier al Bahri there is a picture of Hatshepsut's devine birth which her mother, Ahmose is awakened by the scent of incense fragrance from the land of Punt. The pictures of this expedition have taught us about life in the Land of Punt, its plants, animals and inhabitants. There are also drawings of cone shaped huts, built on piles amidst palm, ebony and balsam trees."(10)

The length and distance traveled by Hatshepsut's ships can be estimated because the above account as well as ancient writings on the subject and finds give a hint as to how far southward her ships went. Statuettes of the Khemite type found in the area of south eastern Africa, show that there had been visits and possibly trade by the Khemites during and before Hatshepsut's time. The Khemites could have gone far around the Cape of Good Hope and up toward the Central Atlantic and West Africa. In fact, Nikau, the Egyptian Pharaoh of about 600 B.C. sent Phoenician sailors to circumnavigate Africa. Perhaps countless such trips were or were not recorded. Hatshepsut's journey to Punt (or of the sailors she sent there for her) and the other mysterious places she went, had been undertaken by other Pharaohs since perhaps, before Egypt's First Dynasty, and back into the 3000 years of civilization and advanced culture that the Nubian-Kushites enjoyed. Who knows how many of the great monuments such as the Sphinx, now suspected to be at least 10,000 years old is actually of the Nubian Civilization. After all, the Negritic features of the Sphinx, including prognathism, thick lips, flat nose and wide eyes are Black African features.

Queen Hatshepsut was one of the greatest women to rule an empire. She ruled disguised as a male pharaoh and wore male clothing, false beard and wig, in order to keep her identity as a female hidden. She acted as regent for Thutmose III, who was the real heir to the throne, but who was too young to rule at the time, and whom some historians believe was pushed aside to the side, thus building in him resentment for Hatshepsut. However, Hatshepsut was effective in some aspects of her rule. She was interested in the increase of trade with other nations and worked very much to achieve it. She improved the military capability of Khemet, built great ships that were faster and stronger to use in trade and travel, as well as military use. She erected great temples, and other projects and sent ships to far-away places and nations to collect, trade and barter goods.

Sewell states that the marriage between Thutmose 1 and his sister Hatshepsut, was part of the traditional system of royal incest practiced by the Khemites. Hatshepsut however, ruled for eight years after which time Thutmose III gained control of the throne. Hatshepsut was both the aunt and the step-mother of Thutmose III, since she was married to her brother, who was Thutmose III's father. She considered the throne to be hers because of her right by marriage to Thutmose III's father, Thutmose I. Her claim was supported by the high priests of Amon Re.

Hatshepsut's first position on her way to the full control of the throne was as that of regent to the young Thutmose III, however she was able to gain the title of Pharaoh of the Two Lands, while the young Thutmose was kept in the background. During her reign she adopted male titles and disguised at times in a male beard in order to appear masculine. She was deposed about twenty years after first gaining control of the throne and was replaced by the young Thutmose III.

Despite her tragic end, Hatshepsut placed an emphasis on trade during her reign and sent her ships to great distances to buy and sell the products of Egypt and other parts of Africa and elsewhere. It was also during her reign that the old style of Khemite ships was radically changed from simple crafts more suitable for river travel, to large ships suitable for sea and ocean travel. These new ships were built stronger and with improved sails and rigs. They were designed to look like the body of swans in order to give them more mobility.

The distance travelled by Hatshepsut's ships on their missions of trade to the southern part of Africa, and possibly around the Cape of Good Hope to West Africa and even the Americas, must be probed. Ancient writings, paintings and wall hieroglyphics clearly indicate that she sent her ships to Punt. Punt could have been an area from the Horn of Africa, to Southern Africa. Some of the products represented in the paintings in Hatshepsut's temple, of her journey to Punt, definitely came from somewhere in Africa, others may have come from somewhere in Asia as well. The racial representations on the paintings show people with features that are Negroid, a racial group which dominated a wide section of Asia, from South Arabia, through India to Southern China and the South Pacific, from Ancient times to the present day. These Asiatic Blacks are Kushitic in origins and are similar in racial characteristics to Africans.

We come to the products mentioned and seen in the paintings in Hatshepsut's temple, such as incence, ebony, animal skins, ivory, baboons, peacocks, goldrings piled on top each other, and people who appear to be captive Africans from the south, along with plants of all varieties and sizes. All of the products mentioned except the peacocks, come from somewhere in Africa, although peacocks do exist in Africa in a spices related to those of India, but with shorter tail and different array of colors. This African peacock also lacks the excessive display of plumage common among the male peacocks found in India, Burma, Sri-Lanka and Indochina. A species of peacock is also found in South America.

Unless the peacock was widespread in Africa during the time Hatshepsut's ships took their journey to Punt and returned with this type of fowl (between 1484-1462 B.C.), or unless the peacock mentioned was the African peacock, then they had to have come from India or parts of Asia, or even South America. The other possibility was that they could have been traded second hand by the people of the East African coast, who originally got them from the merchants of India and the Far East, or may have gone to the Far East to buy them. It must be realized that between the earliest times to the middle ages, the Blacks of South Asia, Oceania, Asia and the South Pacific traded back and forth with each other and ventured into each others' territories.

The case for South American trade with the Egyptians, as well as Mexico, the Caribbean, Central America, the U.S and Canada is now more evident than ever before. Were the peacocks purchased in South America, and were the Egyptians frequent visitors to the Americas? The answer to this question is a resounding, yes! Authors such as Ivan Van Sertima, Gunnar Thompson, R.A. Jairazbhoy, Alexander Von Wuthenau, and a host of other writers, historians, scientists and archeologists have presented irrefutable evidence for the presence of Egyptians and

Nubians in Mexico, South America, Central America and even North America.

The Khemites had ships that were large, strong and sufficiently mobile to go anywhere on earth. The peacocks could have been taken from somewhere like Brazil, Mexico or South America. Furthermore, was a bird such as the quetzal bird of Central America, mistaken for some sort of peacock? With these birds was also large caches of ivory, however ivory is not found in the Americas unless there were elephants there when the Egyptians and Nubian-Kushites visited. Yet, even that possbility is not far-fetched for at least three examples of the images of elephants have been found on stone and vases made in pre-Columbian America. An issue of Ancient American clearly portrays the photographs of pottery cups and plates with the pictures of elephants drawn on them. These cups were of ancient Maya origin.

It is most likely that Hatshepsuts ships got their ivory from African Elephants, then picked up other products along the way. They may have gone to West Africa, where according to Kenneth Caroli in Ancient American (Issue #8, January/February, 1995, p.36), "Documents from both Hatshepsut's and Ramses-III's expeditions refer to Punt as island-like, surrounded by sea, a coastal location, where domed buildings stood on pilings of water. Structures such as these are found in marshlands typical of West, not East Africa."(11) The Pilings and houses mentioned by Caroli are portrayed in the painting in Hatshepsut's temple.

The extent to which travel between Khem (Egypt), West Africa, Canaan (Phoenicia), Nubia-Kush, South America, Mexico and the United States and Canada may be known one day. Records may exist in ancient records which may exist in these lands, in the form of artefacts, etchings, cave paintings and drawings, as well the oral history of the inhabitants who live in these lands today and in the past. Ancient records, papyrus scrolls, ancient trading logs, books such as the bible and archeological sources may give clues. Further research, excavations, decipherment of ancient texts such as the 800 surviving Nubian- Kushite books, Mayan books and stone etched inscriptions, as well as Egyptian hieroglyphic texts and stone etched writings that have not yet been deciphered may provide us with clues that we must have in order to know the complete and true history of trade and contact between Africa and the Americas.

Hatshepsut's ships could have been on a mission of international trade as suggested by the paintings on her temple walls at Dier al Bahri. This expedition may have taken about three to four years, as Pharaoh Nikau ships had taken two to three years around Africa about nine hundred years later. The ships of Hatshepsut may have sailed down the Red Sea to Punt (Somalia, East African Coast to possibly West Africa) where goods were traded. Along the way her ships may have passed at Zanzibar for spices, the East African coast of Tanzania for ivory and apes, plants and ores. The ships may have stopped on the southern coast of Mozambique and Zimbabwe as well as South Africa, for gold. In fact, Egyptian statuettes have been found in that part of Africa. The ships may have sailed around the tip of southern Africa, up the coast of Angola to Cameroon, then the rest of West Africa, where more goods such as gold may have been purchased. From a base in West Africa, her ships could have sailed to Brazil, got some peacocks there, the sailed over to Mexico, where a Black civilization, the Olmec had already taken root. After all goods were bartered and transactions were made, her ships may have sailed eastward across the Caribbean, across the Atlantic, through the Straits of Gibralta, then eastward to the Nile Delta of Khemet. From the Delta, she would sail southward to her home base in No, Memphis or one of the great cities on the Nile's Banks.

Such a journey could have occurred many times. The Khemites and other Africans had no fear of the oceans, nor did they believe that the world was flat, and that they would fall off at the edge, as the Europeans feared during the Middle Ages. Furthermore, many had gone to far away places before Hatshepsut's reign. Journeys of great distances such as those around Africa, to the Americas, and eastward to the South Pacific and Asia, may have taken three or four years to complete. The representation in the temple at Dier al-Bahri of Hetshepsut's ships from a mission of trade may have been of such importance and may have taken such a long time to complete compared to others that she found it necessary to include it on the walls.

The journey of Hatshepsut's ships whereever they may have gone, is an example of the effort ancient Africans put in going to the limit to make sure that trade was carried out. Trade contributed to the wealth of the empire and it is not surprising that Khemet became wealthier during Hatshepsut's reign and the reign of Pharaohs who conducted extensive trade with the rest of the world. Hatshepsut not only improved on maritime activity and trade, but also on construction projects, buildings, and on the naval capability of Khemet.

## Pharaoh Sinefru

One of the earliest Khemite Pharaohs to increase trade outside of the Kushite-Khemite area and Africa was Pharaoh Sinefru who reigned in about 2780 B.C. Sinefru was not only a great trader but he was ruthless in his treatment of the Nubian-Kushites, who by that period, were engaged in warfar for their complete separation from their Black brothers in the north, the Egyptians (Khemites), who had committed the abomination of allowing Asiatics into Egypt, causing the racial mixing that the pure Black Khemites and Nubian-Kushites regarded as an affront to their devine covenent with the Sun God, having black skins. Chancellor Williams discusses this situation in his book, The Destruction of Black Civilization (1976).(12)

Sinefru was a Nubian who conquered northern Nubia in 2730 B.C. By the time he had finished his scorched earth policy on the southern kingdom, the place was almost all wasteland. He almost destroyed a civilization that begun before Khemet itself was fully settled and made an extention of the old Nubian-Kushite Empire which existed as far back as 8,000 B.C. The war against the Nubians/Kushites may have been caused by a major problem faced by the Blacks of Khemet, since the Asiatics were defeated in northern Khemet around the time of AhaMena and Narmer. Semitic invaders had pushed into the region of Canaan from the deserts of Arabia about 3400 to 3100 B.C. These

94

Semites were a mixture of Arabian Black Cushites and white invaders from the northern lands. Blacks during this period, just as the vast majority are today, were anti miscegination and anti integration. They regarded themselves as the Chosen People of the Sun, and their black skins were a mark of great honor and devine blessing. Those who migrated into Nubia, which was pure Black, refused to mix with the hordes of Asiatics who invaded Egypt. Thus, their reason for wanting a complete break from Egypt.

The invasion of Kush by Sinefru may have been related to the need by the Khemites not only to reunite Kush with Khem, but to gain access to Kushite resources such as gold, ivory, silver, ebony, timber cattle, leather, and the many products traded by the Nubian-Kushites. "For one thing, the land to the south of Egypt developed a strong economy continuously enrich by a thriving export trade in paper," according to Chancellor Williams in his book, The Destruction of Black Civilization: Great Issues of a Race From 4500 B.C. to 2000 A.D.(13)

Nubian-Kushite products included to Khemet included gold, ebony wood, emeralds and precious stones, the feathers of the ostrich, and pottery of vivid colors and artistic decorations. Kush had a strong economy and due to that both economic competition and the military threat to Khemet from the Nubian-Kushites was of great concern to the Khemites. The Khemites considered Kush to be a military and economic to their very survival. From the earliest times, the Black Khemites who inhabited Khemet (Egypt), regarded Nubia-Kush as a refuge from invaders and refused to accept alien rule in their kingdom, or the periodic occupations of their area by the Asiatics and others (and Africans today should not accept Asiatic and other foreign settlement or religion and culture in their lands today). The Nubian-Kushites tried to retake Khemet from the invaders and were successful until they were driven out by Ashurbanipal, during the 600's B.C.

Khem's downfall was garanteed as soon as the Black owners of the Khemite Empire began allowing Semites and other Asiatic settlers to become part of the population, or allowing the offspring of the invaders to remain in the empire. Further to the south of Nubia the Kushite Kingdom existed. They wanted to have no part in the integration of the races that was taking place in lower Khemet. Chancellor Williams makes it clear that the pride of the Blacks of Khemet and of Kush was so great that they refused to allow their offspring to be born with Asiatic blood and thus come out with a complexion not as dark as the Khemites.

The greatest hostility towards mixing of the races which occurred in lower Khemet, came from the Kushites who despised the mixed off- spring and regarded them to be impure, and not the chosen, "Children of the Sun," blessed with black skin, which they considered an honorable characteristic. (Chancellor Williams, 1976). (14)

Khemet's dependence on Nubia-Kush for both raw matrials and for the easy and uninterrupted flow of the life-giving waters of the Nile River, was of such great importantce that Khemite control of Nubia-Kush was greatly desired by the Khemites. Due to this fanatical desire which was influenced by the fear of the Egyptians (Khemites), that Nubia-Kush could divert the Nile's waters and cause their destruction, some of their military leadership and Pharaohs did all they could to maintain military and economic domination of the region. This was not easy, however since the Nubian-Kushites were sometimes much more militarily stronger than the Khemites. In fact such was their strength and formidability, that legions of their soldiers fought with the Egyptians and protected them from the invaders from Libya and the northern regions.

Sineferu's attempt to exterminate the Nubian-Kushite armies and population was due to the factors mentioned before. They, the Khemites wanted complete controle of Nubia's resources, lands and people. Their ability to enter Nubia-Kush's territory and exploit the lands and resources was part of their objectives as well as the need to keep the trade routes open. By making Nubia-Kush nothing but a colony of Khemet, Sinefru may have thought that it would have been easier to conquer totally. The resources of that kingdom would then be within easy reach.

That was the intention of the Khemites who wanted to bring their southern Black brothers under their control and keep their rich, fertile lands. Nubia-Kush was highly developed. In many ways the Nubian- Kushite culture was more advanced than that of Khemet and had its own great cities, towns, villages, temples, roads, irrigation projects, dams, tombs as large as football fields in the shape of massive domes, great monuments, and a well established arts and crafts industry. After the Khemites conquered Nubia-Kush and occupied it, they embarked on a program of rebuilding what Sinefru and his people had distroyed, which added to those already built by the Nubian Kushites.

Senefru's reign during the Forth Dynasty (2613 to 2494) B.C., was not limited to the destruction of Nubia-Kush. Among his achievements was the building of a stepped pyramid larger than that built by Zoser. His pyra- mid had eight levels and by filing the sides, he was able to make them as smooth as the Pyramids of Khufu.

The Khemites extended their trade into the Sinai Peninsula and Canaan and their ships had gone to Byblos in the same area since prehistoric times, in search of timber. Issac Asimov examines Khemite trade in the Sinai and Canaan in his book, The Egyptians. "The peninsula of Sinai was occupied by Egyptians for the sake of its copper mines-copper mines that could be used at home and for ornaments abroad."(15) Timber was in great demand in Khemet from the earliest times and they may have gotten a steady supply from the Nubians before Sinefru's invasion and distruction of part of that kingdom.

After that however, they may have restricted their imports of timber to Canaan, since timber of the type they required, did not grow in the Nile valley. Asimov observes, "This was the logs one could obtain from tall, straight trees; logs that could serve as strong and attractive pillars, and which would be much easier to handle for non-monumental structures than would stone which was so heavy and so difficult to carve. The proper sort of trees did not grow in the Nile Valley, where the vegetation was sub-tropical, but they did grow on the mountain slopes along the eastern shore of the Mediterranean just north of the Sinai Peninsula."(15)

"Sineferu's trade with Canaan (Phoenicia) may have not have been easy as far as routes he took to get there. Logs may have been cut in the mountains or hills of Lebanon and loaded on

Khemite ships or barges. His ships were unlike the improved type built by Hatshepsut years later, and could have been designed in a way which made them less seaworthy, but still able to cross the sea. "Sinefru sent out fleets of as many as forty ships to the cedar forests. Such Egyptian ships, strengthened somewhat, crawled out of the Nile into the Mediterranean."(15)

Senefru's trade with the Mediterranean and Canaan was not limited only to the purchase of timber. The Khemites exported gold and other products to the region. Also, this area called Fenkhu by the Khemites and Kushites, was a part of the Khemite Empire in the past before the Asiatics invaded the area. It is no surprise that the ancient Canaanites were of the same racial stock as the Khemites and Nubian-Kushites, that being, Black Negritic people, like the vast majority of the Blacks of the rest of Africa.

The original homeland of the Canaanites was Egypt, from where they migrated northward to what called Canaan, then Phoenicia. The people usually portrayed as being "Canaanites," Phoenicians and others of the region, were later invaders and Semite migrants, or other Asiatics who still dominate the land to this day. From the beginning, this land was part of the Black homelands and Blacks have not and should not give up any claim to it. The Canaanites wore Khemite clothing, used the hieroglyphic script, and the Gods they worshipped were similar in their appearance to the Khemite God, Isis. (Diop, 1991, pp. 92-95; Diop, 1974, p.2).(16)

Khemetic trade with Canaan progressed as the centuries went by and as Black Canaan included some Semites. That trade was spread over the Mediterranean and Africa. Special trading posts were built in Canaan as well as in other places whee they were not refused or pushed out of. The Khemites dominated trade in the Mediterranean area from about the Fifth Dynasty (2494-2345 B.C.), and most probably, much earlier. For thousands of years their ships dominated the region, except when barbarians controlled the sea routes, or when invaders sat on the throne of Khemet, thus causing a regression in trade, building, military strength and culture. However, as the Khemites lost their trading power, other Black nations such as Nubia-Kush,

Elam, the Indisu civilization, Sabea (South Arabia), Abbysinia and others took over and continued the ancient legacy.

It happens that one of the nations that was occupied by Khemet rose to become a world power which began from the time they invaded and reoccupied Khemet, the northern section of their ancient empire about 753 B.C., and continued after they withdrew from Khemet, about one to two hundred years later until the forth century A.D. The kingdom which became an empire larger than Khem itself, was Nubia-Kush.

# CHAPTER NINE

# THE NUBIAN-KUSHITES AND THEIR TRADING

Nubia-Kush was the original civilization in the Nile Valley. It may have been in existence before the Neolithic Age, as early as 10,000 B.C. In fact, new data based on the work of archeologists show that about 8,000 B.C., Nubia had an advanced culture which became Ta-Seti and contributed both the manpower, technological knowledge and culture to what became Egypt. This fact was discussed in the last chapter, when Egypt or Khemet was the northern section of the vast Nubian-Kushite or Ethiopian Empire. At that time, much of the Nile Delta may have been under water and a vast swamp.

Nubia-Kush was the core of Black civilization between 15,000 B.C. to 4241 B.C. The core of the ancient Nubian-Kushite Empire was the portion of land between Aswan and Khartoum. After the Khemites retook nothern Khem from alien Asiatics who were settled in the northern part of the Delta, between 3400 to 3100 B.C. and reunited the two lands, the boundaries of the empire expanded. It began south of Turkey in the north and included Canaan, and the entire region now made up of Lebanon, Syria, Jordan, Isreal and Sinai. Its southern extension included parts of modern Ethiopia and the Lakes Region of East Africa.

There should be no doubt that the civilization of Nubia-Kush was the original civilization in the Nile Valley, for the Khemites, who are supposed to the the first civilization in the region, actually looked to NubiaKush (Sudan) as the origin of their civilization and culture, as well as their people. Nubia-Kush was the source of the Nile Valley culture. The legend of Osirus, who is said to have brought civilization to Egypt from Nubia-Kush points to the south of Egypt as the place of his origins. The Khemites themselves claim that the area which later became Khemet (particularly the Delta area), was still basically swamp, wetlands and ocean during the time the legend of Osirus is said to have taken place. (Diop, C.A. 1991, pp. 103- 108). (1)

Trade occurred frequently between the Nubian-Kushites and Khemites. That trade may have began during the Paleolithic Age and may have been carried out by boat, animals or on foot. The resources of Khem has never been as great as that of its southern neighbors and most of her gold, ostrich feathers, ivory, ebony, animals, food and other commodities came from Nubia-Kush. Kush was not only the mother of Khemetic civilization, but Khemet depended greatly on Kush and the lands further south, for its very survival.

The urge of the Khemites to control or capture all of Kush, had to do with their desire to control the trade routes and the sources of gold and other commodities of Nubia-Kush to the South. Wars between Nubia- Kush and Khemet go back to about 2000 B.C. These wars were wars of resistance from Khemite control of Nubian-Kushite lands after the Nubian-Kushites separated from the Khemites in order to prevent the mixing of the pure Blacks of Nubia-Kush and the infiltrating Asiatics, as had occurred in the Delta region of Egypt.

The Nubian-Kushite desire to retake Khem from the alien Hyksos, Assyrians, Greeks, Persians, Saites, Libyans, Romans and other invaders was motivated by the great need to reunite their ancient empire. Another reason was the need for the Kushites to control the trade routes along the Nile to the Mediterranean. These foreign rulers of Khemet had cut out the flow of goods to and from Nubia-Kush whenever they felt threatened by the Nubian-Kushites, or wanted to destroy their economy. Still, the Kushites found alternative routes along the Red Sea by travelling overland in caravans. Kushite trade occurred inspite of blockades and the occupation of Khem by alien invaders.

Like the Khemites, the Kushites traded with India, Sri Lanka, Mesopotamia, the Arabian Peninsula, South East Asia, East Asia, Europe, the coasts and interior of Africa, the South Pacific and even the Americas. Trade between the Nubian-Kushites and the Chinese, one of Asia's ancient cultures, with an ancient Black cultural origin, began in ancient times, and continued through the Han Dynasty (600's B.C.), into Middle Ages, past the 300's to 400's A.D., into the late Middle Ages. The trade between the Nubian-Kushites and other civilizations in Africa, as well as Asia, is well known and have been documented. Kushite merchants and ships traded directly with nations like India and China.

Philip Snow writes in his book, The Star Raft, China's Encounter With Africa. "According to Chinese scholars, maritime trade between China and Africa was underway by 600 B.C. Their first rulers traded long distance, the Han Dynasty at the turn of the Christian Era were already in touch with to of Africa's most imposing states, Kush and Axum. During that period the kingdom of Kush and Axum in the Ethiopian Highlands were trading through the port of Adulis with ships on their way from the Mediterranean to the Indian Ocean."(2)

The Chinese record in itself does not give a complete picture as to wheather there was trade between the Chinese and Africans before the beginning of the Han Dynasty or even the very first Dynasty of China. Yet, what is known is that Africans from Khem, Nubia-Kush and the Mesopotamian/Akadian civilization established themselves in ancient China and founded China's first two Dynasties, the Xia (2200-1766 B.C.), and Shang (1766-1100 B.C.). According to Wayne B. Chandler, in African Presence in Early America, Africans were in the East by the time of Senefru and way back in prehistoric times. (Editor, Ivan Van Sertima, 1992, pp. 240-308).(3)

The discovery of Blacks in California by the first Spanish invaders in the 1500's, leaves one to wonder whether these Blacks were not part of the ancient traders, who sailed their ships to China, India and parts of S.E. Asia and the Far East in ancient times. Black Californians were among the Native Americans from the earliest of times and Indian legends make mention of them. According to the legend, Blacks with curly hair had been sailing back and forth from California to the Pacific with goods, in their boats. A study of the history of African trade with China and the Far East will reveal that trade relationships may cover over 5,000 years back to a period when China was still in the Neolithic Age, a period in history when China's southern kingdoms were predominantly Black, and Black cultures and civilizations existed over half of China, particularly Southern China.

Armand De Quatrefages in his book, The Pygmies, (1885, p.51) (D. Appleton and Co., New York, 1885, p. 51), explains:

> "The Negro type was originally characterized in southern Asia, of which, no doubt, it was the sole occupant for an infinite period of time. From there, the various representations of the type migrated into various directions. Invasions or infiltrations of various yellow and white races have separated the Negro populations which formerly occupied a continuous area. The Negrito subtype is one of the oldest of the race, and was at least predominant in India and Indo-China when the racial crossing began."(4)

This quotation by James Brunson in his essay 'African Presence in Early China,' (African Presence in Early Asia, edt. Ivan Van Sertima, 1995, p. 121-136) is of the utmost significance. First of all, it reestablishes a fact of history that is known by many African and Africans in the Diaspora, that large parts of Asia was Black, is still Black, and must remain Black lands. Thus, when invaders and occupiers believe they have the right to occupy the lands of Black people in South Asia, South-East Asia, parts of Melanesia and Australia, the right to stop the perpetrators using any means necessary is one that not only just but supported by historical fact.

Apart from these prehistoric Blacks who established themselves in China and other parts of Asia before the Mongoloid invasion from the far North, Nubian-Kushites, Khemites, Puntites and other East Africans and Ethiopians all established themselves in an area from South Arabia all the way to Hawaii and the Australia-NewZeland region.

Kush, the core of a highly populated region and the crossroads of Africa, Europe and Asia, was in a position to gain wealth through trade and commerce. But they were cut off from the Mediterranean during times of conflict with the Khemites or whatever group of alien invaders ruled Egypt for a period of time. Still, Kush was not totally isolated for they had some access to the Red Sea, even during times of conflict.

Nubian-Kushite (Nubian civilization existed as early as 8000 B.C., Kush was the name used by the Jews and Biblical scholars for Nubia, and was the ancient name used by the Kushites to call their lands) products were famous around the world. Their gold, ivory, precious stones, fruits and vegetables, rare woods such as ebony (hbny in the ancient Khemetic language), manufactured such as vases, weapons of iron and bronze, came from Kush. Other products such as timber came from the Ethiopian (Abbysinia) Highlands, Central Africa and the Great Lakes region of East-Central Africa. The Kushites travelled far and wide into the interior of Africa in search of trade goods, or applied middlemen for such work. In parts of Europe and the Middle East, the Phoenicians, who were originally called Canaanites and were Negroid, were used as seamen by both the Nubian-Kushites and the Khemites.

The Nubian Kushites traded with Khemet, however, their relationship was of a love-hate type. When the rulers of Khemet were favorable to the Kushites, there was calm. However, when hostile regimes were on the throne, the Kushites were prepared to defend themselves against hostile policies. In some cases, the Kushites launched attacks on Khemet. These attacks were part of a continuing period of warfare which began about 2000 B.C. Nubian-Kushites felt that they had the God-given right to all of Khem, and wanted to reestablish the ancient empire, and the reunification of all the kingdoms as well as the expulsion of all Asiatics from Khemet. This attitude may still be very strong among Black Egyptians, Nubians and Sudanese today, who would like to eliminate foreign ideologies and Arab influence from their ancient lands.

The Nubian-Kushite desire to overthrow the foreign rulers who occupied the northern half of their ancient empire and to reunite all the lands was quite strong. Yet, so was the Khemite desire to keep NubiaKush as a source of raw materials and soldiers. One of the most ruthless supressions of Nubia-Kush took place about 2613 to 2494 B.C. Despite these conflicts, the

105

Nubian-Kushites were looked upon by the Khemites as their brothers and Nubia-Kush as the place of the origins of Khemetic (Egyptian) civilization itself.

This knowledge of their place of origin and Nubia-Kush's contribution and establishment of their own civilization did not prevent the Khemites from establishing a policy of war against Nubia-Kush, and constant vigil due to the fear of Nubian-Kushite attacks and the retaking of Khemet. Due to these possibilities, the Khemites built forts at places such as Soleb and other areas along the Nile River. They also kept garrisons on the border with the Nubian-Kushites.

The retaking of Egypt (Khemet) from the alien rulers who sometimes ruled Khemet as well as the desire to reunite their ancient empire drove the Nubian-Kushites to have as their policy, the reuification and retaking of Khemet. They also wanted easy access to the Mediterranean and areas north so that they could carry out their trade, without having to get permission, or sign treaties with whoever was in control of Khemet. This issue is superbly analyzed by Chancellor Williams in his book, The Destruction of Black Civilization: Great Issues of a Race From 4500 B.C. to 2000 A.D. (Third World Press, 1974).(5)

# CHAPTER TEN

# PHARAOHS PIANKI AND TARHARKA

About 753 B.C., Piankhi a Pharaoh from Kush, led his armies down the Nile and conquered all of Khemet in one big blitzkreig sweep. He eliminated all the foreign Saite Pharaohs and united all of Nubia-Kush with Khemet. The two Asiatic Pharaohs who ruled Egypt, Tefkakte and Bocchoria, were eliminated. At long last, the Nubian-Kushites had accomplished their long and ancient objective or retaking and reuniting the northern part of their ancient empire, and creating a great superpower from the lands of Khemet, Nubia and Kush. They also retook Fenkhu (Canaan), and reached the borders of Turky (Hattusha) and Assyria (Asshur).

Piankhi took on a building program of great proportions. According to Chancellor Williams in The Destruction of Black Civilization, he built a massive temple complex at Jebel Barkal and worked on many other projects. Piankhi extended his empire to the south, pass the headwaters of the Nile so that he would have access to the resources there. Nubian-Kushite ships as well as alliances between the Nubian Kushites and Phoenicians, sailed throughout the Mediterranean, Indian Ocean (which was once called the Ethiopian Sea), around Africa, into the Black Sea area of Russia, to the Pacific and based on current research, they traveled to the Americas, where their legacy remains in the Olmec Civilization and others which came afterwards in Mexico, Central America and the Southern United States.

They smashed Saite control and the monopoly over trade in Lower Khemet and the Mediterranean Region. Shortly after they had retaken Khemet from the Asiatics, trade was reestablished with many of the Kingdoms and empires of the region. Kushite gold, ivory, ebony, ostrich feathers, manufactured goods and many other products were shipped down the Nile in exchange for timber from Fenkhu (Canaan, Lebanon), grain, amber from

107

Central Europe, lapis lazuli from Central Asia and countless other products such as copper and tin. Trade with the nations of S.W. Asia, Europe, South Asia, the Far East and the Americas, further enriched the Kushites, whose own kingdom, NubiaKush, was already blessed with emmense natural resources as well as a thriving manufacturing and export sector.

This manufacturing and export sector was older than the Nubian Kushite Empire itself, and went back before the Neolithic Age, back to before 8,000 B.C. Phoan Goldman Tarharka writes in Egypt Revisited, (edt. by Ivan Van Sertima, 1995, pp.261-270, "The Nubian Renaissance,"

> "In the space of the ten chapters making up this, Volume One, of Black Manhood--which might fittingly be subtitled, The Building of Civilization by the Black Man of the Nile we have shown that many of the most salient developments and the cardinal personalities in the maturation of the human species and civilization effloresced along the banks of the Nile including the anufacture of tools, the beginnings of agriculture and man's control of fire. These flashpoints in man's creative growth and the pace setting, ingenious builders of Egypt's civilization have finally been credited to the pioneer folk of mankind's premier continent-Africa."[1]

Nubian-Kushite military power and control of the of the Mediterranean, which they had control of as early as 1000 B.C., when Nubians controled the armies, navies and parts of the monarchy of Khemet, opened vast opportunities for the Nubian-Kushites. There were no restrictions to their movements and on their trading activities. At that period in history, Nubia-Kush was the world super-power, with their arch enemies the Assyrians being their competitors.

Every commodity on the market found its way up and down the Nile River to and from cities like Napata, Merowe, No (Thebes), Memphis, Hikuptah and others. Open and free trade between the Kushites and others as far away as India and China, helped make the NubianKushites, very wealthy. That wealth was used to establish an even more glorious culture in Nubia-Kush and Khemet, as well as in far-away lands such as Mexico, where the Nubian-Kushite cultural influence florished between the period of 1100 B.C. to 200 A.D., with the establishment of the Olmec civilization, with its architecture, culture, people, and religious culture strinkingly similar to that of West Africa, Khemet and Nubia-Kush between a historical period of 1100 B.C. to this very day.

Ancient records of Nubian-Kushite trade by sea may exist in the form of ancient Nubian scrolls (of which 800 still exist), temple hieroglyphics and other forms of documentation. Trade with West Africa by Sea was carried out by the Khemites. Pharaoh Nikau's ordering of Phoenician to sail around Africa about 600 B.C. is well known. As for the Nubian-Kushites, their sea voyages and journeys of trade as well as settlement, though not widely known, did occur. In fact, their domination of the Mediterranean and the Indian Ocean, the North Atlantic and most possibly the waters of the Americas and the Pacific has been studied, is being currently studied and has produced positive results, which point to a Nubian-Kushite presence in all these areas in pre-historic and ancient times, up to the Middle Ages.

There was also extensive overland trade between Nubia-Kush, Khemet and the Ethiopian Highlands, West Africa and the Western Sudan Region. Still, it is highly possible that the Kushites sailed southward along the western coastline of Africa, down to ancient Ghana and scattered kingdoms of the West Coast of Africa. The Kushites may have used sailors from Phoenicia as well as their own. Considering that in ancient times, many trade sources and routes were kept secret, it is possible that the Kushites may have been very suspicious of allowing foreign seamen on their ships. However, the Phoenicians, though foreign, were vassals of the Nubian-Kushites and Khemites. Arnold H. Heeren explains the relationship between the Phoenicians, Carthaginians and others in his work, Historical Research Into the Politics, Intercourse and Trade of the Carthaginians, Ect...(Oxford, 1832, p.411).(2)

Nubian-Kushite influence on the ancient culture of West Africa may go back to about 800 to 500 B.C., and as far back as 2,000 B.C. Some Kushites migrated to West Africa from Nubia-Kush, the nation today called Sudan, now under the occupation of a Semetic cultural influence and religion. The Kushites may have began a migration to West Africa during the time of their wars with the Khemites, and particularly during the period of Senefru's war against the Nubians, during the Fourth Dynasty (2686 to 2613). Apart from these early migrations, there were occasional migrations from Sudan (Nubia-Kush) to West Africa. Among the Yorubas of West Africa, it is believed that their people migrated from Egypt during the time of Moses.

Ivan Van Sertima speaks of a migration from Egypt of Black Jews to West Africa during the time of the invasion of Egypt by Cambysis, the Persian King. The descendents of these Black Jews still exist in West Africa today and are called the Puel. Alexander Von Wuthenau writes in the book, African Presence in Early America, edited by Ivan Van Sertima. His comments were made concerning the great similarities between Olmec terracotta art and that of the West Africans of about 1000 to 400 B.C.

"People living in New York might still remember the splendid exhibition of Nigerian archeological treasures in the Metropolitan museum, where amongst the beautiful Black Terracotta heads, belonging to the Nok period, some excellent Jewish heads were on display. The dating of these artifacts dovetail perfectly with the time of Cambyses invasion (525 B.C.) In Egypt and the destruction of Memphis. The Jews, remembering the appalling fate of their compatriots in Jerusalem, could not escape via the Nile, guarded by the Persian soldiers. So they tracked through the whole African coast. It stands to reason that, on this trip (Vasquez mentions several African Kingdoms the migration had to cross) they had contacts and friendships not only with the Nigerians but also with the experienced river navigators. ("Unexpected Pre-Columbian Faces in

Ancient America," A.Von Wuthenau. African Presence in Early America, edited by Ivan Van Sertima, 1992, p. 92). (3)

The Nubian-Kushites, ancient ancestors of the Yorubas, the Black Jews and others all migrated to a region with a flourishing culture and civilization, the Nok Civilization, which was began by migrants from the Sahara, and whose artefacts have been dated to about 2700 to 3000 B.C. by Nigerian archeologists. Cultures similar to the Nok Culture were spread from the Southern Sahara to the Bight of Benin, and from the Cape Verde region to Chad. The migrations occurred in both tricles as well as in waves, depending on the period and problems which were occurring in the regions where the migrants were fleeing from.

The Nubian-Kushites also sent their trading ships down the coast of East Africa, around South Africa to West Africa. Considering the many grand projects undertaken by the Nubian-Kushites, as well as their zealous attitude toward trade, commerce and military domi- nation and strength, voyages to the south and east of Nubia-Kush had to have occurred. In fact, this fact is mentioned already and according to Chinese scholars of the Han Dyasty (600's B.C.), both the Nubians and the Abbysinians (modern Ethiopians), traded with China. Such being the case, then the Nubian-Kushites were very proficient in their use of international trade and commerce, and such trade and commerce may have begun before 8,000 B.C., when Nubian-Kushite civilization is now proven to have been established.

## Tarharka's Objectives

Tarharka may have been Piankhi's son or nephew. The African matrilineal system of inheritance made it possible for the King's sister's son to inherit the throne or to be given first priority. After Piankhi's death, Tarharka inherited the throne about 686 to 688 B.C. During that period, Kush was the most powerful empire on earth. They controlled about one quarter of the continent of Africa, all of Canaan, up to the Turkish border, and colonies and settlements from Egypt to Mexico in the West,

111

and from South Arabia to Southern China in the East. The Red Sea was also under direct Nubian-Kushite control as well as the Ethiopian Sea (Indian Ocean), to the East. Their ships also travelled the Atlantic towards the British Isles, where according to Van Sertima, they mined tin at Cronwall with the Phoenicians, in order to make bronze weapons.

Tarharka continued the policies of his predecessors, of encouraging trade with faraway lands. He pushed for economic improvements and improvements in culture and religion, as well as building and construction. He had friendly relations with Syria, Lebanon and Palestine. Tarharka's friendship with the Jews was so important to him, that he attempted to protect them against his arch enemies, the Assyrians.

Like his father before him, Tarharka took on a building program in both Nubia-Kush and Khemet, something not accomplished since the control of Khemet by the last Dynasty of Black, native Egyptian Pharaohs, the Ramsids. Tarharka built more massive temples all over Nubia-Kush and Khemet to the Gods, Osirus and Ptah. He built the massive temple at Jebel Barkal, by having it carved out of the granite hillside, southwest of the fourth cataract and south-east of Dongola on the northern bank of the Nile, as it curves to the north-east.

Tarharka and those before him created a Nubia-Kush that was even more magnificent that Egypt (Khemet). The lands to the south of Nubia-Kush, pass the Sudd region of present-day Sudan, towards the East African lake region and eastwards to Ethiopia, were all part of the Kushite sphere of influence. It was from these lands to the south, that some of the wealth of Nubia-Kush and Khemet came from. Commodities such as ivory, gold, timber, ebony, monkeys and apes, plants, precious stones and metals and other important goods. The value of the lands south of Kush had been realized earlier by Piankhi, who wanted to extend his empire further south.

Tarharka continued the spread of Nubian-Kushite influence throughout the Mediterranean that his father had begun. They kept friendly relations with nations like isreal and used sailors from Phoenicia to travel in some of their ships. Tarharka led expeditions past Sicily, through the Strait of Gibralta. He may have visited the British Isles and parts of Europe, and wanted to lead an invasion of Spain (Tarshish), at a time when there was an indigenous Black population on the Iberian Peninsula, who were concerned about the encroachment of groups such as the Phoenicians. According to Phoan Goldman, "Erastosthenes, the Third Century, Greek geographer and librarian at Alexandria was quoted in Strabo as saying that Tarharka was, "...a warrior who...penetrated into Europe as far as the 'Pillars of Hercules' (Gibralta)-that is a great conqueror."(4) (Arnold H. Heeren, Historical Researches into the Politics, Intercourse and Trade of the Carthagians, Ethiopians and Egyptians (Oxford; D.A. Talboys, 1832), 1, p. 411). This quotation of Erastothenes by Phoan Goldman in Ivan Van Sertima's (editor) Egypt Revisited, says very much about the power and influence of the Nubian Kushites during their five hundred years of military and economic power between 1100 B.C. to 600 B.C.

There is no doubt that the Kushites went into both the Iberian Peninsula and Western Europe in search of raw materials and metals. The search for and the mining of tin in Britain by the Kushites is highly possible. The Phoenicians or better yet, the Canaanites, were a Negroid people who existed in Fhenkhu (Canaan), and were the original inhabitants of the region. Between 753 B.C. to 688 B.C., the Phoenicians were under the employ of Kushites, just as they had been under Khemite control before the reunification of Nubia-Kush with Khemet. The British Isles was well known as a source of tin, and the Khemites as well as the Nubian-Kushites needed it in order to make bronze utencils and weapons. Other sources of tin, such as the rest of Africa, India, China or even the Americas, may have been explored as well.

# CHAPTER ELEVEN

# CONFLICTS WITH ASSYRIA

The Assyrians invaded the the Levant, then pushed into Egypt in an attempt to conquer Egypt and install their own puppet regimes in place of the Nubian-Kushites. Although the Nubian-Kushites had defeated the Assyrians in many wars and battles, under the leadership of Ashurbanipal, the Assyrians were able to push the Nubian-Kushites back towards their own Kingdom, Nubia-Kush. Some historians blame the ability of the Assyrians to push the Nubian-Kushites out of Egypt to the descision of the Nubian-Kushites to protect the Isrealites, as well as their refusal to change from bronze weapons to iron ones. The Assyrians were well armed, with iron weapons which proved to be no match for the bronze weapons of the Nubian-Kushites.

After the Kushites were pushed out of Khem by the Assyrians, their trade with the Mediterranean may have decreased, yet their trade with the rest of the world was hardly hampered for long. The Nubian Kushites found other routes to the sea, such as the port of Adulis on the Red Sea, where they conducted trade with lands as far as India, China and lands to the Pacific Ocean. The fact that the Nubian-Kushite kingdom continued until the fifteen hundreds A.D., means that they had a large and extensive trade during this long period. It is quite possible that after the Assyrians were pushed out of Egypt, they retained their access to Egyptian ports. Even more likely was that they found other routes, such as the Red Sea from which their ships sailed in all directions.

The involvement of the Kushites in the wars of the Syrians, and Jews against the Assyrians may have contributed to their being attacked by the Assyrians, thus causing the occupation of Khemet by the enemy. The continued use of bronze weapons as mentioned already, was another factor, although the Nubian-Kushites and Egyptians were making use of iron on a small scale as early as 1500 B.C. The Nubian- Kushites being somewhat conservative in cultural traditions, failed to put their ability to make iron products to the use of weapons. Their adversaries were using iron in every facet of their military.

The history of the Nubian-Kushites show that an aggressive attitude towards trade, ensuring sources for buying and selling products, manufacturing and making things for export and defending the routes of exporting goods were all part of their trade philosophy. It may have been the policy of the Nubian-Kushites not only to keep a large army but to have a large population had to have been much larger. As for Kush, their population may have been too small about 2686 B.C. to stop the Khemite invasion of their territory, and perhaps their army was also too small to stop them.

About 1200 B.C., the Kushites had reached a high level of military and economic power. Their soliders protected Egypt and many served under their own Generals during the time of the Ramsids. By 753 B.C., the Nubian-Kushites may have reached a high level of population, as well as military and economic strength. This positive change in their historical circumstances, their large, formidable army and their determination to achieve their political and imperial objectives, prompted them to send their armies to conquer Khemet.

The importance of trade to the Africans of Nubia-Kush and Khemet was one they held with even more zeal and importance than they did religion. Such zealousness was shown by the actions and measures they took to ensure that trade routes, customers, supplies and goods were within their reach and control. When goods were far from their immidiate grasp, they sailed on ships and went to the sources to retrieve them. The Khemites and Nubian-Kushites' need for trade was greatest at the places where the Nile Valley did not produce too many commodities, such as the area from the city of Aha-Mena (Memphis) in the north, to Dongola in the south. This area of the Nile Valley was not as richly blessed in resources as either the Nile Delta, or the fertile lands of Nubia Kush. In fact, the entire length of the Nile Valley south of the Delta had only a thin strip of fertile land, compared to the rich, fertile lands of upper Nubia-Kush, where they had an abundance of timber, crops and a wide variety of resources.

The discovery of metals such as copper and tin, which produced bronze, of iron which was put to extensive use after the 700's B.C. by the Nubian-Kushites helped them and the Khemites produce better tools and weapons after the Assyrian invasion. Thousands of years previously, when Assyria and much of Mesopotamia was inhabited by Black nations, iron was being used in Khemet on a small scale as ornamental jewelry. At that time, the idea that iron would determine whether the NubianKushites would continue their rule of Khemet was probably not considered. They learned a very good lesson (which Blacks worldwide today must also learn). That lesson was that they should lead in all aspects of technology and be ahead of their adversaries. And so, they took on the systematic and rapid development of their iron industries, making the city of Meroe, the largest and most proficient manufacturer of iron weapons, wagon wheels, utencils, tools and other manufactured goods, after the 700's B.C.

Both the Kushites and Khemites realized from the earliest times, that trade and manufacturing was essential in keeping their wealth, power, civilization and longevity. In retrospect, trade helped the Nubian Kushites and Khemites to create the first and greatest two civilizations on earth, at a time when much of the world lived in the Stone Age, or various levels of the Neolithic Age. They, the Nubian-Kushites, were also the first inventors of technology, art, mathematics, astronomy, city building and planning, irrigation and irrigation machinery, hydralics, medicine, surgery, and a host of technological aspects still used in today's societies. They made certain that they created what others wanted and manufactured some of the best products on earth. This is the example that Blacks and Africans worldwide must follow today. Lessons must be learned from the accomplishments as well as the failures of the ancestors, so that we shall return to greatness as we enter into the Twenty-first Century and the new Mellenia.

# CHAPTER TWELVE

# ANCIENT WEST AFRICA (ANCIENT GHANA)

The western part of Africa from Congo to Chad and from Liberia to Mauritania contained two major areas of culture before 3000 B.C. The first the area around Gabon and Cameroon and the Chad Basin, as well as the southern part of West Africa. The second was in the area where Mauritania, Mali, Niger, Burkina Faso, Nigeria, Ghana and the rest of West Africa is located. These areas were the places where one of Africa's oldest civilizations and cultures, that of the Nok figurine culture, existed.

Ghana was the first imperial civilization in West Africa, however, its history began more than one thousand years before the 700's A.D. when the Arabs first visited the area. In fact, Ghana was part of an extensive culture dominated by a Mende speaking peoples who had developed agriculture before 5000 B.C., were spread in parts of the Sahara when it was fertile, and included among them master shipbuilders and sailors, who may have taken the African cotton to the Americas as early as 5000 to 4000 B.C.(Ivan Van Sertima, They Came Before Columbus, "Plants and Transplants," 1976).(1)

Apart from Ghana, which is considered to be one of the earliest civilizations of West Africa, there were a number of others, particularly in the South of the Ghana, Mali, Songai and Kanem-Bornu cultural area. Most of these kingdoms and civilizations have not been properly dated by European historians, who have treated them as cultures who suddenly appeared in their respective areas, when the Europeans first saw them. However African scholars who live in the areas where some of these ancient civilizations have introduced more accurate dates.

According to Goddy WichenDu, Art Director for The Afrikan Magazine (edt. Chief Ani Dike Egwuonwu, Afrikan Publishing Co., Jamaica, New York, 1994, back cover), a map of ancient African kingdoms and empires of West Africa show that the Ashanti Kingdom existed from 1600 B.C. to 1823 A.D.(they are still a cultural force in Ghana today). The Benin Kingdom flourished from 1200 B.C. to about 1457 A.D., the Kingdom of Kanem-Bornu florished from 1200 B.C. to 1400 A.D., (and up to the 1800's). The Igbo Kingdom florished from 870 B.C. to 1200 A.D. The Ife Kingdom florished from about 864 B.C. to 1200 A.D.(2). All of these kingdoms continued into the 1700's to the twentieth century, however their deterioriation during that period was caused by Arab slave traders and their allies, European slave traders and religious as well as wars of expansion. These cultures according to Michael Bradley may have all originated from the core Nok culture, which was extensive throughout West Africa from a very early period. (Michael Bradley, The Black Discovery of America, 1981, pp.26-27, 33).(3).

The discovery of advanced civilization in Nok, Nigeria and other parts of West Africa, related to the Nok culture is an example of what may be hidden beneath the soil in this part of Africa, which includes parts of the Sahara. Moreover, the part of West Africa which includes the Sahara, was fertile land between 3000 B.C. to 2000 B.C. According to Michael Bradley (1981, pp. 19-20), the Nok culture may have been part of an extensive and widespread culture which included a number of cultural aspects, from architectural styles to the types of terracotta made by the inhabitants. Bradley writes in regards to the Black migrations from the Sahara. "Some went directly south into the tropical fringe of West Africa around the shores of the Atlantic. They established themselves in the forested region of West Africa as early as 3000 B.C., and they brought a relatively high Saharan cultural level with them."(pg. 20) (4)

The ancient people of West Africa seems to have come from various parts of northern Africa and the Sahara. Others came from the east of Chad, and possibly from the south. Some were descendents of the earliest inhabitants of West Africa Negroid Pygmies as well as the tall, more robust Black African Negritics who predominate in the region today. These Blacks have been in the region for more than ten thousand years. Other Blacks left the Sahara due to the movement of sand into the area and the drying up of its water supply. According to M. Posnansky, in

General History of Africa, Vol. II, (1990, pp. 297 to 298), the elephants and other large animals were among the first creatures to leave the Sahara when the food supply started to become (5) scarce. The Pygmies and Bushmen as well as fishermen, farmers and those who consisted of the Sahara's aquatic civilizations were among the first to leave the region.

The West Africans had developed civilizations similar to that of Nubia-Kush and Khemet, which in turn were similar to the early Black civilizations of the Sahara. The absence of Egyptian or Nubian type pyramids in West Africa is not even a factor when comparing the ancient civilizations of West Africa with those of the Nile. Moreover, ancient Pyramids exist in the Lake Debo area of Mali, along the Niger River. These pyramids were made of mud brick. Cheikh Antah Diop discusses these pyramids as well as other monuments found at Lake Debo in Mali, as well as the ancient Ghanian city of Kukia, which existed during the time of the Pharaohs.(6)

In the central part of the Ghana Empire, the ruins of the ancient city of Kumbi-Kumbi has been found. This city was first seen by Arab traders and travelers about 700 A.D., the period of time that Western historians seem to enjoy giving Ghana, as its date of origin. On the other hand, they ignore the high cultures that existed in the region that was Ghana as early as 3000 B.C. Ghana was a great civilization thousands of years before the Arabs saw it and invaded the area (they are still occupying Mauritania today, the exact place where part of ancient Ghana existed, and have been accused of making slaves of the Africans living there today). When they reached Ghana, they encountered an ancient civilization that was more ancient than China, Greece, Rome, and Isreal. Only Egypt, Nubia-Kush, Mesopotamia and India's Indisu civilizations were around when the Sahara migrants established the prehistoric civilizations of West Africa. Moreover, the fact that the Mende who had a thriving agricultural society about 5000 B.C. in the exact regions where the Nok figurine culture is located, clearly attests to the great antiquity of sedentary civilization in West Africa.

The West African agriculturists of the period prior to 5,000 B.C. and as early as 10,000 B.C. may have had extra time due to

121

the change from hunting and garthering, and probably fishing, which may have occurred before 10,000 B.C. in the region, when it was covered with more water than it presently possesses. They were able to develop the terracotta and figurine culture, create art out of stone, terracotta and bronze which is considered among the world's finest examples of prehistoric art, and establish a thriving culture. Arts and crafts, building and other allied industries developed and progressed. There was more time to create things while they waited for crops to become ripe enough to harvest.

The development of agriculture in West Africa contributed to the proper use of time. Thus, spare time was used to create crafts, weapons, weave cloth, make houses, caste bronze and create a number of things that would not have been possible, had they preferred to maintain the lifestyle of hunters and garthers, or pastoralists. Leisure activities as well as new types of industries developed. This is what occurred West Africa after the establishment of and development of agriculture. Furthermore, the use of women in agriculture and the strict division of labor allowed men who continued to hunt and fish, to develop new industries, or widen what they already had, such as pottery making, terracotta artwork, bronze casting, carving, making weapons, jewelry, and weaving valuable purple and multicolored gold and silver threaded cloth and fabrics. That's a skill that is practiced by men in West Africa, as Goran Burenhult shows in his book, Traditional Peoples Today, 1994, p. 133) (7)

The making of terracotta figurines and the planning and building of giant projects like dams, cities, roads and others, helped build a great civilization and continue what had been created in the Sahara, Khem and Nubia-Kush before and was still taking place during the period of 3,000 to 500 B.C. When one examines the arts and crafts of West Africa, from as early as about 3,000 B.C. to the current time, one will notice a steady development from naturalistic art to highly sophisticated abstract art, as if a form of artistic evolution had taken place. In other words, by about 600 B.C. and afterwards, the African artists' minds had become too sophisticated to depend only on copying

122

naturalistic art to express themselves. They were experts in the production of naturalistic art as their works clearly show. They began to express their inner souls through abstract art. By 1000 A.D. An example of ancient Olmec art which closely resembles West African abstract art practiced both in ancient times and today is seen in Ivan Van Sertima's book, African Presence in Early America, (1992, p.90, fig. 7) (8)

It seems that by 500 B.C., the West African artist had developed a philosophy to go with his art. This philosophy had been engrained in the African subconscious from the beginning of human history. Abstract art in the later eras became the norm and was based on the mental and spiritual as well as the physical.

The age of anthropormorphic art in West Africa and of advanced civilization and culture in West Africa is over seven thousand years. In fact, it bagan with the development of agriculture and sedentary living by the Mende speaking peoples of West Africa, who were also spread out in the southern Sahara in prehistoric times. According to Nigerian anthropologists, cultures such as Nok of Nigeria have produced artworks of great skill and craftsman with an age of 2700 B.C. Iron may have been used in the area about between 1500 B.C. to 1000 B.C., much earlier than the 500 B.C. period that some historians usually suggest. The book, History of Africa, Volume II, edited by G. Mokhtar, discusses the early age of iron. M. Posnansky writes in, "Introduction to the Later Prehistory of sub-Saharan Africa,"

"The suggestion has recently been made that iron working may have developed indigenously in Africa. A strong proponent of this view is C.A. Diop, who is supported by Wai Andah in Chapter 24 of the main edition. It is further suggested that as many of the early sites for iron technology in West Africa, such as those associated with the Nok culture, or in Burkina Faso, are associated with stone tools, then the possibility must remain open that iron working took place in predominantly Late Stone Age contexts." (1990, p. 301).(9)

This is clearly a facinating revelation and pushes the history of civilization, arts and crafts production and the production of iron implements back to a considerable period of time. This very old period has already been discussed, due to the fact that historians place the establishment of sedentary agricultural culture among the Mende of West Africa to about 5,000 to 6000 years Before Christ. The use and working of iron in West Africa means that ironworking and the culture that created fine artistic works connected to the Nok civilization of Nigeria, is about 10,000 to 20,000 years old. This very ancient period for the possible use of iron in West Africa is no surprising, considering that very little is known about the cultures of the Sahara. Yet, it is known that in the region, a Black aquatic civilization existed. It was one of the regions from which Egypt received some of its cultural benefits.

Africans of West Africa and the rest of the continent became tired of creating the same type of naturalistic art, over and over again. In their minds, their Gods, spirits and ancestors, were too important to take on the look of mere humans. Furthermore, their minds began to develop a sense of abstract creativity that can only be expressed by creating what was not in existence to the eyes, but only imagined in the mind. The origin of the changes in the way artists expressed what they actually saw, with what they felt or wanted to portray can be seen in Egyptian art, where people of typical Negroid features are portrayed in a highly stylized, stiff form, without curves, which gives them the features of works done by people who had no time to perform a good job. Some of these are carved with straight noses, bulgeless arms and straight, curveless bodies.

This art style occurred until the time of Akenaton, who went out of his way to have his features portrayed exactly as he looked. Even some of these appear stylized. Abstract art done during the time of Akenaton as well as present-day Africa, and the rest of Africa between 1500 A.D. till today is an advanced development in an artistic tradition that was well developed way back in the Paleolithic age and during the time the art of the Tassalli are of the Sahara was occupied. Rock paintings going back to about 7000 B.C. and continuing up to 1500 B.C. show naturalistic paintings of Africans placing their nets in a lake or river. These paintings are so naturalistically done, that they can be compared to art today done in the same school.

# CHAPTER THIRTEEN

# WEST AFRICAN TRADE AND COMMERCE

The West Africans developed a trade network which included Nubia-Kush, Khemet, the Sahara, North-East Africa, the Congo Basin and the Americas. The trade routes by carmel caravan from West Africa to the Maghreb and North-East Africa in the later years are well known, however the first traders may have used horses and ot her draft animals before the carmels were brought over from S.W. Asia, hundreds of years later. Donkeys were used as well.

The vast network of trade which existed in the the Sahara during the late Neolithic and early iron age period (5000 B.C. to 2500 B.C.), was a continuation of a network that was in existence thousands of years earlier. This network began in West Africa and criss-crossed the Sahara to points north, south, east and west. Thus, during this period, it was West Africa that was one of the primary sources of trade and commerce and not necessarily the Sahara. B. Wai Andah, a Nigrian archeologist with the University of Benin, in Nigeria explains in General History of Africa (edt. G. Mokhtar, 1990, pp.337-338), "Prehistoric Trade and the Earliest States in West Africa." (1)

"Recent archeological research thus clearly shows that an important element of long-distance trade in prehistoric times was carried on with the peoples of the Sahara and North Africa. But this by no means justifies claims such as those made by Posnansky that 'to discover the origins of long distance trade in West Africa our search has to begin in the sands of the Sahara.' However well intentioned such a claim may be, the emphasis is wrong and the far-reaching implications false. For one thing, it ignores the fact that an internal system of long-distance trade existed in West Africa which much preceded (and indeed made possible) the development of trans-Saharan trade.

In the view of this author, existing evidence points to the existence from Early Iron Age times of a complex and extensive network of long-distance trade, thriving on local complementary craft industries, especially (e.g. in fish and salt) between coastal peoples and inland farming peoples on the one hand, and also between the latter peoples to the south and more pastoralist societies to the north on the other. Important local products traded included iron and stone (for tools and weapons), leather, salt, grain, dried fish, cloth, pottery, woodwork, kola nuts and stone and iron personal ornaments.

The patterns of internal trade and crafts (industry) developed within West Africa shaped and sustained trade routes between the West African and the Saharan worlds. Such internal trade also fostered the growth of larger villages and towns in the Late Neolithic and Iron Age times. Archeological information which is now accumulating, even for the forest areas of West Africa, continues to indicate that the subsequent emergence of the Asante, Benin and Yoruba states, as well as the Igbo-Ukwu culture, depended essentially on a highly successful exploitation of their environment by earlieriron-using (and in some cases non-iron-using) peoples."(1)

No one could have stated the West African development and spread of trading activities better then B. Wai-Andah. His statements clearly show that despite the lack of courage by some archeologists and anthropologists to lay the facts concerning the West African development of trade, culture and civilization in their region, the fact remains that indeed, they participated in that development and spread their ideas as well as their products over a wide area of Africa. In fact, it was from West-Central Africa that the Bantu speaking peoples migrated to the rest of southern Africa, bringing with them the techniques of agriculture and iron-making. They also spread from West Africa to Eastern Africa and up to the southern parts of Somalia.

Much of the reasons for the migrations of Africans from West Africa may have to do with their need to find new lands to plant as well as to graze their livestock. However, trade may have also been one of the catalysts which prompted the great migration of Bantu-speaking West Africans from Eastern Nigeria and the Cameroons southward to the rest of Africa. These migrations and trading trips were most likely carried out in canoes. Trade from all areas may have also used canoes, draft animals, sailing ships and human porters for transportation.

Canoes well stacked with goods coming from the east, west or any region where rivers were navigable and led to towns, villages or cities may have gone in and out of ancient prehistoric West Africa, particularly to ancient, pre-Christian kingdoms such as Ghana, Ashanti, the Ife, Benin, Igbo-Ikwu, and others. Boats or canoes sailed eastward along the Niger to the area of present-day Sokoto, then from there by caravan to Kano where boats could have transported goods to Lake Chad. From lake Chad down the Chari River and up on the Bahr Salami, caravans could have been used to carry the goods to Bahr El Arab river to Malakal, where boats could have taken goods along the Nile in various directions.

Although these routes may sound far-fetched due to the distance of 2,500 miles covered in what today may be traiterous terrain, in ancient times, these routes may have been much more navigable and frequently used. In fact, some of these ancient routes were used by slave traders and kidnappers of Africans between the 1500's to the 1900's. Furthermore, trade between West Africa and the civilizations of the ancient North and North-East did occur, so taking these routes would not have posed any great difficulty. Goods were moved from one place to the other on draft animals (where using them was not hampered by the tstse fly or 'sleeping sickness'), by boat or by potters. There were villages, towns, cities and places to rest along the trade routes. At these points, animals were exchanged or fed and rested, while new boats were purchased or used.

West African trade with the Nile kingdoms occurred and did use the sea routes as well. That means that as early as 3000 B.C. to 400 B.C. B.C., the Khemites, Nubian-Kushites, West

Africans, Puntites, Abbyssinians, Canaanites, Carthaginians, and others were sailing to West Africa and West Africans were sailing to some of these places, in the very same way they had been sailing to the Americas. They used longboats, ships and other means of sea travel. The West Africans may have used the easy route of sailing westward, then northward, hugging the western coast of Africa, through the straits of Gibralta, then eastward towards Khemet, Nubia-Kush, Canaan, and some of the nations of the Mediterranean. Their ships could have cruised down the Nile River to cities such as No, On, Armana, Elephantine, Napata and Merowe.

Khemite and Nubian-Kushite ships could have sailed in the opposite direction, down the Red Sea, southward to the tip of South Africa and northward to West Africa. The Saite occupier of Khemet, Pharaoh Nekau, sent ships to West Africa. They sailed around Africa about 600 B.C. The Phoenicians or Carthaginians took the same journey about 450 B.C., with Hanno who spent some time in parts of the coasts of Africa. Among these places visited was probably southern Africa. Cameroon and other parts of West Africa was also visited, where Hanno and his men witnessed what may have been the earliest example of the celebration of the harvest festival (Kwanzaa).

According to B.H. Warmington in General History of Africa, Volume II, (1990, p.247, "The Carthaginian Period."), a report by Herodotus concerning Hanno, leader of the Magnoid Family, discusses the gold trade between the West Africans and Carthaginians about 450 B.C.

"At Cerne, the Phoenicians (i.e. Carthaginians) anchor their gualoi, as their merchant ships are called, and pitch tents on the sland. After unloading their goods they take them to the mainland in small boats; there live Ethiopians with whom they trade. In exchange for their goods they acquire the skins of deer, lions and leopards, elephant hides and tusks...the Phoenicians bring perfume, Egyptian stones (faience) and Athenian pottery jars." (p. 251). (2)

Many types of trade goods were exchanged between the West Africans and other parts of Africa, particularly Nubia-Kush, Khemet, Carthage, Ethiopia, the Sahara, Central and Southern Africa. Ivory, ebony, copper, gold, silver, iron and iron tools and weapons, ostrich feathers, foodstuffs, tools, weapons, cloth, salt, leather, and other goods left West Africa on ships, animal caravan, or foot for the lands mentioned above. From the north came products such as amber, salt, alabaster and ceramic wares, turquois and other products including some manufactured goods. Although West Africans were major manufacturers of goods who made their own cloth, weapons, utencils, tools, wood products, furniture, jewelry and ornaments of gold, iron, bronze, copper and ivory, they had no objection to importing foreign manufactured products.

## West African Trade With The Phoenicians

There is no doubt that the ancient Phoenicians or better yet, the Canaanites, were members of the Black race. The Biblical writers themselves state that Ham was the father of the Black race (after the flood, although this is unlikely scientifically, since all humans came from the Black race, the original Homo sapiens), and that Canaan was a son of Ham, thus Canaan was Black, if we believe in the biblical account. The name 'Phoenician,' itself should not even be used to refer to these ancient Negroid Black people, for it says nothing about their racial or ethnic origin. It is a fact of history that the Canaanites, regardless as to whether the biblical tale is accurate or not, were of the same race as the Egyptians before the Semites infiltrated Canaan and began mixing up the peoples there. Furthermore, it is very likely that the Canaanites migrated from Egypt, where the the ancient Maobites who entered Canaan in prehistoric times also migrated from. Thus, by the First Dynasty, the ancestors of the Canaanites, who were pure Black Khemites, migrated to Fhenkhu (Canaan) and established a culture similar to what they left behind in Egypt.

The name Phoenician does not tell too much about these Black Africans from Khemet who were the first settlers of

Palestine and whose original Black forefather Canaan, gave the land its name. The word 'Phoenician,' originated from the Greek word, 'phoenikes,' which means purple or refers to the purple and reddish-purple color of the dye the Canaanites used for their cloth. The name may have also been used to refer to the dark-black to reddish brown complexion of the Phoenicians, in the same manner that the blue-black skin color of some West Africans, caused them to be called 'the blue-skinned men,' by outsiders. These Africans who were so called, are not to be mistaken or confused with the Tuareg, a Negroid people with some Semitic admixture, who were also called the 'blue men' because the blue dye of their cloth gave the appearance of blue skin even though they were either dark brown, reddish brown, or of black complexion.

The proof that the Canaanites or so-called Phoenicians were originally Black people, similar to those of Africa, goes beyond the fact that they were descendants of Ham. African civilization itself is tens of thousands of years older than the story of Noah and his sons, and the scientific proof has shown that African Negroids were the original people on the planet. And so, the history of Black Negroid people go back hundreds of thousands of years, compared to the 6,000 years of biblical history.

The original people of Canaan were stone age farmers descended from Black Africans who first migrated out of Africa beginning between 200,000 to 150,000 years ago. These included the original Black Homo sapien and the later Grimaldi Negroids who also passed through that are to Europe about 40,000 years ago. Semitic invaders from the Arabian peninsula who were a mixture of the original Negroid inhabitants of the area and Caucasian invaders from the north, arrived in Canaan between 3000 to 2000 B.C. and afterwards. In fact, they occupied the entire area and mixed with the Blacks of the whole Middle East region, to create the mixed race dominant in the region today.

Black people from Khemet had already established a culture in Canaan thousands of years before the Semitic speakers invaded the area. After the Semites arrived, there were many conflicts between the two peoples, particularly over religious beliefs and land rights. The Bible has accounts of these conflicts such as the worship of Baal, who was a copy of the Khemite God, Amun or Hathor. In fact, the Canaanite God wore clothing identical to the Egyptian ones.

Although the Canaanites left no records on paper about who they were, there is evidence in stone, ivory, gold and wood, which portrays the racial characteristics of the Canaanites. The most ancient evidence shows the features of Negroid Black people, such as the picture of a female with Negroid features and hair styled in the braided, beaded style of the Blacks of ancient Egypt, looking through a window. This picture can be found in the National Geographic Magazine, on page 171(3) of volume 142, no. 2. The female has all the features associated with Negroid African people such as flat nose, full lips, round face, curly hair and so on.

Another work of art, an ivory carving inlaid with gold shows a lion attacking an African dressed in a Khemite kilt, without a shirt, among lotus plants. This African is not only wearing his curly hair, well portrayed in gold, but his Negroid racial features are as plain as daylight. A stone carving of a child show Negroid features, although the outline of the flat nose seems to have been cut or broken off. Other sculptures show bass reliefs of Semetic people dressed in long, Semetic styled dresses and with racial features typical to the Semitic people at the time, such as aquiline hooked noses and long straight hair.

Exactly when did the Semites occupy Canaan? It is known that Asiatica had occupied parts of Lower Egypt before 3100 B.C., and that Aha-Mena, or Menes defeated them and reunited Khemet with the Delta, which had been occupied by Asiatics. This unification zrocess failed to expel the Asiatics, and was a grave mistake since the descendents of these Asiatics opened the door for further invasions and are today the majority of the people who live in the northern part of Egypt today. It is possible that the same Semites who invaded from the Arabian deserts may have been the ones Aha-Mena defeated. They may have remained in northern Egypt after they were defeated. Yet, the Semitic people as a large and significant group may have not been powerful enough to take on a war with Egypt, or to flood northern Egypt with any amount of people whose presence would be of any great significance. After one branch of the Semites, the Hebrews who may have been Black or mixed Black people were freed from Egypt by Pharaoh Merneptah about 1200 B.C., prior to staying in Egypt for over 700 years before they were freed with Moses, they went directly to the 'Promised Land,' Canaan, a land that rightly belonged to the Black Canaanites.

According to the Bible, prior to the journey of the Hebrews to Egypt, there were only a few family members. Abraham's twelve sons, their wives and children, Abraham himself and his wife. Four hundred years later when they left there were many hundreds of thousands including Black Egyptians, Nubians and other Africans who joined the family Isrealites out of Egypt. When Aaron reached Canaan, the land was already occupied. In fact, they had to fight their way into one of the first towns they reached, or as the Bible accounts, "They marched around it till the walls came tumbling down." Abraham's family was one of the many Semitic pastoral families who migrated to Khemet during the periods of famine and drought in the region.

The first people with whom the Phoenicians traded was the Khemites, since the Phoenicians or better the Canaanites, were an extension of Egyptian civilization into SW Asia. The trade was carried out at the port of Byblos. At the period before 3100 B.C., timber and wood were the primary products exported by the Canaanites to the Khemites and Nubian-Kushites. The Khemites may have also imported large amounts of papyrus from Byblos, (the word Bible comes from Byblos, where much wood and papyrus flowed from in ancient times). Before 3100 B.C., and afterwards, timber and wood were the primary products exported by the Canaanites to the Khemites.

Among the other goods the Canaanites (Phoenicians) traded with the Khemites or exchanged for Khemite products were copper, which was mined in Khepra (Cyprus), grain, inscense, spices, animal hides and precious stones. Ships from Khemet transported piles of timber logs from Canaan to help them in their ship building and building programs, long before 3100 B.C.

134

They took manufactured goods from Khemet and sold or bartered them at the port of Byblos.

One of the biggest errors ever made during the interpretation of ancient history occurred during the 19th Century, when scholars from Europe misinterpreted the biblical story of the origins of the races. All races are said to come out of Noah and his sons and his sons wifes, it is said. The Phoenicians or Canaanites were said to be Semetic, even though they came out of Ham who was Black and of the same racial group as the ancient Egyptians and the Black people of Africa and the African Diaspora, today. The people of the north of the Mediterranean were classified as Japethic or "white."

Gerhard Herm is also confused by this story of human origins. He asks, in his book, The Phoenicians, The Purple Empire of the Ancient World, "Who in fact were the Semites? History, which is not a very exact 170 science simplifies matters considerably. It lumps together under this collective name all the major races which from 3,500 B.C. onwards, migrated from the deserts of Arabia towards the flourishing civilizations of the Nile and Euphrates. Thus, the Akkadians who occupied Sumeria are called Semites and also the founders of the Assyrian and Babylonian Empires. The Arameans who settled in Syria were also Semites, as were the Jews and Arabs."

"What seem to have distinguished these groups from each other was both their racial characteristics such as a hooked nose and their speech. In the 18th Century Europe, Shem, the eldest was promoted as the father of the Semites, Ham was the father of the Hamites (Blacks) and Japhet for the Japhetic (white) race or the people of Asia Minor. However, Canaan and Sidon, two symbolical figures connected with Phoenicia were held to be descendents of Shem, yet according to the biblical story, the Phoenicians were descendants of Ham."(4) It seems that if Canaan was the son of Ham who was Black, then Canaan was also Black, moreover, if the Semites did not migrate to Canaan before 3,500 to 3,100 B.C., when Canaan was already settled by Black people from Khemet (Egypt), then the Phoenicians or Canaanites could not have been Semetic or even Caucasian, nor

135

could they have been the original inhabitants of Canaan. It was probably after 3,100 B.C., that the Semites appeared on the scene and even they could not have totally absorbed the native Black population of the region, after they (the Semites), invaded the area. Thus, a conclusion can be made that the Phoenicians, who traded with the Mediterranean and West Africa up to the Roman period, were Black people for the most part, until the massive invasions by Semites, Greeks, Indo-Europeans, Romans to the area.

By 3,000 B.C., the Canaanites had established a lucrative trade with the Khemites. The Phoenicians controlled some of the sea routes by 1200 B.C. By then, the Semitic element had gained a partial foothold among the native Black Caanites, although the Canaanites still dominated the region as well as the trade. From then onward, the Phoenicians became wanderers of the sea, trading, bartering and selling on all coasts around the Mediterranean. From Byblos, papyrus continued to be shipped to Khemet, and copper continued to come from Cyprus and other places. More Khemite and Nubian-Kushite manufactured goods and raw materials continued to filter into the Mediterranean region. Some historians that the Phoenicians not only sailed throughout the Mediterranean, but they went to the east to India in later years. The southern coast of Spain know as Tarshish, was among the places the Phoenicians, the Nubian-Kushites and the Khemites went to carry out trade, settle and mine for minerals. It is said that the Phoenicians founded the city of Cadiz, in the south of Spain. From that port, they may have gone into the rest of Western Europe, Britain, and Africa in search of metals such as tin.

The Phoenicians (Canaanites) were the movers of goods not only for the Khemites but also for King Solomon of the Jews, who brought gold from Ophir. The location of Ophir has always been mysterious, but the products from that land brought back to King Solomon were products such as wine, precious stones, peacocks, emeralds, honey, oil and ivory. These products could only have come from Somalia, India, anywhere around Africa, and as far away as the Americas.

The Phoenicians or Canaanites built the city of Carthage about 814 to 813 B.C. after they left their original homeland and decided to establish settlements on the north-west coast of North Africa. They extended their trade not only to Tarshish (Spain) and the rest of the rest of Europe, but along the N.W. coast of Africa, down the west coast to Benin, the Ghana coast and the Ivory Coast area. The Phoenicians traded with the 'Libyans' according to the Greeks, who used the term to refer to the Black people of Africa who lived on the northern coast of Africa and in fact, throughout all of Africa. The name 'Libyan,' was the Greek word for Black Africans and had nothing to do with the Asiatics who migrated there much later, and who continue to occupy the land to this day. The Phoenicians had a method of trade they used when conducting business with the Africans that was later used by Arab traders to Ghana in the 700's A.D., and afterwards.

Trade was carried out in the following manner: Gold and other goods were placed in a specified place by the "Libyans" who afterwards retreated to a faraway area so that the Phoenicians could examine the gold and place goods of equal value next to it. If they were not satisfied they left the gold and their goods there, until more gold was placed next to it. Upon being satisfied, they took the gold and other products, and left the goods they brought for the 'Libyans' to take.

The Phoenicians traded with the rest of Africa, particularly West Africa and that is documented by ancient writers, as the past quotations in this text clearly shows. The Phoenicians sailed around Africa by going eastward and sailed westward around the Western Bulge of Africa, down to Cameroon, further southward, and back to the Mediterranean. In the area of Cameroon a journey led by Hanno mentioned meeting native people and seeing hairy apes called 'gorillas,' by the West Africans. It is said that the Phoenicians went beyond the Straits of Gibralta, into the open Atlantic, a feat that had already been accomplished by the Nubian-Kushites, and the Khemites hundreds of years before. The West Africans also accomplished the same feat by sailing to the Americas and it may have been from these people that the Phoenicians may have heard about land across the Atlantic Ocean.

Latin historian Diodorus of Scicily wrote in regards to the lands across the Atlantic (called The Western Sea) by the ancient Africans. "In the deep of Libya (Africa) an island of considerable size, fruitful, much of it mountainous, through it flow navigable rivers."(5) The Phoenicians had discovered it by chance after they had planted colonies throughout Libya amassed great wealth and assayed to voyage beyond the Pillars of Hiracles into the sea that men call, "the ocean." The Island could not have been Madagascar, since the Pillars of Hiracles is in the west, whereas Madagascar is in the south-east and close to Africa. Therefore, unless the writer was referring to the Azores or Cape Verde Islands, then the Americas is the most likely place that the Phoenicians sailed to.

## Phoenician And West African Relations

The relationship between the Negroid Africans of Northrn Africa and those of West Africa during ancient times is one that has seldom been written about, except in the case of the ancient trade between Khem and Kush, and West Africa. The trading pattern and and the relationship between the Black Canaanites and the West Africa. needs to be established.

By the time the first Phoenician ships sailed around Africa, West African civilization, particularly in the Savannah areas, was quite ancient, moreover, much of the forest areas of West Africa may have been sparsely settled before three thousand B.C., but not after that period, when migrants from the drying Sahara as well as parts of West Africa entered into the area. The Savannah regions of West Africa served as a crossroads for people moving between the Sahara and West Africa. So, the establishment of settled and advanced culture in the forest regions of West Africa may go back to a period between 10,000 B.C., when Negroid Blacks certainly lived in the area alongside the pygmies and 2600 B.C., when the early Iron Age was beginning in West Africa. It is important to note that the use of bronze in West Africa was mainly in the production of utencils and ornaments, while iron has been used from a very early period of time, for weapons cooking utencils, and other purposes.

The Phoenician impression of West Africa about 450 B.C., when they accompanied Hanno to the Cameroon, in West-Central Africa, may have been incomplete because by that period, civilization in the area was in full bloom. Cultures such as the Nok Culture, were well established throughout West Africa. Such cultures existed in the forest areas as well as the savannah area. As for the settlements and kingdoms of the interior, the Phoenicians made no mention of them, and perhaps they did not see them.

This is the account given by Hanno who sailed as far south as Cameroon about 450 B.C. This account was told by the Greeks and may have been somewhat altered. Hanno gives this account about the coastal region of West Africa up to the farthest point east he sailed along the West African bulge, before turning back toward the north. Hanno gave a description of how he sailed through the Straits of Gibralta (The Pillars of Hiracles) with sixty ships and a large group of about 30,000 men and women.

The Phoenicians may have had trading posts along the West African coasts as early as 600 B.C., when Nekau's ships sailed around Africa, however, it seems hardly likely that thirty thousand people from the Mediterranean area would have been able to colonize any part of West Africa, where the native Black population were well established, as well as militarily capable. Furthermore, in this tropical area, close to equator, the average temperature was probably 105 to 115 degrees average. Moreover, malaria, the tsetse fly would have made it difficult for people who depended on draft animals, or who were not protected or accustomed to malaria to survive. West Africa was also one of the heavily populated areas in Africa, even thirty thousand people armed with swords, spears and weapons similar to what the Africans had would not have been able to take over the areas they landed at, unless there were no people to challenge them.

Any settlers who came and tried to settle in West Africa during that period could have died out sooner or later, due to the various obstacles to outside settlement there. If the Phoenicians settled anywhere, it was not the forest regions of West Africa, along the Bight of Benin, but somewhere between the Senegal River and the Atlas Mountains. Then the possibility that the Phoenicians of 450 B.C. were still basically a Negroid people with black to brown complexion, who were able to suit well into the West African enviroment is possible, so that if the settlers were primarily Blacks, they would not only have survived, but some of their descendants may be some of the people who live in West Africa today.

Hanno's account continues. "On the second day of his journey he founded the colony of Thymiaterion, and on the fifth day, Karikon, Gytte, Akra, Melita, and Arambys, then he came to the mouth of the  River Lixus where he took interpreters on board probably among the existing Phoenician settlers. We sailed for two days to the south paralell with a desert shore and then eastwards again, and found a small island of about five stades (one kilometer, or about two-thirds of a mile) in circumference at the far end of the bay. We founded a settlement there called Cerne, then we sailed up a river called Chretes and reached a lake, in which three islands bigger than Cerne, lay. We sailed on for another day and reached the end of the lake. Some very high mountains towered over it which were inhabited by 'savages' (my quotations) wearing wild animal skins who threw stones at us and prevented us from disembarking."(6)

The description given above of where the Phoenicians were, could have been any number of places along the west coast of Africa. If one calculates the amount of time a ship during Hanno's era (450 B.C.), sailed per knot, a conclusion can be made concerning exactly where they landed. Hanno had been sailing for six days (either exact daylight days, or twenty-four hour days), before he founded his last town. Arambys then came to the mouth of the River Lexus. Ships during that period sailed an average of about five knots per hour. With twenty-four hours per day at five knots per hour, and one mile per knot a ship could have traveled about one hundred and twenty miles per day, without stopping.

Hanno did stop in a few places of course, but how long he stopped is not known. But if he let out settlers upon each stop and sailed again, then he may have spent an average of six to ten hours per place on each site where he disembarked supplies or people. He continues, they, "sailed for two days," he writes, "parallel to a desert shore, which means it would have had to have been somewhere between Cape Timiris and Sidi Ifni. So as we can see, these first colonies may have been built on the shores of the desert regions around Mauritania and northward. From that base he travels towards the south for a few more days, "and eastwards again and found a small island of about, "five stadts (one kilometer, three quarter of a mile)." This area could have been anywhere from Senegal to Cameroon. It takes a day to reach the end of a lake they sail into by river, suh a lake may have been Lake Chad, further to the north-east of Cameroon, or the lake south of Timbuktu, which is part of the Niger River.

If it took one day to reach the end of the lake at a travel of about 100 miles per day of sailing, then the lake had to have been Lake Chad, the only lake about one hundred miles long from the mouth of the Yobe River, to the eastern shore and with islands in it. It could have also been a lake in the present area south of Timbuktu along the Niger, or anywhere along the coast that has since been reduced due to changes in the physical characteristics of the land or topography. The lake is described as having, "some very high mountains towered over it." That description would rule out Lake Chad or the inland lake south of Timbuktu as the place since there are no tall mountains in either area. The most likely place would have to have been anywhere along the coast from Senegal to Cameroon, but most likely, the area around Cameroon.

The discription by the Phoenicians of having seen "many fires," by night, heard the sound of flutes and cymbals and wild voices. We were seized with fear and our interpreters bade us sail away." This account gives a hint of what was probably an established trading relationship, for it takes a while for one group of people to learn the language of another, unless they had some sort of relationship with each other, or went out of their way to learn the other's language. As for the fires they saw, that could have been the burning of the grain fields which occurs during the harvest time in West Africa every year. The sound of flutes and cymbals hints that metal was being worked and musical instruments were being used to celebrate a festival.

The Phoenicians' description of man-like creatures as 'gorillas,' certainly leaves a lot to ponder. The word "gor," "vir," means "male" in the Wolof language, a language spoken around the nation of Senegal, in West Africa, "gor gwne," also means "young man," in the same language, according to Cheikh Antah Diop (General History of Africa, 1990, p. 31). Hanno's account states, "We chased some of them but could catch none of the men, because they were used to climbing the rocks and pelted us with stones from there. But we caught three of the women. They bit and scratched those who carried them because they had no desire to come with us, so we killed them, and skinned them and brought the skins back to Carthage. We sailed no farther, because our supplies had come to an end."(6)

This account of what may or may not have been humans is puzzling. Who exactly were these 'gorillas,' and from what language did the term originate, or was it a misinterpretated word. The similarities between the word gorilla and the Wolof words gor, which means male in Wolof, and gor gwne, which means 'young male' in the same language, clearly shows a connection. Thus, the language spoken by the local people could have been wolof or a related language. As for the so-called, "savages," they could have been chimpanzes or some type of ape, but definitely not humans. It would be very unlikely that these creatures were any human type in that part of Africa, for Africans and particularly Negroid Africans are not hairy, furthermore, to some people, the first sight of chimpanzees, would make them wonder whether these were some type of humanoid.

The Phoenicians knew of Negroid people quite well, since they were partly Negroid, worked for Negroid people of Egypt and lived in an area where Negroids were a large part of the population. As for the Pygmies, it is unlikely that these "savages" were Pygmies because Pygmies were known to some of the North Africans. They were hired as entertainers by the ancient Egyptians, the same ones who hired the Phoenicians to sail some of their ships. African culture in West Africa was also at a high stage of development when Hanno reached the area, after all, the ancient settlement of Nok, where most of the iron age culture and terracotta works were created was about 350 miles from the coast. The ancient kingdom of Ife, where some of the most magnificient artworks ever produced, as well as well as Benin, Oyo,and the Ashanti, ancient kingdoms and cities which existed as early as 1600 B.C., florished during the time of Hanno's visit to the area. These kingdoms and cities or settlements were no more than about one hundred miles or less from the coast of West Africa, along the Bight of Benin. Thus they would not have regarded these advanced Africans with whom they traded as "savages."

Had the Phoenicians journied further inland where the Africans had established high civilizations and cultures since before 3000 B.C., their account would have been totally different. Then again, who knows what accounts they told and whether these accounts are known and are simply being hidden, like thousands of facts about Black African history.

The Phoenicians would have had some difficulty landing 30,000 people on the territories of one of the ancient kingdoms of West Africa. The Africans of that period were very secretive about where their gold was coming from, hence the use of "dumb barter" as a vehicle for trade. That system was still in use during the 700's A.D. when the Arabs went into the area to trade and acquire the region's gold.

The possibility that the 30,000 people who travelled with Hanno included a large number of Black Carthaginians is very likely, although by 450 B.C., the original Canaanites and Phoenicians who were Blacks, became partly racially mixed with Semitic types. In fact, the vast majority of people of Northern Africa and parts of the Levant, before the invasions of the Hyksos, Greeks, Jews, Assyrians, Romans and Arabs were Negroid Black people who were in their aboriginal homelands. here had not been any mixing on the level there would be later in history. So, some of the 30,000 people who left Carthage, may have been similar in appearance to the millions of Blacks who already lived in West Africa and founded the early civilizations there such as Ghana, Ashanti, Benin, Nok, Ife, Oyo and others.

It is also possible that even while African civilization and kindgoms florished in the interior during the time of Hanno's visit to West Africa, Black Phoenicians as well as other could have settled on the coast without causing too much of an uproar at first. However, these settlers would have been found out, captured, and sold off. In fact, some writers familiar with West African history point out that this is exactly what happened to some of the Phoenician settlers.

Another problem is the location of the place where the Phoenicians would have settled, was it West Africa along the Bight of Benin. The coast of West Africa acts as a barrier to the interior and the savanna lands, except along the river valleys that empty into the sea. The lands from Gambia to Cameroon is mainly highland covered with thick forests, highlands, high mountains and thick fly and mosquito infested jungles, where malaria and other infestations caused death to animals and to those who were not accustomed to the enviroment in the region. This type of land area go inland for about two to three hundred miles or more, before the savannah lands and sparsly vegetated forests begins.

There are similarities today between Africans who live in Africa and the ancient African cultures and civilizations of northern Africa. Similarities between the Akan or Ashanti of Ghana an the Carthaginians or even the ancient Greeks and Khemites, as well as the Jews can be pointed out. The Ashanti clothing is one example, with its robes which resemble the togas worn by the Greeks and Romans, as well as the males of Carthage and Numidia. These North African and South European cultures were greatly influenced by Egyptian and Nubian-Kushite civilization and culture.

Many West Africans such s the Ashanti and Wolof claim to have originated in the North, however both the Ashanti and Wolof may have come not from near the Mediterranean, but around the area of Mali during the early Middle Ages, and perhaps the Sahara in earliest antiquity. Also, the Ashanti seemed to have been in West Africa at least one thousand years Before Christ, when they had a kindgom in the area, although it was not in the present location of the Ashanti today, in Ghana. The Wolof may have Khemetic origins, since their language has a large amount of Khemetic words. Their migrations, along with that of other Blacks from Egypt and nations of the Middle East such as Morocco, Tunisia, Algeria, Libya, Sudan and Canaan, all formerly Black nations, were caused by invasions, upheavals and other problems in these nations.

Yet, in West Africa, particularly along the Bight of Benin, no Phoenician towns have been unearthed, although traded Phoenician like artifacts have been found in some areas. As far as towns and cities go, the only city which sounds in name like one of the towns built by Hanno's settlers, is the city of Accra in Ghana, which sounds like the Akra of Hanno. However, Hanno's Akra was built north of Cape Verde, perhaps along the west coast of Morocco, Spanish Sahara or Mauritania.

### Ancient West Africa: Wealth And Resources

The trade carried out between the Africans to the south, and the Phoenicians had to have increased about the time when Pharaoh Nekau the Saite, sent his ships to sail around Africa about 600 B.C. He like others before him, may have known of earlier voyages around Africa taken by Sahure, Snefru, Hennu and Hatshepsut. Did Nekau wanted to match their accomplishments? It was Nekau who rebilt an ancient canal from the Mediterranean to the Red Sea, something former Pharaohs had done in the central part of Khemet, from the Nile eastwards to the Red Sea, from No (Thebes). Sahure took the eastern route through the canal to the Red Sea in 2500 B.C. Hennu did the same in 2000 B.C. and Hatshepsut in 1493 B.C. All used that route by passing through a canal that led to the Red Sea. Herodotus, the Greek historian recounts that Nekau had ordered "Phoenician men to sail home through the Pillars of Heracles into the Northern Sea (Mediterranean Sea), and so back to Egypt."(7) It seems that that the Phoenicians and those who sailed Nekau's ships, were ordered to sail eastward, then

145

southward around Africa, then up northward along the western coast of Africa, around the western bulge of West Africa toward the north. The ships would have sailed northward along the coasts of Mauritania, Spanish Sahara and Morocco, through the Straits of Gibralta (or the Pillars of Hiracles), into the Mediterranean Sea, to the Nile River's estuary, then southward to No, or the other cities of Khemet.

Herodotus' account continues. "They launched forth from the Red Sea and sailed across the Southern Sea. When autumn came round, they landed and sowed their crops, finding themselves in Libya (Africa) each time and there they waited for the harvest. When they had brought in the grain, the sailed on, so that after two years, they came in the third year through the Pillars of Hercules and back to Egypt again. They said which I do not believe, but many others do, that on the voyage around Libya, they had the sun on their right."(7) The sailors were correct in their observation, the sun is on the right when sailing in the far south and going in the direction they were sailing in, when they discovered this phenomena.

The circumnavigation by Nekau's ships around Africa is well documented, yet nothing is said about what products they may have traded with the Africans, particularly in West Africa, apart from the exchange of African gold for Egyptian products that may have occurred. Being among the most proficient sailors and traders in the Mediterranean (along with the Egyptians and Nubian-Kushites), the Phoenicians who worked for Pharaoh Nekau may have attempted to trade with the Africans for their gold as well as other products the Africans had, particularly manufactured iron products such as tools and weapons.

Some historians are aware that as early as 1500 B.C., Africans from West Africa were engaged in trade and exploration in the Americas. It is also known that from about 3,000 B.C., Africans on the west coast of Africa and those in the empires of Khemet and Nubia-Kush were involved in cross continental trade by using the networks of rivers and trails along the southern edge of the grasslands. It is also known that Africans had been involved in trade among themselves and with others who lived in all directions from West Africa, as early as

10,000 B.C., and earlier, particularly during the aquatic phase (20,000 to 10,000 B.C.). Knowing these historical facts, African trade with the Phoenicians who came late on the African scene compared to the long history of African civilization, was probably not very facinating to the Africans. After all, they had traded across West Africa and the Sahara by using their ships to move from region to region as early as 20,000 B.C.

The Africans with whom the Phoenicians traded could have been the ones in the areas where they planted their grains and waited for the harvest. If they planted wheat and it grew sufficiently enough to harvest, then they may have stopped on or near the southern tip of Africa, near or on the highlands of East Africa, or the northern part of Western Africa. Wherever the sailors of Nekau stopped to plant and harvest grain, they could have traded with the inhabitants there.

Taking the lands from Cape Verde to Cameroon as one of the places where the Phoenicians traded with the West Africans, it is highly possible that there was a very fruitful trade in that area from 600 B.C. onwards, with the Phoenicians, although earlier trade most certainly occurred. Africans in this area were already involved in trans-Atlantic trade with the Americas, therefore, extra trade with the Phoenicians would have only been more profitable for them.

Gold was the most important product traded by the West Africans along with commodities such as cotton cloth, steel and iron tools and weapons, manufactured leather goods, glass beads, leopard skins, ivory and ivory products, tin, precious stones, and wood and stone products. Gold came in the form of nuggets and ignots although most traded gold was in the form of gold dust. Copper, bronze and iron ornaments and implements were also traded. Copper X-bars, ignots and rings were the most famous of the processed copper raw materials. The sale of bronze statues, ornaments, weapons, cooking utencils and other products also occurred.

West Africa has been a source of gold and iron as well as gold iron, brass and bronze products from the earliest of times. Compared to other parts of the earth, West Africa has been richly blessed with such valuable raw materials, as well as ingenous craftsmen and craftswomen, who initiated the earliest Iron Age (2600 B.C.), and metal products manufacturing process. Yet, from the earliest times, the West Africans kept their gold producing regions secret, and conducted silent barter on the beaches miles away from the sources of their products.

The elaborate system of measuring and weighing gold and gold dust existed among the ancient West Africans, similar to these same types of methods applied during the Middle ages by the Ashantis and others. In fact, Ashanti weights, measures and scales continue to exist. This elaborate system of trade brought great wealth to the West Africans, thus by 600 B.C., when Nekau circumnavigated Africa, African artists, craftsmen and the entire material culture improved greatly. It was at this period that the Ghana Kingdom experienced a new era, as it improved and developed into a glorious empire. The forest kingdoms along the West African coasts also experienced a period of improved wealth and development, as well as artistic improvement.

The actual age of the West African kingdoms such as Ashanti, Igbo-Ikwu, Ife, Oyo, Benin, Kenem-Bornu and Ghana is very much older than the invading Arabs and Europeans have told the world. These civilizations were in existence as early as 1600 B.C., according to West African historians and writers. In the case of Ghana, the earliest civilization in West Africa and the one recorded by Arabs during the 700's A.D., it did not simply pop on the scene about 700 A.D., as Western and Arab historians like to point out. In fact, this was the period when the Arabs came to prominence in the Middle East, then began expanding their empire and religious empire towards Africa. Ghana's history was began in prehistoric times, probably by Mende and Soninke speaking farmers, who had an established agricultural culture by 7,000 B.C., and who spoke part of the Niger-Congo languages, said to be about 10,000 years old. The people in the region of Ghana were also the first people to use iron and iron products (2600 B.C.), after the Swazis and people of Southern Africa, who are documented to have mined iron and red ochre as early as 40,000 years ago.

By 2600 B.C., the early Iron Age began in West Africa. Iron was being used in West Africa while neither bronze nor iron was in significant use anywhere else. In fact, there was no "Bronze Age," in West Africa, or the rest of sub-Saharan Africa, for that matter. Yet both bronze and brass were used extensively for tools, weapons (for example spearheads) and ornaments. The Africans went from using stone tools, to using both stone and iron, to iron, without passing through a bronze period, similar to the Middle Easterners.

In the area of exports, bronze and iron products was sent far and wide. One of these places was the Americas. The West Africans may have exported their artwork and artworking techniques with those of their people who migrated to Olmec Mexico between 1800 B.C. to 500 B.C. The type of art produced by the Olmects of mexico originated in West Africa, at least some of their carving and sculptural techniques. In fact, much Olmec art is identical in racial characteristics, style and technique, to the West African Nok Culture's artwork, which flourished from as early as 3000 B.C. down to the Middle Ages, when the West African kingdoms of Ife, Benin, Ashanti, Oyo, and Igbo-Ikwu continued to produce versions of these ancient styles of art and sculpture.

In his book, The Destruction of Black Civilization, Chancellor Williams writes, "Ghana's actual history goes far back beyond its known record. That record listed forty-four kings before the Christian Era and that alone would extend Ghana's known history beyone the 25th Dynasty when the last Black Pharaohs ruled Egypt."(8) This evidence shows that somewhere before 800 B.C., Ghana was a well established kingdom with an organized and civilized society equal to that of Khemet and Nubia-Kush. This may have attracted people such as Nekau, Hatshepsut, and others who wanted to share in the trade of this powerful and wealthy kingdom of West Africa.

## IVORY

Ivory was one of the products traded extensively between the West Africans and others, including the Phoenicians, since ancient times (Warmington, p. 251: General History of Africa, UNESCO, 1990).(9) Elephants may have also been traded. The western part of Africa was much more heavily populated with elephants than the northern part, where elephants were in great demand as beasts of burden and later on for purposes of warfare. There were countless animals on the savannas of western Africa about 500 B.C., compared to today. Tons of ivory could have left West Africa along the coast for cities like Carthage, Tyre, Byblos, Sidon and the cities of the Nile Valley. The Carthaginains were known for their use of the elephant in their cavalry, during the 300's to 100's B.C.

Hanibal, the Carthaginian general used them in his conquest of Rome, while the Romans used horses and were astonished by these huge beasts. It is possible that some of the elephants used by Hanibal may have come from the savannas of West Africa, traded to them by the West Africans. These elephants may have been led upon ship, then sailed up north to Carthage. On the other ;hand, the elephant was also widespread in parts of North Africa in these areas not taken over by the desert. They roamed the northern and western coasts of Africa then all the way east, down the Nile Valley to Sudan and back west to the Atlantic. All Africa had elephants, except the arid desert areas of the Sahara.

The elephants of northern Africa during the time of Hanibal were less in number than those of West Africa, and so there may have been a need for those of West Africa, as well as for the ivory these elephants produced. Trading in West African elephants may have also occurred if they were a better breed, or better suited for warfare than those of North Africa.

## TIN

West Africa may have also been a source of tin for the Phoenicians, the Khemites, Nubian-Kushites and Carthaginians. For thousands of years, the people in the northern part of Africa and the Mediterranean longed for tin in order to make bronze weapons, utencils, tools and other things. The Phoenicians themselves had already sailed to the British isles for this metal, under Khemite and Nubian-Khemite financing and direction. The Phoenicians sailed as far as India in search for this metal. Going to West Africa for the same metal, or trading in it there would have been only a matter of asking the West Africans whether they had any to barter. Tin had always been very essential in the production of bronze and was wanted by most nations at the time. Yet, iron was being used in West Africa as early as 2600 B.C. (the early beginnings), for making tools weapons and other impliments. Whenever tin was available, it was used to make bronze artworks, jewelry, gold weights and utencils. It was also used to cast bronze figures of humans as late as the 1500's A.D., in the Kingdom of Benin. The West Africans may have had an abundance of tin, but since they did not use much of it to make weapons of bronze, (iron was used instead), they may have sold some to the Phoenicians and others.

## IRON

Iron may have been traded by the West Africans to the Phoenicians and others. Iron was in great demand about 600 B.C. to 450 B.C. due to the need for stronger weapons among nations of the Mediterranean. These nations had not forgotten the Assyrian push of the Nubian-Kushites out of Khemet, due to the stronger, iron weapons of the Assyrians compared to the bronze weapons of the Nubian-Kushites. Chancellor Williams states in, The Destruction of Black Civilization (1976, Third World Press), that the Assyrians were able to capture Egypt from the Kushites, because the Kushites were not armed with weapons of superior quality, but with bronze, while their enemies had iron weapons. The attack on the Kushite occupied Egypt was carried out by Esarhaddon, the Assyrian, who achieved victory near Memphis, one of the greatest Black cities in the ancient world.

After appointing puppet princes from Khemet to collect tribute, Esarhaddon settled down but Tarharka, Shabaka's nephew, mounted another attack from the south and wiped out the forts put in place by his enemies. In 669 B.C., Esarhaddon died on the way to invade Khemet. He was succeeded by his son Ashurbanipal who continued the invasion. Tarharka retreated to

151

Kush after a fierce fight and Tanutamon contunued the struggle against the invaders and their Khemite allies. The Nubian Kushites were finally driven back to their kingdom, Nubia-Kush about 661 B.C. Their great Khemite city of No (Thebes), was burned by the Assyrian invaders.

The retreat of the Nubian-Kushites from Khemet as the Assyrians advanced southward, was a lesson to the Nubian-Kushites as well as those who watched from the sidelines, such as the Jews, Syrians, Libyans, Carthaginians, Puntities and the emerging Greeks, the Black Elamites who were enemies with the Assyrians and wanted to crush Assyrian hegemony in parts of Mesopotamia. To them, iron weapons was the most effective type of weaponry available if they did not want to be defeated. The Black people of Elam, an ancient empire in the south of present day Iran and Iraq, were at war with the Semites and the Indo-Europeans who had invaded their territory. To all these people, West Africa where iron was used as far back as 1100 B.C., was the most reliable source of iron, where the metal was also abundant.

At the same time however, the West Africans of about 600 B.C. to 400 B.C., may have kept the source and manufacture of iron a secret, refusing to sell or trade it with outsiders. That had been the policy of the Kushites who discovered the use of iron long before the Indo-Europeans began using it for the first time in Anatolia, about 1500 B.C. However, its use was not applied on a large scale to weapons. Iron ornaments and some tools and weapons were being manufactured, although on a small scale. In West Africa however, iron tools, weapons and ornaments were being produced on a mass scale earlier than 2000 B.C. By 1100 B.C., the West Africans had developed an iron industry, while the rest of the world, except for a few nations, used bronze. The invention of steel making and of the blast fernace to produce steel, has been documented to have existed in East Africa about 300 to 200 B.C., in Kenya. It was merely a continuation and progressive evolution of thousands of years of using iron in Africa, and may have been carried to East Africa by the Bantus, who migrated from West Africa as early as 1000 B.C.

Ironmaking may have been a tightly kept military secret in ancient Ghana and the rest of West Africa, in the same way it had been a military secret in Kush before the Assyrian invasion of Khemet. In fact, the West Africans carried out trade with the Phoenicians in complete secrecy, refusing even to speak during trading transactions, and exchanging goods miles away from the source of materials they exported, so that these materials would not be taken by outsiders.

The book, Africa and Africans by Paul Bohannan, examines this attitude toward ironworking. "Ironworking in Meroe was probably closely associated with the priesthood as a source of power The priesthood had the kingship in Egypt had scarcely been separated. The process were probably secret, at least for a long period. Even today in West Africa, smithing is associated with social groups that are disassociated from the rest of the clans or tribes, and in many of them, there is a correlation between high rank and ironworking and in a few between low rank and ironworking." (10)

The high amount of secrecy associated with the production of iron was not limited to West Africa. The Kushites, who began developiing their iron industries long before the Assyrian invasion, back to a period when the Khemites were using iron for jewelry and ornaments (1500 to 1100 B.C.), may have decided not to apply iron to weapon-making on a large scale. Chancellor Williams gives the Nubian-Kushite preference for developing their copper and bronze industries over iron as one of the reasons for their defeat. They lacked weapons strong enough to defeat the Assyrians, who attacked with the use of iron weapons. Williams points out that iron was not unknown to the Kushites who had it in abundance, and who also knew how to smelt it and make use of it. They preferred to invest in their bronze industries instead of putting iron to use in their military, and they suffered the consequences.

The policy of not being up to date or above the rest of the world by the Kushites should be a lesson to Pan-Africans today, for many Black nations are doing the same thing by not inventing and investing in new technologies, some which are invented by African-Americans. At the same time, nations such as those of Europe and the Far East cash in on American and African-American technologies, some which were first invented by Africans in Africa, and redone by African slaves since the era of slavery in the U.S.

The slowness of the Kushites to develop their iron industries for military use led to their loosing their ancient empire, which still has an effect on Blacks today, since Egypt (Khmet) and now Sudan (Nubia-Kush) is still occupied by the descendants of the invaders, those who invaded afterwards, and their religious and political domination. In fact, the destruction of the Nubian kingdom during the 1500's by the Arabs, and the continued enslavement of Black Africans today by the very same people responsible for the enslavement and sale of Africans in the region since the 1500's is one of the most important issues facing Africans today. In fact, this problem can and will be solved when the Africans themselves, eliminate all vestiges of foreign domination, culture and religion from the Holy Lands of the Black race, Sudan and Khemet.

Had the Kushites defeated the Assyrians, Egypt could have remained pure Black throughout, down to this very day. Nubia-Kush itself, regained its military strength and lasted up to 1500 A.D., through the smaller kingdoms of Mukuria, Alwa and Nobatia. They indeed learned their lesson, realizing then that in order to stay at the top, and not allow the rest of the world to move ahead of them, they had to develop and improve their technologies. In this era, Blacks worldwide must have the same mentality. One group of Africans, say African-Americans and those in places like the Caribbean, Europe, South America, India, the South Pacific and Australia, must combine their scientific, industrial and economic power in order to create and exchange technological knowledge for the benefit of all our people.

## The International Ancient West African Iron Connection

West Africa was a source of iron and it was being worked in the region as early as 2600 B.C., during the early Iron Age. During this period, cultures such as the Nok Culture had already been in existence and were spread from the southern parts of the Sahara, which may have been fertile, to the Bight of Benin. The first people to use iron according to European historians and anthropologists were the Indo-Europeans of the Anatolian region of Turkey, or somewhere near the Caucasus mountains. They began using it about 1500 B.C.

The Assyrians continued to use iron and used it in weaponry. Still, the Indo-Europeans were latecomers when it comes to the use or even the discovery of iron. Africans were the first to discover, use and turn iron into steel and as early as 2600 B.C., the early start of the African iron industries age, was beginning. This age brought about an industrial revolution in all of Africa, including the southern part of Africa where the evidence clearly show, that iron ore and red ochre were being mined in Swaziland as early as 42,000 B.C., a period in history when European Homo sapiens did not exist in the Caucasoid stage, but were Negroid.

So, inspite of the writings of European scholars and historians giving the Indo-Europeans the credit for being the first to use iron, its first use was in Africa. Michael Bradley in his book, The Black Discovery of America, states this on the civilization of West Africa which led to the first use of iron. "The Nok figurine culture of Central Nigeria shows indisputably that by 3000 B.C., people somehow related to the Sahara culture of Tassili were established in West Africa. By 1200 B.C. bronze had already been brought by the Africans who lived in the drying Sahara to the western part of Africa. Gold was also being worked. By this time, the lost wax method of casting was known and used. Cotton was being woven." (11)

The period given for the first use of iron by European scholars is about 500 to 600 B.C., which is the age that figurines discovered in Nok, Nigeria were dated back to. However, evidence already discussed in this text pushes the use of iron back to a period that is even older than 2600 B.C., back to the end of the late Neolithic to the early Iron Age period (between 5,000 to2600 B.C.) Apart from the evidence given by the people who should be the most qualifiably authority on the Nok civilization, the Nigerians who say that the Nok civilization

155

produced masterful works of terracotta as early as 2700 B.C., there seems to be a direct connect between the Nok civilization of West Africa and the Olmec civilization of ancient Mexico. The Olmecs have produced Negroid artwork and sculpture identical to some produced by the Nok cultue of Nigeria, which existed from about 2700 B.C. to 400 A.D.

Apart from West Africa, South America was also a source rich in iron ore, particularly the northeastern part of Brazil, which fits snugly into the West African bulge. Both areas are very rich in iron ore and both places could have been mined for the ore by West Africans. The same iron could have been sold to the Phoenicians and others who could not find iron in large quantities in the Mediterranean area.

Paul Bohannan examines Africa's richness in iron ore in his book, Africa and Africans:

"Africa is almost a solid chunk of iron ore, most of it low grade obviously, though in some areas of Liberia and Guinea, the content runs as high as 84 percent. When mining in the Nimba Mountain area on the boundary between these two countries was begun in the early 1960's, the technique was merely to clear off the trees, let the thin topsoil wash away and use surface mining methods on the naked rusting hills."(12)

Brazil, the largest nation in South America also has enormous quantities of iron, and iron is easily retrieveable there as it is in West Africa. Thus, it seems that the ancient West Africans could have mined iron ore in West Africa as well as Brazil, particularly if that of Brazil was of a similar or greater quality, despite the steady supply in West Africa. The attitude of the ancient Africans could have been similar to that of many modern nations who take control of the same types of valuable resources, such as oil, uranium, iron ore, titanium or other strategic metals and precious metals. In fact this may very well have been the case, since both Phoenician and Roman coins were discovered in Brazil during this century. Furthermore, a Black nation of African origins called the Chuarrus, do exist in Brazil, they have lived in the region since before Columbus. Therefore, the fact that the Africans were among the earliest people to mine, smelt and use iron, due to the thousands of clay and brick smelters of pre-Christian origins found all over Africa, it is very possible that they may have gone far and wide to find top grade iron ore.

It is believed that the Native Americans did not use iron, nor did they use bronze, yet, we find massive basaltic stone sculptures carved out in one of the hardest types of rocks known, carved to perfection. Moreover, these carvings portray Black African Negritic features of the West African and Nubian (Sudan, Egypt) so distinctly, that no mistake can be made about their racial origins. These basalt stone heads average seven feet high and about eighteen feet in circumference. These heads were not carved out with bronze, although copper may have been used. Yet, it is very likely that iron may have been used in their creation.

The clue that iron tools were used were found in the ground next to one of these giant heads. Bags of well made iron beads were discovered, and they were made with a high degree of skilled craftsmanship. Therefore, if one had the technical ability to produce iron beads of such great quality, which also seems to be portrayed in the helmet of one of these basalt heads, then why not iron tools, weapons, and other articles, including perhaps chain mail and nets of iron beads. What is facinating is that these collosal heads date to about 1100 B.C., some were carved before, and others were carved hundreds of years afterwards. Whoever carved these heads during that period, were using iron in tools and for other implements. The Africans were experts in both carving in stone as well as working iron, and they represented their features with the utmost skill. Iron tools could have been used to build all the temples, monuments, and other structures such as pyramids in the Meso-American region and elsewhere along with copper tools as well.

Those fromWest Africa who mined iron and other metals in in Brazil and Mexico, may have been the same people who sold iron to the Phoenicians and others and it was from them that the Mediterranean traders heard about lands to the west. On the other hand, the West Africans may have kept all sources of iron ore a secret, although the only enemies they may have had, may have been the surrounding kingdoms who also knew of the source of iron across the Atlantic.

To conclude, West Africa was one of the main sources of iron and tin for the Phoenicians, Khemites, Nubian-Kushites, Carthaginians, and others between 2600 B.C. to the early Christian Era. According to the ancients themselves, tin was mined in England and to get there, their ships had to pass through the Pillars of Hiracles (Straits of Gibralta), yet, that may not have been the only direction in which they traveled in search for iron and tin. They also sailed to West Africa, and West Africans may have sailed to them with these metals.

## COTTON

Cotton and cotton products have been exported from West Africa and the Southern Sahara as early as about 4000 to 6000 B.C. In fact, the earliest evidence for the presence of West Africans in the North American continent, involves the presence of an African cotton found in the United States. This cotton was brought to North America most likely by prehistoric African merchants or traders, who crossed the Atlantic to North America. Cotton products were also among the merchandize sold to the Phoenicians, Khemites, Nubian-Kushites and others by the West Africans.

Although the most reliable evidence for Phoenician or Khemite trade by sea with West Africa goes back to 600 B.C., West African trade with the Mediterranean may have gone back as early as the time of Pharaoh Sahure about 2600 B.C., moreover, trade across the Sahara between West Africa and the Nubian-Kushite-Egyptian region, as well as North and East Africa may have been as old as the time of the aquatic civilizations of 20,000 to 10,000 B.C.

In regards to the age of cotton and its use as a trade item by West Africans, Michael Bradley writes in his book, The Black Discovery of America, "Henri Lhote's work at Tassili, revealed a rock drawing of a charioteer showing what may be a woven kilt on the human figure. It may be that the center of Old World cotton cultivation was originally the Sahara, and refugees from increasing drought brought knowledge of cotton cultivation with them to their adopted havens. Cotton would have come to West Africa at a very early date." (13)

No one knows the exact date when cotton was first domesticated and woven by Africans in antiquity, but if representation of cotton garments appear in the Tassili rock drawings which were began about 7000 B.C. to 4000 B.C., the cotton would have had to have been spun and woven by Africans who inhabited the area at the time, and where it was being cultivated. Having migrated southward after the Sahara dried up, Africans would have brought the cotton south with them. Still, the cotton plant also grew in parts of West Africa, therefore, it may have always been there, and was probably first used by the West Africans who had always been in the region, such as the Mende speaking agriculturists whose language in the region goes back to 10,000 years.

By the time the Arabs visited West Africa about 700 A.D., they mentioned the use of cotton cloth by the West Africans. Both weaving and the dyeing of cloth are mentioned as well, but these industries were in fact very, very ancient when the arabs mentioned them. To what extent cotton products were exported to the rest of Africa is not known but it is well known that West Africans traded in cotton cloth. These cloths were of various types and dyed in a myriad of beautiful colors, identical to today's kente cloth and purple, royal cloth. In fact, West African was sent as far as the Aztec Empire, during pre Columbian times. Such cloth is mentioned by the Aztec Emperor, Quaquapitzuak, who ruled in Mexico sometime between the 900's to 1100's A.D.

## The Phoenicians: Masters Or Servants

Various articles have been written over the years, concerning the possibility that the Phoenicians sailed to the Americas and that the people represented in the collosal basalt stone heads were slaves of the Phoenicians. Moreover, since the Phoenicians traded with West Africa from their base in Carthate (modern Tunisia), then the Africans portrayed in the collosal heads were slaves of the Phoenicians. This idea is not totally wrong, it is also illogical, considering the stature of the Blacks in ancient Mexico as ordinary citizens, shamans, kings and working people. Some were even worshipped as Gods, as one of the collosal stone heads, used as an oracle clearly indicates. Furthermore, the Africans portrayed in the collosal, stone heads may have been from the Nubian-Kushite Empire, which included Egypt and parts of the Levant, as well as Egypt.

It is unlikely that the Phoenicians got slaves from the West Africans. Many accounts of Africans having voyaged to the Americas on Phoenician galleys as slaves are most likely false, particularly if these Africans were forced to make such a voyage, as occurred later in history, during the European slave trade. It is possible that there was some trading of captives in Africa, as some Khemetic paintings and hieroglyphics on temple walls in Egypt and Nubia clearly show, however, many of these were prisoners of war captured during periods of warfare.

The Africans represented in Olmec art are represented in all facets of life. Some of Alexander Von Wuthenau's photographs of Olmec art show Africans and Blacks in general in all walks of life, particularly in(14) his book, Unexpected Faces in Ancient America. In Olmec representations of Africans, the Africans are placed in a position of dominance over people who seem to have "Semitic" characteristics, such as "hooked," aquiline noses, beards, turned up shoes, and other characteristics. Representations of Semitic looking people have been found carved on stalaes and in other mediums.

Bill Mack discusses the African position among the Phoenicians in Fate Magazine:

> "For a long time, archeologists have been puzzled by the diversity of physical types portrayed in Olmec art. The Olmecs, first of ancient America's true civilizations, were the precursors of the Mayans. They sculpted figures that are strikingly Negroid in feature. To further confuse the already murky picture they also portray what

archeologists call the 'Uncle Sam' figure, men with aquiline features and chin wiskers."

Early archeologists concocted theories that these portrayed Phoenicians and the Negroid featured portraits were either slaves or crew, or both. As is usual in such schorlarly guessing games, the balance tipped the other way when a number of stalae were found where the 'Uncle Sam' figure were shown groveling in submission to the Negroid featured men. To add to the considerable confusion, some Olmec statuary depicts a combination of the two Negroid features with chin wiskers! Many of the Mexican state and university museums have taken the bull by the horns and labled their exhibits as having been introduced or at least influenced by contacts with Africa. Perhaps the most striking example of why Mexican officials made their decision is found in the state museum of Jalapa. A terracotta bust approximately ten inches high is definitely the portrait of an African right down to the 'cornrow' hairstyle. The clincher is that the sculptor, to insure that there was no doubt painted the face black." (15)

The observations of Bill Mack and that of the Mexican officials throw doubt into the innacurate belief that the Blacks portrayed in Olmec art and in the collosal stone heads, were slaves or even servants of the Phoenicians. No enslaved people, would be bowed to, nor would their portraits be carved in gigantic boulders, many times bigger and more massive than portraits of their so-called masters. Furthermore, one of the collosal heads was used as an oracle or talking God. It has a hole in one ear, through which a priest may have uttered words to represent the God. This same technique was used by the Ancient Egyptians and Nubian Kushites, who made use of 'talking Gods.

We are left with what is actually the truth and the reality, that the Blacks portrayed in the collosal, basalt stone heads were both representations of Gods or kings, or God-Kings similar to those of Egypt and Nubia-Kush. These great Black Olmec kings ruled Mexico for perhaps one thousand or more years, beginning about 1100 B.C. to about 300 A.D. In fact, about twenty-two of these gigantic stone heads have been found in Mexico, and there may be more.

The so-called Semites portrayed among the African Blacks were probably Phoenicians or Canaanites, for these were people who were a mixture of Semitic and African, with a predominance of African features. This type is clearly present in Bill Mack's description. Also, the similarities between the pure Blacks portrayed in Olmec art and West Africans and the pure Blacks of Sudan, and Nubia-Kush of ancient times is stunning. Thus, a ship under the control of Black Egyptians and Nubian-Khemites could have hired some Phoenician sailors, as was their custom and sailed to West Africa, where African sailors accompanied them in West African boats, for a trip that had been planned. After all, the Nubian-Kushites, Khemites and Phoenicians traded with the West Africans. Logic says that due to the very ancient relationship that the West Africans had with the Americas, (earlier than 4,000 B.C.), then the Khemites, Nubian-Kushites and Phoenicians would have heard about lands beyond the Atlantic from the West Africans, in the same way that the African sailors of Cape Verde told Christopher Columbus about the Americas and their trading relationship with the American Indians there.

In retrospect, the history of West Africa was as fruitful, rich and glorious as that of Khemet, Nubia-Kush, Elam, Sumer, Punt (Negau), India or any of the Black civilizations on the north-eastern portion of Africa, West and South Asia. All these regions made great accomplishments. While the Nubian-Kushites and Khemites spread their trade and influence throughout the Mediterranean, the Indian Ocean (called the Ethiopian Sea as late as the 1500's A.D.), the Atlantic, Asia, the rest of Africa and Europe, the West Africans spread their trade and influence to the Americas, the Sahara and North Africa, the Nile Region, Central Africa, the British Isles and the Iberian Peninsula. There are records which proves an ancient African connection between the Africans in the area of Cameroon and the ancient Blacks of Mesopotamia as well as ancient China.

162

Wayne Chandler discusses this facinating topic in the book, African Presence in Early Asia, edited by Ivan Van Sertima (The Principle of Polarity (1995, pp. 360-370).

The West Africans traded in gold, silver, tin, iron products, colored cloth, spear heads of metal alloy and gold, weapons, manufactured goods, leather goods, wood products, ivory and ivory products, pottery, food products and fruits and a wide variety of goods. The evidence for the transfer of crops from West Africa to other areas and vice versa exists in the availability of crops and plants found in places like the Americas, that were there before Columbus, yet were also in Africa from ancient times.

Crops such as peanuts were planted in the Andes mountains about 800 A.D., yet the peanut was also in Africa during that period. Plantains and cotton were found in the Americas as well as Africa before the time of Columbus, with the crop having been transported by Africans to the Americas in ancient times. Various crops such as rubber, were found in both places. Rubber had been planted by the ancient Ghanians long before the eighth century, when Arabs wrote of seeing it in the area, however, it was also grown in pre-Columbian Mexico. In fact, the word "Olmec," used to call the ancient Blacks Of Mexico, came from the Aztec or Maya word, "olli," which means rubber. Within the ancient boundaries of the Olmecs included areas widespread with rubber trees.

# CHAPTER FOURTEEN

# PUNT (SOMALIA, EASTERN AFRICAN COAST, SOUTHERN AFRICA AND THE AMERICAS, WHERE WAS IT?)

It is believed that the ancient region of Punt was restricted to an area from Southern Arabia to Somalia, regions where Blacks inhabited and organized great civilizations, both before and after Christ. But that restricted area is not all there was to Punt if one carefully examines various texts and comments by ancient sailors who traveled to the region. For example, during the reign of Amenenhat II, and for centuries before, Khemite Pharaohs had sent their ships to Punt, which actually included the entire East African coast from Somalia, pass Tanzania as far south as Mozambique. There is even those who believe Punt may have included parts of the Americas.

However, the tale of a sailor who shipwrecked on an island off The Land of Punt, where spices were plentiful gives an idea of the distance between Punt and Khemet, as well as its overall size. Moreover, while Punt included southern Africa, journeys to Punt may have also included journies to the Americas, which the Khemites called "Manu," and "The Land at the Bottom of the World." Still, it is quite likely that when taking a voyage to Punt, which was southern, eastern and western Africa, the Khemites and Nubian-Kushites also voyaged to the Americas and other places.

Still, in regards to Punt or eastern, southern and western Africa, the tale of the shipwrecked sailor gives a clue to where exactly Punt was. The location of one area, an island where spice has been traded since very ancient times, is off the east coast of Tanzania. This island is called Zanzibar. The island is referred to as being in Punt (or part of Punt), by the "King" of the island who welcomed the sailor. If that was Punt or part of it, then Punt may have stretched from Somalia to the coast of Tanzania. It is off the Tanzanian coast that there are three islands that cover an area from the border with Kenya, to the north of the Rufifi River south of DaresSalaam. These islands are called Pemba, Zanzibar and Mafia Island.

Zanzibar has been world famous for its cultivation and export of spices and has been involved in the exchange of spices for other products since the time of Sahure, about 2500 B.C., who sent ships to Punt for trading and commerce. The island mentioned in the book, The Shipwrecked sailor, had to have been Zanzibar Island. If that was the case, then Punt was much larger than previously thought (as being only Somalia, Southern Arabia, ect...), and the Puntites controlled a much larger land area than Somalia. This area would have included Kenya, Tanzania, Northern Mozambique, Zimbabwe, down to South Africa. The extent of the Kingdom of Punt, or 'God's Land,' as the Khemites in Hatshepsut's time called it, can be found out without much difficulty if the story of the shipwrecked sailor was derived from some event which actually occurred.

The story of the ship-wrecked sailor deserves careful analysis. This story is the inspiration for the Adventures of Sindbad. This analysis is necessary in order to find out how far down the coast of East Africa the Puntite Kingdom, or region went. If Punt was infact a Kingdom or empire similar to Khemet and Nubia-Kush, then there is no doubt that archeologists have not done a proficient job in finding where it is, writing its history, and proclaiming its glory.

The story begins with the sailor who has just arrived from Punt and is met by a Khemite official. Cyrus H. Gordon states in his book. "The noble courtier said: "Let your heart be hale, O captain!" The captain has just returned from a distant merchant maring mission and is about to report to the Pharaoh. A well-meaning courtier is trying to prepare the captain for facing the anxities of the situation by reminding him of his return for which he should be thankful. "We have reached the residence (where the Pharaoh is), the mallet has been seized and the mooring stake driven in the prow rope fastened on land. Give praise and adore God, for every man is hugging his fellow. Our crew has come back safely, without loss of our personnel. We have reached

166

Wawat and Senmut.  We have returned in Peace and reached our land." (1)

Wawat was a part of a greater Khemite Empire about the time that Khemet and Nubia-Kush was one giant empire, centuries before 3000 B.C.  It may have been somewhere to the west of the Ethiopian Highlands, or it may have been on the shore of the Red Sea, south of the canal now called, Wadi al Hammamat, whih was used by Hatshepsut, Hennu and Sahure between 2500 B.C. to 1493 B.C. as a waterway to enter into the Red Sea.  As for Senmut, it may have been further South in the area of Erithrea.  By the wording of the account, both Wawat and Senmut may have been regional areas or kingdoms, passed by along the way to the Nile and to cities like No, On and Hikuptah.

The courtier continues.  "Listen to me, O captain!  I am devoid of exaggeration was to yourself put water on your fingers.  Then you will answer when you are addressed you will speak with poise to the Pharaoh, answering without faltering.  The mouth of a man can save him; his words can get indulgence for him.  But you will do according to the dictates of your heart.  It is tiresom talking  (this way) to you.  I'm going to tell you something similar that happened to myself.  I was going to the mines of the sovereign."(1)

During these ancient times, the mining of gold, copper, tin, silver, and other important metals was sometimes carried out in secret and the mines were kept secret, so that others would not infiltrate them.  This was the policy, unless the people who owned the land whcre the mines were kept, did not think bringing others too close to the source of the metals would be a dangerous threat.  This in fact, was the policy and attitude of the ancient Ghanians, who kept the Wangara Gold Mines a secret, and refused to carry out trade near it, with the Phoenicians and others.

The mines mentioned may have been anywhere from Somalia to Azania (South Africa).  The sailor continues, "I went down in a ship, a hundred and twenty cubits long (150 feet) and sixty cubits (90 feet) wide." A crew of a hundred and twenty, the

167

pick of Egypt manned it. They had seen the heavens and seen the earth. Their heart was braver than lions."(1)

The people selected for the journey, "the pick of Egypt," who "had seen the heavens and seen the earth," describes people who were experienced in sailing, and who may have been chosen for a special journey, hundreds or thousands of miles south of the Horn of Africa, or all the way around the tip of South Africa, to places as far up as West Africa, and possibly across the Atlantic, to the Americas. The journey was of great significance and the mining of metal, its purchase or barter and the exchange of goods was of primary importance.

The story continues. "They could predict a storm ere it came; a hurricane ere it happened." The effects of moonsoons on the east coast of Africa, though not as disasterous as in regions like the Far East, was still quite dangerous. Sailing when one was due to come, was a risky and disasterous affair. "A storm arose while we were at sea before we could reach land, driven by the wind, (which) kept making wave(s) of eight cubits (12 feet). A beam of wood hit me; the ship fondered. Of those who were in it, not one was saved. Then I was lost by a wave of the sea on an island. I spent three days alone with my heart as my heart as my (only) campanion. I lay down on an arbor of wood, embracing the shade. I found figs and grapes there, and all sorts of excellent vegetables. K'w fruit (kiwi?) was there together with Nqwt (loquat?) fruit and cucumbers like those cultivated. Fish there were, together with birds. There is nothing that was not in its midst. Then I satisfied myself and put (the rest) on the ground for it was too much for my hands. I carved a wooden drill, produced a fire and made burnt offerings to the Gods."(1)

The Shipwrecked Sailor gives the sailors next surprise. "Then I heard a noise (like) thunder and I fancied that was a (tidal) wave of the sea. Trees were breaking, earth was quaking. When I uncovered my face, I found it was a serpant coming, thirty cubits long (45 feet long). His beard was over two cubits long (3 feet). His body was plated with gold, his eyebrows were pure lapis lazuli."(1)

168

Part of the above account, particularly that dealing with the snake appears to be nothing but fiction, while the rest appears to be more reality. Serpants, including boa constrictors do not grow as long as thirty cubits, which is about forty-five feet long, in fact, they usually grow an average of about fifteen feet long. The Python, an African snake similar to the boa constrictor, does not grow much longer than fifteen feet, either. The snake in this story may be a metaphor for a Pharaoh or king, and the jewels worn by the serpant, may have been the king's jewels. Otherwise, the serpant could have been the ruler, given the attributes of a serpant, in order to make the story more mysterious. In fact, ancient Khemite Pharaohs were sometimes called, "Serpant Kings." The serpant may have also been a long boat with the head of a serpant, painted, or clad in metal to resemble a giant snake, as it emerged from the interior on the backs of people going out to sea, or sailing on the waters with men rowing it to shore. Did the sailor see a python somewhere in a tree or on the ground and developed his story after that?

The story continues with the serpant asking the sailor who brought him. The sailor gives a long account obout how he ended up shipwrecked on the island. The serpant describes the island as having borders surrounded by water and calls the island, "Ka," a place not found on any modern map as yet, but may be on some ancient Khemite and Nubian-Kushite texts. The serpant bestows upon the sailor generosity for which he the sailor, "extended on my belly and touching the ground in his presence, I said to him, "I shall declare your might to the sovereign (Pharaoh) and cause him to know your greatness. I shall have the finest spices brought to you, and temple inscence wherewith every God is gratified. I shall tell what happened and what I have seen of his (your majesty's ) power. God shall be praised for you in the city before the majestrates of the entire land. I shall slay oxen for you as a burnt offering and sacrifice fowl for you. I shall have ships brought to you laden with all the luxuries of Egypt as is done for a God who loves men in a distant land which men do not know."(1)

The sailor accounts that the Serpant King thought his remarks were foolish, laughed and said. "You have no abundance of myrrh and every fine spice and incense. But I am the ruler of Punt. I've got myrrh and that spice you said you'd bring is plentiful on this island. It will happen that when you depart from this place, this island will never be seen again, for it will become water." (1)

The mention of Punt in this story gives an idea of where Punt actually may have been. The 'ruler' lived on an island where spice and other good things were plentiful but he was also the ruler of Punt, which may have been along the East African coast, west of the island of Zanzibar or further south. It is important to note that Zanzibar or some other island further south. It is important to note that Zanzibar may have been the seat of an ancient king who used the island as a place to plant, harvest and collect spices. The Africans used the island for thousands of years as a trading base before the Persians, Omanis, and Arab invaders of later centuries used it as a slave dealing port and established a sultanate.

The amount of time it takes to make the journey from that island to Khem (Egypt) was 'two months' according to the story. During that period, the Khemites used the solar calendar, therefore a month was thirty days, which means they took sixty days to make it back to Khemet. A ship from Khem traveling at five knots per hour (which was about the amount of time a ship traveled in these days) from No (Thebes), through the canal, Wadi al Hammamat, then southward would have to reach somewhere on the coast of southern Mozambique to Swaziland, before the two months was complete. That is if the ship traveled for twenty four hours per day, and sixty days without stopping.

This vast area may have been the Punt mentioned in Hatshepsut's paintings and the logs of the sailor and those who ventured in the region before the reign of Hatshepsut. There are two significant island groups along the east coast of Africa; the isles of Zanzibar and the Comoro islands. Madagascar is a massive island itself, but it is unlikely that it is the island referred to in the story. It may be easy however, to determine exactly where the sailor was shipwrecked and what the island was used for during that period. That has already been analyzed.

The story contains the following information about the raw materials exported from Punt. These very materials attracted the Khemites and others to the region. It says about the gifts given by the ruler of Punt to the sailor. "He gave me a load of myrrh and assorted fine spices, mascara, giraffe tails, a bundle of incense, elephants tusks, hounds, monkeys, apes, and every fine luxury. I loaded it on that boat (a boat sent from Egypt after he had stayed in Punt for four more months) prostrated myself on my belly to praise God for him. Where upon he said to me, "behold you will reach the Pharaoh's residence in two months." (1)

The description of the products given here points not only to one area in Eastern Africa, but a larger region from Cape Guadafui on the African Horn, to Swaziland. The climate in this vast area makes it possible to grow grapes. Giraffes and elephants, monkeys and apes are found in the area. Spices are found in Zanzibar and perhaps other areas of East Africa, where this story may have taken place. Incense is found in the area from Tanzania to Somalia, and most of the region. The story would have been meaningless in an essay about Puntite trade had these clues not been mentioned concerning the goods produced there.

Mention of Puntite trade with Khemet, Nubia-Kush, and other lands can be found in ancient historical texts, as well as modern history books. It is very likely that the Puntites also traded with others, apart from the Khemites and Nubian-Kushites. Being located on the east coast of Africa, they most probably traded with the inhabitants of India, the Arabian peninsula, China and the Far East, S.E. Asia, and other lands in Asia.

Puntite ships sailed to places in the east as well as to the north and south, and also to the west to the Mediterranean. Chinese or Indian texts concerning Puntite journeys to their region may exist, as well as Puntite and Egyptian accounts of journeys to these lands. Trade goods were shipped back and forth between Punt and all the regions mentioned on both the ships of the puntites and on that of those they traded with.

Trade may have been tried out between Punt and the East, just after it was tried out with Khemet and Nubia-Kush, or Phoenicia. The civilization of Punt was in many ways similar to that of Khem, their people were the same Negroid type found elsewhere in Africa, and their languages may have been similar, as the language of present-day Somalia is similar to ancient Egyptian, belongs to the Kushitic branch of African languages, and is not related to the so-called Semitic languages. Moreover, the ancient empires and kingdoms of Khemet, Nubia-Kush, Shoa (today's Ethiopia) and others, may have stopped at Puntite ports on their way to and from the Far East, making northern Punt the crossroads between Africa and the Indian Ocean and Far East. In fact, the ruins of an ancient Puntite (Somalian) port city called Sukim, exists.

Trade between Khemet, Nubia-Kush and Punt were among the earliest heavy networks of trade between the Khemites, Kushites and Puntites outside of their immediate borders. The National Geographic book, Into the Unknown; The Story of Exploration, contains an article by Ian Cameron about Khemite and Puntite trade in the essay, Early Quests:

> "The Egyptians were the first people to make any records of their travels. From hieroglyphics and temple reliefs we can put together accounts of their voyages to a distant and mysterious land they call Punt. "The Egyptians began building ships of cedar about 2600 B.C. when Pharaoh Snefru sent his new fleet to search for Punt, the legendary Land of the Gods so called because the Egyptians believed it was the home of their earliest ancestors, and because it was said to abound in all those treasures Egypt longed for. Ebony and ivory, silver and gold, and incense to burn on itsalters." (2)

> "When Sahure's fleet returned, the ships were laden with 80,000 measures of myrrh; 6,000 bars of electrum, a gold silver alloy; and 2,600 logs of wood, probably ebony. Around 2000 B.C. Pharaoh Mentuhotep sent a court official named Hennu on another expedition to Punt to bring him fresh Myrrh..."I went with three

172

thousand men. I made the road to be even as a river, and the desert even as a sown field. To each man I gave a leather bottle, a carrying pole, two jars of water, and twenty loaves of bread...I dug two wells in the wasteland, and three more in Idahet. I reached the Red Sea. I then built this ship I dispatched it laden with everything." (2)

It already has been determined that Punt was located anywhere between Cape Guadafui on the Horn of Africa, to South Africa. Now it may make one curious to know how wealthy Punt was and how advanced its civilization was. By the accounts given, it appears that Punt was a rich kingdom as well as an entire region. It was very large and there were villages, towns, and cities all along the coast. The distance from Khem to Punt, in relationtion to the amount of time a ship traveling at five knots per hour, for two months took to get there, shows a distance of about seven thousand miles to Southern Mozambique and north-east South Africa.

Cameron states that the Khemites recorded one of their voyages to Punt, and one of the final voyages was taken by Queen Hatshepsut's official, Nehesi in 1493 B.C. She sent five ships to find the land called Punt, or "The Land of the Gods." Nehesi built his ships and set sail southward from some port on the Red Sea. After two years, he returned with the, "marvelous things of Punt." (3)Hatshepsut had a record of the journey carved on the walls of her mortuary temple near No (Thebes). Among the goods and products shown in the relief style carving on the walls are, incense trees in tubs, black ebony wood, elephant ivory, "cinnamon, monkeys, dogs, panther skins." According to the hieroglyphic writings which accompany the reliefs, "nothing was the like of this brought for anything since the beginning."

The location of Punt is shown by the reliefs, and among the carvings are the five ships that Nehsi led on the exebition with about thirty oarsmen, and a heavy cargo of Khemite products to be bartered. In the same relief, these ships are shown at anchor on the shores of a village (or small coastal town), composed of huts of reed built on poles. In the same relief, a scene of Nehsi's men taking Puntite goods back to their ships as they walk on the gangplank is just as clear.

In this series of reliefs the people are clearly shown. Cameron points out that a Khemite official meets with the Puntite queen and her entourage. This queen has the features of an overweight African similar in physique to some South African women, including Kong-San types.

Cameron suggests that because of the Physical features of these Blacks, they may have come from an area close to Mozambique, and since Nehesi had a cargo of antimony, a red substance used in cosmetics by the Khemites was found only in Mozambique, then that nation may have been where Punt was located.

So, when the story of the shipwrecked sailor is compared side by side with the actual recorded accounts of journeys taken by Khemites a parallel is clearly found concerning the whereabouts of Punt. The culture of the Puntites, since it was in southern Africa as well as from Somalia southward, needs to be examined. First, the Puntites were traders and were engaged in commercial enterprises with the Kushites and Khemites, and other nations, which was trade. The Puntite had towns and cities, palaces and other structures, even though the depiction of a village on stilts is what is shown by the temple drawing. Such villages were usually close to a swampy or harbor area and not inland where the rest of the culture was located.

Secondly, the ancient towns such as Sofala and others on the eastern coast of Africa, from Cape Guadafui to southern Mozambique may be very ancient, and were began much earlier than the period of 700 to 1500 A.D., when the Swahili civilization again emerged to create a similar coastal civilization of the area where Punt once was. Extensive excavations in these areas may reveal that indeed these towns are much more ancient than the period usually given for their age.

Thirdly, the Puntites by their dress, hair style and some of the adornments show a similarity with that of Khemet and Nubia-Kush, as well as Canaan, and other Black civilizations of very ancient times. It shows that the Puntites unless they had been portrayed in Khemite costume had a high culture and their

174

cultural influence may have spread all along the east coast of Africa from Somalia to Southern Africa. Moreover, the ancient cities of East Africa credited to the Swahili may have been started by the Puntites long before the journey of Hatshepsut and back during the time of Sahure.

The Ndabele, a people of South Africa, build their houses in a style that may have been the norm for the people of the region during that period, particularly those who lived just off the coast away from the swampy or sea areas. Ndabele houses are made of clay and mudbrick. They are build in the rectangular form, unlike that of some of the other nations in the region who build fences of brick, which are also beautifully painted around them. This type of settlement may have been built in Southern Africa in ancient times, just as they are still built in the area today. These early trading towns and villages may have developed into the large cities of the Swahili, during the Middle Ages. 224

The Puntites which included the people of Southern Africa, mined gold in what is today Zimbabwe and South Africa and exported that gold to the north, and the rest of Africa. They also mined red ochre which they exported and had been doing for at least 40,000 years in Swaziland, where the earliest mines for iron and red ochre, or any metal exists.

In retrospect, the Puntites were not only the people of Somalia but the Africans who settled the whole region of eastern Africa from Cape Guadafui to the tip of Africa to the South, and their entire area including the inland of Africa to Zimbabwe, South Africa and Swaziland, was include in the region loosely called Punt. Punt was not merely one kingdom, but may have been a number of small and large kingdoms with towns, cities and villages scattered over them, with kings and queens, and with high culture. The ethnic make up of the Puntites may have been a mixture of two types of Black Africans, the Kong-San people, and the taller Negritic peoples who inhabited the area before the migration of the Bantu speakers about 1000 years ago. In the ancient African trading network, Punt was among the most important sources of both manufactured and raw goods for Africans, and for those whom the Africans sold or bartered their goods, including China and India.

175

# CHAPTER FIFTEEN

# TRADE BETWEEN THE SUMERIANS AND ELAMITES WITH THE NUBIAN-KUSHITES, KHEMITES AND PUNTITES

The country occupied by the Sumerians can be described as a land that was both dry and subtropical, with a climate suitable in some areas for crops and farming, due to the fertility of the Tigris-Euphrates river valley. The country resembled what it looks like today but with much more greenery and cropland and probably less desert areas, compared to today. In his book Ancient Iraq, George Roux describes the landscape of Iraq in ancient times:

> "Not only do bare mountains, stony deserts, fields of barley palm groves, reed thickets and mud flats form the landscape which ancient texts and monuments suggested, but the living contitions outside the main cities are reminiscent of those days of yore. On the hills shepherds grazed sheep and goats; in the desert, tribes of bedouins endlessly wander from well to well, as of old in the plain. Peasants live in mud houses almost identical with those of the Babylonian farmers and often use similar tools, while fishermen in the marshes dwell in reed-huts and punt the boats of their Sumerian "ancestors."
>
> "The plain watered by the Tigris and Euphrates River is rich in farming land, and was even richer in antiquity before extensive salinization of the soil took place. The entire population of 'Sumer' could easily feed on the country and barter the surplus of cereals for metal, wood, and stone which had to be obtained from abroad. Though wheat, emmer, millet and sesame were grown, barley was and still is the main cereal, since it tolerates slightly saline soil. Agricultural methods were

177

as might be expected, primitive: Ploughing and sewing were performed at the same time by means of a wooden seeding plough which barely scrached the surface of fields, and the furrows were wide apart."

"There were two or three irrigations in Sumer; the main harvest was usually in April but a cash crop was often possible after the winter rains. Yet, so fertile was the land that a figure of three hundredfold given by Herodotus and strabo for the yield of corn do not appear to be grossly exaggerated. On the basis of cuneiform texts, it has been calculated that the yield of wheat in the extreme south of Iraq about 2400 B.C., could favorably compare to that of modern Canadian wheatfields. The hot and humid climate of southrn Mesopotamia, and the availability of ample water supplies in that region also were conditions highly favorable to the cultivation of the date palm which grows along rivers and canals."

"We learn from ancient texts that as early as the third millenium B.C., there were in the country of Sumer extensive palm groves and that artificial pollination was already racticed. Flour and dates the latter of high caloric value-formed the staple food of ancient Iraq, but cattle and sheep were bred and grazed in the non-cultivated areas and in the fields left fallow, while rivers, canals, lakes, and sea provided fish in abundance. A variety of fruit and vegetables were also grown in gardens shelteredby the palm trees and watered by means of a very simple water-lifting instrument (dalu) which is still used underits old name."(1)

The above passages give an idea of what the land of ancient Sumer may have looked like, yet one of the most deliberately hidden historical facts about mesopotamia, which included Sumer, Elam and later Assyria, was the presence of Blacks in these lands who were the original owners and builders of the first civilizations in the area.

Sumer was the most ancient civilization in the Fertile Crescent and they had both a racial and trading relationship with

Khem, Kush and Punt. In other words, the Sumerians were part of the Negritic Black race of the Nubian-Kushitic empire of ancient times. George O. Cox observes in his book, African Civilizations and Empires that the Sumerians entitled themselves, "The Black Headed People," and they were descendants of Nimrod, the mighty hunter who was similar to Osirus of Khemet and Nubia-Kush, and may have been him. The historian Gerald Massy decleared that, "In Kam or Kush, the Black Aethiopic center was the primeral parentage, and they branched out to found the civilization of Egypt, Kush, Mizraim, Phut and Kanaan, represented by the four different directions and Nimrod is the typical leader of the Sumeri-Nimrod, the son of Kush, or the Black race."(2)

According to Ephorus, "The Ethiopians occupied all the southern coasts of both Asia and Africa."(3) Drucilla Dunjee Houston felt the same way, and quotes Diodorus Siculus who said, "The Cushite Ethiopians were the absolute governing class in politics. They commanded the armies and held the offices of state. From them came the ruling families of Babylon." (4)

George O. Cox examines the political, social and racial domination of the Kushites in Mesopotamia. "Kush colonized Mesopotamia around 2800 B.C. Kushite subjects now settled in Babylonia as overlords of Mesopotamia and introduced there what the world has since come to know as Babylonian civilization."(5) The Babylonians were colonists from Egypt according to Richard Lepsius the German Egyptologist who stated. "In the oldest times within the memory of men we know of only one literary development viz those of Egypt, and we know of only one contempory people which could have knowledge of this culture appropriated its results and conveyed them to other nations, this was the Kushites, the masters of the Erythreas Sea to its farthest limits. It was by them that Babylonia was colonized and fertilized Egyptian culture." (6)

There is no doubt that, apart from occassional famines due to war or natural disasters, the Mesopotamians generally enjoyed a rich and varied food and were much better off, in this respect, than their neighbors of Syria, Iran and Asia Minor. Having been richly endowed despite the lack of many mineral and natural resources, trade between the Sumerians, Elamites, Nubian-Kushites and Khemites flourished. As already discussed, although the country was baren in some areas, the southern parts were fertile. Crops were planted and harvested, and surplus was exported. The barter of wheat, barley and other grains such as millet for export to places such as Khemet and Nubia-Kush, who also produced grains, was carried out. Sometimes gold was used in exchange. Turquois and lapis lazuli came from the area of Mesopotamia and was exported to Khemet and Nubia-Kush, along with precious stones.

The Sumerians and Elamites began trading with the world outside of their immediate area quite early in their history. Yet, they were quite poor in mineral resources, therefore they traded massive amounts of grains for metals and the other products they needed. Bitumen, a substance related to petroleum was the only mineral product produced in great quantities. That mineral was used in many ways such as for "caulking boats, as fuel and even as a drug, there is some evidence that at least during certain periods in their history, they exported it."(6)

There were hardly any metals or solid rock and stones, or wood suitable enough to build in Mesopotamia, however their agricultural land produced a bountiful of products. From very ancient times the people of Mesopotamia had been involved in trade and commerce in which they imported products from other lands, and exported their locally produced goods.

The lack of metal ores essential in the production of weapons, or timber for building pushed the Mesopotamians to import from the outside. The first use of copper in that region came from ore that was discovered and mined in the area of the Caucasius Mountains. Copper had been in use in Africa, thousands of years before . Later other sources of copper suplies included Anatolia, Cyprus and Oman. Tin came from Persia or Afghanistan before the Canaanites began bringing it to the Mesopotamians from areas such as Spain. Silver came from the Tauras Mountains and gold came from Nubia-Kush, Khemet and India.

Sumerian traders followed the same directions that the invading Semites would follow after the Sumerians became overwhelmed by them. "Traders moved up the Euphrates beyond Mari, along the Tigris into Assyria and through the Zagros Mountains to Iran and Elam. Voyages were made into the Persian Gulf to Magan (the Oman coast of Arabia)"(6) states Carl Roebuck in the book, The World of Ancient Times, "where Sumerians exchanged textiles, vegetable oils, wool, and leather for copper, ivory, and semiprecious stones. Tilmun (probably Bahrein Island) was becoming a clearing port for these goods and for incense and spices southern Arabia. There was also trade by sea with Melukkha, the identity which is obscure. Some scholars identify it as African Somaliland, others with Balichustan or north western India, with which the Sumrians had trading and perhaps even closer cultural relations." (6)

The Sumerians and Elamites who were each other's enemies, at intervals during their history, may have traded with Punt, along the coast and inland areas of East Africa, as they had traded with Khem and Nubia-Kush for gold, ivory and other valuable products. Due the large area under Puntite control and at their disposal, and from which to draw raw materials, they could have had a trading system whereby their ships may have sailed to the foreign ports to sell goods (as their descendents the Swahili did from about 200 B.C. to the the 1600's when their large ships carried goods to China, including an elephant and other wild animals). Gold, copper, tin, metals, ivory, animal skins, timber, iron tools and utencils, gold ornaments and jewelry, cloth, and a wide variety of weapons were traded by the Khemites, Nubian-Kushites and Puntites in exchange for Sumerian and Elamite goods such as lapis lazuli, turquois, amber and others.

The ancient kingdoms of Elam, Sumer, Khem and Kush, as well as Punt (also called Negau), were both racially and culturally related and had maintained this relationship for thousands of years, although there were infiltrations of Caucasians from Central Asia into these regions, particularly Elam and Sumer. All the early people, including the inhabitants of the Black Indus Valley civilization of Harappa and Mohenjo Daro in the Indus Valley of India were Blacks who originally migrated from Nubia-Kush and Khem, and established trading stations in the lands where they settled. This migration was not the earliest migrations which has led to the settlement of places like India and the Andaman Islands with Black Negritic people, but the migrations during the early stages of Khemite and Kushite civilization about 8,000 B.C. to 5000 B.C.

The ancient Africans of Harappa and Mohenjo-daro kept themselves racially intact, and their cultural traditions strong till the coming of barbarians. These barbarians had a very hypocritical policy (similar to racist Euro-policy today in the U.S. and Latin America, whereby they oppress, create despair, and constantly lie about so-called Black inferiority, while at the same time, using Blacks as a means to pro-long their lives, stay looking young, and for other reasons. The Black Dravidian-Africoids and Afro-Asiatic Negroids of India were able to maintain their ethnic self-preservation, although the barbarians had already began to mix a small segment of the population, giving rise to a small by growing number of people who were of mixed heritage, and who were used, even in India to fortify the racist caste system. These mixed offspring were usually in the middle, being lighter skinned than their Black Indian parent, yet darker than the barbarian. This mixing helped consolidate the caste system.

## Elam: The Black Empire Of Ancient Southern Iran And Iraq

Trade was one of the reasons why the Sumerians remained strong, yet an even stronger kingdom in the southern part of today's Iran and Iraq (where black peoples still exist particularly in the marsh areas), arose. The kingdom was Elam (mentioned in the Bible), continued to grow from what had been the ancient Black Sumerian civilizations. However, between 1000 B.C. to about 500 B.C., they were threatened by the Assyrians, whom they defeated many times in battles.

The Elamites strengthened their position by building a mighty army that kept the Semitic invaders of Babylon at bay. The Assyrians, who were originally a pure Black people, began to become more mixed by the time of Sargon 1 of Akkad (2340

B.C.), thus, the establishment of kingdoms such as Elam, where the inhabitants were mainly pure Negritic-Australoid (as some of the Black people of Sri-Lanka, and South India) as well as pure Negritic-Africoid, began to protect themselves from further Semitic and Indo-European incursions. The Elamites and other Blacks in the Mesopotamian region were prepared to defend themselves and their territory and took the measures necessary to do so.

Elam was one of the earliest civilizations on earth and was a direct offshoot of Khemite and Nubian-Kushite civilizations as well as Sumer. Its people came originally from the Nile Valley and were part of a migration of people from the area which began between 5000 B.C. 8000 B.C. The capital was Susa (Sush). Some of the other cities were Awan, Simash, Madaktu and Dur-Untash.

Elam was one of the earliest civilizations and the people were related to Blacks in Africa as well as Asia. Elam's history can be considered part of or a continuation of the Black Sumerian civilization, and extends into remote antiquity. Runoko Rashidi quotes Gaston Maspero in The Journal of African Civilizations, (edt. Ivan Van Sertima, Transaction Publishers, N.B., NJ 1982)

"Gaston Maspero describes the Elamites as 'a short robust people of well knit figure with brown skins, black hair and eyes, who belong to that Negritic race which inhabited a considerable part of Asia in pre-historic times." (7) French archeologist Dicn La Fag, one of the first to excavate at Susa, referred to ancient Elam as a preogative of an Ethiopian dynasty.

George Rawlison, once again, records that. "In Susiana where the Cushite blood was mentaned in tolerable purity, there was if we may trust Assyrian remains, a very decided prevalence of a negro type of contenance. The head was covered with short, crisp curls; the eyes large, the nose and mouth nearly in the same line, the lips thick." (8)

"Herodotus regarded Elam as Eastern Ethiopia, and believed as did other greek writers that it was the home of Memnon, the great Black warrior king who is credited by Quintus with, "bringing the countless tribes of his peoplewho live in Ethiopia (Africa) land of the Black man," to Priam's Troy in support of the war for survival against the hostile coalition of Greek city states. Memnon came to help them. Memnon was lord over the dark Ethiopians, and the host he brought seems infinite. The Trojans delighted to see him in their city."(8)

The accounts given by those who knew the Elamites personally show that they were of the Black race and they went beyond their immediate borders. Like the Sumerians, the Elamites occupied an area where the soil was sandy and composed of silt. They used hardened brick for their buildings and may have imported stone from the mountains of Media (northern Iran, Iraq) or from Africa. Trade between the Africans and the Elamites took on the same pattern taken by the Sumerians but they may have used the sea routes much more. They were cut off from the north by Assyria, the hostile invaders who wanted to stop the Elamites from remaining a powerful nation in the region.

Elamite ships travelled from the shores of Elam, on the Tigris Euphrats estuary, eastward to Oman and around the bend southwest to Africa, then up and along the Red Sea to Khem, Nubia-Kush and Negau (Somalia) and Punt. The Elamites traded down the East coast of Africa where gold, ivory, tin, iron, spices, herbs, manufactured goods and countless other raw materials were being traded with the Kushites and Khemites. A much shorter route by which trade was carried out between the Elamites and their brothers and sisters in Africa could have been up the Euphrates and southward to Khem by passing through Syria, Lebanon and Isreal. These lands howevever became occupied by the Assyrians, between 750 to 600 B.C. In these places, trade also occured as well.

Later in history between 750 B.C. to about 450 B.C., the Assyrians began to feel the military pressure of the Elamites who invaded and sacked a number of Babylonian and Assyrian cities, carrying off their golden idols, and defeating them. The Assyrians grew more powerful after they were able to cause the retreat back to Nubia-Kush of the Nubian Dynasty of Tarharka, who fought a bitter war with the Assyrians. The Assyrians then controlled much of the seas and land area from Assyria through the Levant, to Egypt. They prevented the movement of ships and controlled much of what came in and left the region.

Elamite trade with Khemet could have suffered a major setback during these periods. The elamites then, would have no choice but to turn east for their raw materials, or to sail southward to Punt, or have Puntite ships bring goods to their ports on the esturay of the TigrisEuphrates river. The trade with nations like India and Nations of the Far East, would have been easier as well, during times of war in the Mediterranean. Their trade with Harappa and Mohenjo-daro, or the culture that developed there at the time, was being carried out long before the Aryan barbarian invasions about 1700 to 1500 B.C.

# CHAPTER SIXTEEN

# HARAPPA AND MOHENJO-DARO THE BLACK AND FIRST CIVILIZATIONS OF INDIA

The first civilization of India was the Black empire of the Indus Valley, whose origins like that of Sumer and Elam was in the ancient prehistoric Nubian-Kushite empire which extended from Turkey to parts of the Lakes Region of East Africa, Southern Sudan and Ethiopia. Egypt was part of this great ancient Empire, called by the Greeks (and by Chancellor Willams, The Destructrion of Black Civilization, 1976),(9) The Ethiopian Empire. This empire was began in ancient Nubia, where civilization was in existence as early as 10,000 to 8,000 B.C. (an article in Time Magazine, points out a period of 8,000 B.C.).(10)

These Nubian-Kushites migrated down the Nile and established civilization in Egypt, the Mediterranean, South Arabia, Mesopotamia and India. It was these Blacks, as well as an Australoid Dravadian type who also originated in East Africa who contributed to the civilization of the Indus Valley.

Wayne Chandler discusses the origins of the ancient Blacks of the Indus Valley Civilization, in African Presence in Early Asia;

"At this juncture, clarification must be made as to the racial stratification arranged within Indian history. As previously noted, the original layer consisted of Ethiopian Blacks (Nubian-Kushite, East African) known as Negritos, the second element later introduced was that of the proto-Australoid (such (as the Munda of India, and other pre-Dravian Blacks), Bharitya describes these people as Black and platyrrhine (havinga broad nose with widely separated nostrils). With the Negritos this race may once have covered the whole of India; a geneological offshoot would later generate the aborigines of Australia. The merging of these two culturally diverse but monoracial groups the Ethiopian Negrito and the Australoid--produced the people of the Indus valley civilization."

These Africoids built one of the most glorious and magnificent civilizations on earth, which was further developed by Black Dravidians coming from East Africa and the Mediterranean. Stanly Wolpert writes in A New History of India:

"In the river valley of the Indus, an urban civilization had deveoped in the course of the third millenium. Its history is more obscure than that of Sumer and Egypt for it is known only through archeological excavation made since the 1920's. The people of the Indus Valley had invented a script for writing but the language is unknown and the text still untranslated (perhaps when this statement was written, P.A.B.). Apparently, urbanization organized in environmental conditions essentially similar to those of Mesopotamia and the economy depended on intensive cereal production based on irrigation from the Indus River. These cities were developed by 2500 B.C., among which the best known centers were at Harappa and Mohenjo-Daro. These two are about four hundred miles apart, but their remains show remarkable similarity of culture. The cities were regularly planned on a checkerboard layout using blocks of uniform size, and the chief architectural features was a citadel enclosing palaces, and temples. This civilization flourished until about 1700 B.C., when a period of stagnation set in, which was followed by destruction about 1500 B.C."(12)

According to Wayne B. Chandler, "Mohenjo-Daro and Harappa, the greatest examples of Harappan architecture, were built between 3000 and 2500 B.C.; these masterpieces of Harappan city planning were the calmination of towns and villages which date from 6000 to 7000 B.C." Chandler describes the civilization of the ancient Blacks of India's Harappa and Mohenjo-Daro:

188

"The population of Mohenjo-Daro and Harappa are estimated to have been 40,000 apiece. The discovery of these two cities has given us a new opportunity to increase our understanding of the earliest human settlements. The most striking aspect of these city ruins is their undisputable evidence of sophisticated city planning. The founders of the Harappan cities are undeniably the world's first urban planners. The two major cities are similarly laid out, again demonstrating the Harappans deliberate city planning. As one author puts it, the city was "Built in a gridlike fashion with a large main street; it seems almost a minute version of Manhatten Island."(Mario Rossi, Christian Science Monitor, "A Lost Civilization Vanishing Again? 1984, pg.25). Both capitals were masterpieces of urban planning."(13)

Drusilla Dunge Houston is far from shy on who the original builders of Indian civilization (Indus Valley Civilization) was. She states in Wonderful Ethiopians of the Ancient Cushite Empire, that the name "Hindu is Ethiopian, and the name 'India' means 'Black.' She further states that according to ancient records, Hind and Sind were sons of Kush. She proceeds further on this issue and points out that, Philostratus, (the Greek Sophist of 217 B.C.) Wrote in Vit. Apollon (lib) II, that "The Indi are the wisest of mankind. The Ethiopians are a colony of them, and they inherit the wisdom of their fathers."(14)

Dungee states that the Indians (pre-Aryan Black Kushitic Indians) were Kushites who separated from the original African stock, ages before the invasion of the so-called Aryan of India. She points out that according to Ephorus, the Black Kushite type occupied all the southern coasts of Africa and Asia, and they introduced metalworking and the arts to the aboriginal tribes. These Kushites made iron weapons, pottery, gold ornaments and built circular tombs for their dead, both in Africa and in India.

On the racial type of the Dravidians and Australoid Blacks of India, Houston points out that they are Ethiopian (Kushite) in ethnic type, and India's civilization came from them. She states that Megathenes considered the people of India and Ethiopia (Africa particularly Sudan), during his time to be similar in skin complexion and features. Houston describes them as a short race similar in form to the ancient Iberians and Chaldeans, with skin color ranging from brown to black, long heads, and broad nose and full, crispy hair. These ancient Black, according to Houston, are the descendants of Blacks with short, woolly hair who were the most ancient inhabitants of Media, Susiana and Persia.

Runoko Rashidi examines the racial and cultural origins of the people of Sumer, who may have had a direct relationship with the people of the Indus Valley civilizations. "Joint excavations conducted by the field museum and the Oxford University conducted in 1926 and 1928. Their findings are key to the concrete physical identification of the regions inhabitants. At the conclusion of the digs pronounced: "The earliest historical crania (hyperdolichocephalic) are from Jemdet Nasr, 18 miles northeast of Kish and those from "Y" trench at Kish...the forehead is retreating, the browridge are always prominent, and the cheekbones rather wide. The nose is braod, in some cases inclining to extremely platyrhine, although the face has seldom survived. This is the type described by Sergi Giuffrida-Ruggeri and Fleuve and named the "Eurafrican" type." (15)

The Sumerians, a Negritic people who were related to the ancient Khemites and Nubian-Kushites (of Africa) included people who migrated from these ancient civilizations between 8,000 B.C. to 3,000 B.C., at varying intervals. They established civilization in Mesopotamia and may have blended with Asiatic Blacks who lived in the Indus Valley area and who were of prehistoric African origins. However, the earliest Black population in India and the rest of Asia may have arrived there between 200,000 to 150,000 when humans left Africa to populate the rest of the world.

Stanley Wolpert comments further. "The winds that anually bring revitalizing rain to the south (of India) probably brought the first humans to peninsula India by sea from East Africa. There are no skeletal remains, only tools to inform us of human nomads to the South India during the Paleolithic Age, but here the tools are core stone impliments, rather than flakes. Crude hand axes have been found in western, central and eastern sites across the Deccan, but since most of these early finds were located in Madras, on the peninsula's eastern (cromandal) coast, this stone core production is called Madras Industry. Its techniques and products are identical with those found in South Africa and Southern Europe."(16) This brings to mind that the earliest people on earth, Black people, migrated from Africa, from the southern and central regions as well as the Rift Valley and the Sahara, to populate the rest of the world.

This passage suggests that the first inhabitants of India, and the rest of Asia for that mater, came from Africa. They were the original inhabitants of South, South-East and East Asia, according to current data. These ancient Blacks may have been of a type similar in features to the dimunitive Blacks who continue to exist today such as the Pygmies, Kong-San, Agta and others. Remains of these types of Blacks have been found all over the world. It has been determined that these Pygmoid types whose carvings of bone and ivory have been found worldwide, sowed the first seeds of Homo-sapien culture on a world-wide scale.

Stanley Wolpert comments:

"There seems to have been a second great wave of human migration to South Asia from East Africa or Southrn Europe sometime after the final receding of the glacial ice that had so long paralyzed human during the Mesolithic Age which began around 30,000 B.C. Numerous microliths have been found scattered across the face of the Deccan and up into central india and even in the Punjab. These tiny stone weapons called Pygmy tools, so closely resembles those found in France, England, and East Africa, that it would appear they were brought to India by hunters and food garthers who were quite different from South India's Paleolithic pioneers." (17)

Although this passage makes one wonder what would Pygmies be doing in Southern Europe during the Ice Age, or soon after the receding of the ice, it cannot hbe discounted that the Grimaldi Negroids, said to be the migrants from Africa who established themselves in Europe about 40,000 years ago giving rise to the Cromagnon, were in the area. In fact, these so-called Cromagnon were the ancestors of the Caucasians of today. It is rather ironic, that in today's climate of racism, that the very ancestors of whites were Blacks from Africa, who changed in hue and racial features in order to adapt to the cold climate.

## Black Civilization, Trade And The Alien Invasion Of Black India

The first barbarians to invade India were from Eurasia. They were called "Aryans" and were a hodge-podge of predominantly Caucasian, barbarian nomads, who followed a pastoral, nomadic and warlike way of life. These barbarians were a very backward people, compared to the Blacks of the Indus Valley civilizations. The barbarians infiltrated and conquered parts of India and established a "varna" (color) based caste system, after they could not totally conquer the resisting Blacks of India, who were the aboriginal inhabitants. They invaded the civilizations of Harappa and Mohenjo-Daro and after establishing themselves, established a religious philosophy which contributed to the keeping of the Blacks in a position of utter inferiority. Vertual slaves were made of the Blacks, whom they called "Dasas" a term synonymous with the word, "Black," or "slave," in the same way in which the term "slave" is usually connected with Black in the United States.

V.T. Rajshekar, editor of Dalit Voice and author of a number of books on the Black Dalit situation explains in his book, Dalit: The Black Untouchables of India (Clarity Press, Atlanta GA, 1987, p.43):

"The Dalit were the original inhabitants of India and resemble the Africans in physical features, (according to a Nigerian genetic scientist, their genetic structure is identical to that of Africans; P.A. Barton, the author). It is said that India and Africa were one land mass until

192

separated by the ocean. So both the Africans and the Indian Untouchables and tribals have common ancestors. Some portion of these came to found the Indus Valley Civilization. These original inhabitants of India put up a strong fight against the Aryan invaders. However, the latter, working through deceitful means, defeated the innocent but hardworking original inhabitants who had built the world's most ancient civilization in the Indus Valley."

Rajshekar continues by quoting Runoko Rashidi. "According to Rashidi, the Aryans enforced the caste system on the Black population (the original inhabitants of India) "with a coldbloodedracist logic with Whites on the top, mixed races in the middle andthe mass of the conquered Blacks at the bottom." (18)

Despite the racist attitude of the invaders, which continues to this very day as if their world stopped three thousand years ago, the Indus Valley civilization was a pure Black civilization and included Ethiopic and Kushitic Blacks from East and North-East as well as West Africa (for example the Bak People who contributed to Akkadian, Elamite and ancient Chinese civilization is said to have migrated from West Africa in the Cameroon region, where some of the words, names of people as well as villages and towns have names similar to those in the Chinese language, for example, Anyang is a town in Cameroon, as well as the ancient Black Shang Dynasty Chinese capital. For more on the Bak Tribes, see Wayne Chandler, African Presence in Early Asia, ed. I.V. Sertima, 1995, p. 363 364).(19)

One group of people important to the history of Indian civilization including the Kushitic and Ethiopic Blacks from Africa, were the Australoid-Negroid branch of the Black race. They are also called Veddoid, or Tribals in India. The ancient Greeks called this branch, including the Black Dalits, the Eastern Kushites. In East Africa, they are regarded by many as a branch of many tribal Kushitic groups who currently reside in the region, and speak languages related to Tamil, Kannada, Malaylam and others.

According to Stanley Wolpert, remains of Veddoid people were "found at cemeteries at Harappa and more recently at the port of Lothal and Kalibangan. Careful analysis of the skeletal remains of one hundred people indicates that the people of Harappa were a mixture of predominantly proto-Australoid (Asiatic Negritics such as the Tasmanians, P.A.B.) and Mediterranean physics, as in modern peninsula India, ranging in height from five feet to five feet, nine inches." (20)

What is described as "proto-Austroloid," as well as "Mediterranean," are simply euphamistic terms for people who were of Black African origin and racial make-up, who existed and continue to exist in hundreds of millions, from the Arabian Peninsula, through India and South Asia, to Australia and the South Pacific. These two branches of the Black race both originated in Africa and have lived in Asia longer than any other racial group, including the Mongoloid stock.

The Australoids migrated from Africa during the Paleolithic era and retained most of their racial characteristics. A period of about 200,000 years before the present, to 100,000 years is about the approximate time that the Australoids, who were Homo-sapiens when they left Africa, migrated to Australia. A few minor changes occurred during the tens of thousands of years since the first migrations. For example, a change in blood grouping among some Australian aboriginals and others may have been due to mixing with other races while living in East Asia, where people related to the Australian aboriginals once lived throughout the south of China along with Blacks of Negritic type from Africa, who migrated to the area later in history (between 50,000 to 20,000 B.C., before the existence of the Mongoloid race), perhaps the second massive wave, with the first being about 200,000 to 100,000 years ago.

A large number of Australoid Blacks have a wide range of texture of hair. These types include straight black hair, curly black hair, or kinky black hair which range in color from jet black to blonde. In fact, a large percentage of Blacks in the South Pacific have blondish hair. Most Australian aboriginals are born with blonde hair, which darkens as they get older. Yet, these characteristics can be found among pure Blacks in Africa

194

as well, where pure black Negritic features and blondish hair is found among some tribal groups.

Some Veddoids and Australoids are much darker than some Africans. For example, there are both Australian aboriginals and South Asians who are darker in complexion than Africans such as the KongSan (Bushman), and a number of Southern African groups such as the Zulu, Swazi and others. This is due primarily to climate differences.

As far as the "Mediterranean," type found among the remains of the Indus Valley civilization, they may have been pure African similar to the types who resided in Egypt and parts of the Mediterranean region before the invasions of the Aryans, and the blending of white and Black to create the Semitic race about 3000 to 2,000 B.C. Thus any so-called "Mediterranean physics," found at Harappa and Mohenjo may as well be mixtures of the invading Aryans and Blacks, which occurred after the 1500,s B.C., or Blacks from the Mediterranean region, who are usually referred to as "Mediterraneans" by some historians and scientists in order to cover up their true Black identity.

### Wealth, Trade And Invasion

Black India of the Indus Valley civilization was highly advanced long before the coming of these savage barbarians from Urasia, "whose only 'civilized' advantage" according to Stanly Wolpert, "seem to have been some superior weaponry and the use of harnessed horses."(21) 248 In fact, the horse was first harnessed and used on chariots by Blacks from the Sahara, according to Michael Bradley, in his text, The Black Discovery of America ( 1981, p.21).

Indus Valley civilization was one of the most advanced and glorious on earth particularly between 6,000 B.C. to 1500 B.C. (the period of steady development, before the invasions of hordes of barbarians from Eurasia. It has already been discussed that the Indus Valley civilization was a mixture of Blacks from East Africa as well as the indigenous Black population of India, which included Negritic and Australoid Blacks, whose place of

195

origin was Africa. Yet, what was Indus Valley civilization seem to have been a long and wide belt of Black civilization in ancient times which began in West Africa, and extended eastward to Sudan (Nubia Kush), Khemet (Egypt), Negau Punt (Somalia, East Africa), Sabean (South Arabia), Mesopotamia (Elam, Sumeria, Akkad,) Indus Valley Civilization and the Xia and Chang Dynasties of ancient China. These were all Black civilizations that were later invaded and occupied by Eurasians and Mongoloids.

Although there seem to be a similarity between the people represented in some of the art of Sumer and that of Harappa and Mohenjo Daro, which has been deliberately promoted to show what seems like Caucasian types, these racial types may have been the same barbarians and tenders of cows and sheep who invaded the region after 1500 B.C. These invasions brough about great conflict with the original Black inhabitants, which still exists today.

The desire to find new sources of raw materials or new people with whom to trade contributed to the migrations of Blacks from Africa to the rest of the world, including India. These traders came from continental Africa, Mesopotamia, Elam, South Arabia, and the Mediterranean area. Upon their arrival in the Indus Valley, the Blacks merely contributed to what was an already established Black culture by adding some of the culture existant in Africa and the areas mentioned. Still, the high level of culture in the Indus Valley took on a level of uniqueness and high quality. Stanley Wolpert examines this. "Indus civilization now represented no fewer than seventy unearthed sites, extended over half a million square miles of the Punjab and Sind from the borderlands of Baluchistan to the desert wastes of Rajasthan, from the Himalayan foothills to the tip of Gujarat, probing the limits of its ecosystem during the half millenium of its mature survival. Recently discovered Harappan outposts along the Makran coast, including that of Sutkagen Dor near the border of modern Iran, clearly attest to brisk and continuous trade with Sumer, especially during the reign of Sargon of Akkad (2334-2279) B.C.

196

Thanks to Sumerian dig at Ur in 1932, we know that the merchants from Harappa and Mohenjodaro were trading with their Sumerian counterparts between 2300 to 2000 B.C. The huge graneries beside the river at Harappa seem to indicate that Indus merchants exported their surplus grain to Sumeria and possibly elsewhere." (22)

Trade between Harappa and Mohenjo-Daro with Africa took on the same pattern as it took between these Indus Valley civilizations and Sumer. They traded metals similar to what the Khemites, Nubian-Kushites and Puntites traded, such as gold, tin, iron, wood, stones and precious stones, animal products and others. India had its share of elephants, so ivory was probably not traded on a grand scale. Trade from Khemet and Nubia-Kush, Punt and other parts of Africa was carried out by boat. About 3000 B.C., Khemite boats were already capable of making trips to Crete, Byblos and other parts of the Mediterranean. Nubian-Kushite vessels had been sailing the Mediterranean and the Indian Ocean since prehistoric times. By 2600 B.C., the Khemites were already making regular trips to Punt. Sahure's ships were capable of sailing about 7,000 to 8000 miles each way to Punt (South Africa). A journey to India or China would have been no big difficulty, at about half the distance.

A journey by Khemite or Kushite, or Indus Valley ship may have taken the same route through the Wadi el Hammat, back and forth through the Red Sea to the south western tip of the Arabian Peninsula, and then sail from there to the north-east and to Harappa and Mohenjo-daro, back and forth. These early maritime journeys occurred at a period in history when Africans were also taking journies to other lands to barter their products for the products of others.

The high level of civilization reached by the Indus Valley Blacks as well as their trading relationships with Africa and other nations, needs to be further examined in order to establish the importance of trade and commerce to the earliest Black civilizations and how it was carried out. The appearance of cotton in the Indus Valley, in an area where it did not originate testifies to the distance that products from Africa traveled to get to area. "By 2,000 B.C.," Stanly Wolpert states, "the Indus people had begun to spin cotton into yarn and weave it into cloth. A dyed fragment of which was found at Mohenjodaro." (23) The cotton plant did not originate in India, but was brought there from Africa.

Wolpert observes in his book, A New History of India, "Henri Lhote's work at Tassili revealed a rock drawing of a charioteer showing what may be a woven kilt on the human figure. It may be that the center of old world cotton cultivation was originally in the Sahara, and refugees from increasing drought brought knowledge of cotton cultivation with them to West Africa at a very early date."(24) (Actually, some Nigerian archeologists and scientists date the use of cotton in West Africa among the Mende Peoples, very much earlier) (25)

Michael Bradley brings more light to the use of cotton in Africa before anywhere else, in his book, The Black Discovery of America. "No one knows when cotton was first domesticated and woven by the West Africans of antiquity. Cotton production and fine weaving and dyeing are casually mentioned by the first Arabic writers of West Africa. This would lead to the conclusion that it was not considered remarkable and that knowledge of cotton domestication and use has been long known among the Black Africans when Arabs came in contact with them. It seems that cotton may be a recent addition to East Asia, although it was found in India from about 2,000 B.C. Radio carbon analysis shows that cotton cultivation did not reach China and Indonesia until 700 A.D.

The conclusion from this observation is that cotton may have not been preferred by the Chinese and Indonesians due to the availability of silk, therefore, cotton remained widely used in India and not China. Still, cotton is a versatile fabric and its use goes beyond the making of clothing. Still, one fact remains, that is that cotton originated in Africa and was carried to India by Africans in ancient times.

Robert W. July explains in his book, A History of the African People. "The cotton of Mohenjo Daro came from a cultivated plant that had undergone much genetic and structural change but was nonetheless identifiable as the descendant of a wild ancestor still growing in Southern Africa. Historical botanists have speculated at great length about the formidable question of how, where and by whom cotton was domesticated, and what means were employed for transporting thousands of miles by land and sea from its homeland to a far-off civilization apparently unconnected to Africa (with that I disagree, for in fact, ancient India and Africa were connected culturally and racially, and cotton may have been brought to India by the ancient Africans, or sent through trade). Whatever may be the answers to these difficulties, it seems clear that a very long history of travel and cultivation must have preceeded the fact of a flourishing cotton cloth industry in the Indus Valley fully five thousand years ago." (27)

Cotton cloth was among the trade items that the ancient Africans exchanged for the goods of Elam and the Indus valley civilizations. Cotton appeared in India between 3000 to 2000 B.C., about the same period people from Africa who had settled in Mesopotamia migrated and began the Indus Valley civilizations. The cotton, if it came via Sumer and Elam between 3000 to 2000 B.C. was part of the countless amounts of cotton that had been exported from Africa to other lands. Tools, weapons, gold silver, animal skins, precious stones, and other products were shipped from Khemet, Nubia-Kush, Punt and Shoa (Ethiopia), to India.

The Indus Valley civilizations like the Indians afterwards, exported a variety of goods to other lands and to Africa. L.S. Stavrianos states in his book, A Global History, The Human Heritage. "Most Indian exports were probably luxury items of relatively little bulk or weight such as etched carnelian beads, shell and bone inlay goods, ivory combs, and possibly even peacock feathers, and apescommodities later imported from India by King Solomon, including precious wood products. It is unclear whether spices were yet used and traded though green amazon stones found at Indus sites, we do know that the merchants of Mohenjodaro imported products from as far as south of the Nilgiri Hills in Southern India and may h;ave established commercial relations with the Malabar coast. The presence of Tibetan jadeite at the sites indicate the probable northern limit of Indus commercial contact, while silver, turquois, tin, and lapis lazuli were imported from Persia and Afghanistan." (28)

The vast network of trade first established by the ancient Africans and Veddoid peoples expanded throughout the subcontinent and may have reached Central Asia before the barbarian invasion of the Indus Valley civilization. Stanley Wolpert states that the hunting and garthering, fishing and small scale agriculture which depended on the rising and lowering of the river, which made it possible to produce food for a large population. The people of the Indus Valley civilizations also kept domesticated animals such as the, "dog, cat, camel, sheep, pig, goat, water buffalo, zebu, elephant, and chicken." (29) Wolpert further points out that the clay figurines of horses found at sites in Harappa or Mohenjodaro may have been brought by the Aryan invaders.

Although the horse may have been brought to India by the barbarian tribes from Eurasia, the importation of the horse could also have from the Sahara or East Africa, just as the cotton plant had come from that region. The horse is usually not regarded as being in Africa before before the time of the Hyksos, another barbarian people invaded Khem, yet we find cave paintings of horse-drawn chariots in the Tassili culture of the Sahara that predates the barbarian invasion of India and Khemet between 1700 B.C. to 1500 B.C.

Bradley explains. "Two wheeled chariots with horses shown in flying gallop of later Cretan style," were portrayed among the paintings found at Tassili by French explorer Henri Lhote in 1958. The age given for the drawing of these horses and other types of art is somewhere between 7,000 to 1500 B.C. This is during a period when the Sahara may have been turning from thick forests to savannahland. Furthermore, it could be that the first horses were domesticated in the Sahara, before it was in Europe. Bradley states, "we should not forget that the Greeks claimed that they had learned to hitch for horses to a chariot from the Libyans, (their term for Blacks) (30)

So, the horse could have been introduced to India as a draft animal from Africa, even though it was well known and used in Eurasia. The ancient Africans used the horse before the Hyksos barbarians invaded Egypt, although the Egyptians themselves did not use it as a method of making war. The early Greeks, the Dorians and others are part of the barbarian hordes who swept into Greece and other parts of Europe and Asia from Central Asia and Eastern Europe. Which group of Greeks learned to "hitch a horse to four chariots from the Libyans," (31) and did they learn it before or after they left their place of origin, is still a question.

There is no doubt that the ancient speakers of the Aryan languages were culturally influenced by the aboriginal Black who lived in Eurasia and northern India, Pakistan and perhaps the Tamrin Basin area, since prehistoric times. Blacks had ventured into Eurasia when they were the most powerful racial group in the region. Their objectives were finding rare precious stones such as lapis lazuli, amber and metals. Their cultural influence in the area was unavoidable, since near to areas where the barbarians lived (north of India, Sumer, Elam, ect...), the great Black civilizations existed. These magnificent civilizations were attractive to barbarians, who wanted to invade and control.

James E. Brunson discusses the variety of ancient Black nations who existed in Eurasia before the emergence of the barbarians. These Blacks existed in the region as the aboriginal groups and it is very possible that the so-called Aryan speakers were influenced culturally by the Blacks, who entered Asia during the Upper Paleolithic.

"Skeletal remains from Neolithic period peoples similar to AustricVeddoid types were found at Anau (Turkistan), submerged regions along the northern Black Sea, the Caspian Sea, and the Sea of Azov. These Aurignacian Blacks eventually occupied a vast area extending beyond the Ural Mountains to Lake Baikal. The writers of antiquity noted three nations of blacks known to inhabit the area. Successive invasions diminished these nations, which had once included the

Caucasias and Afghanistan, and portions of India. By 6000 B.C., Asia was sufficiently differentiated into Africoid, Europoids and Mongoloid populations. It seems that an eternal battle, as indicated by the written traditions, existed between nomadic and sedentary populations." (J. Brunson, "Unexpected Black Faces in Early Asia: A Photo Essay, ed. I.V. Sertima, African Presence in Early Asia, 1995, p.205). (32)

The word "Aryan" itself used to refer to a collection of languages spoken by a group of people who lived in a region called Aria, by the ancient Greeks and others. These people were barbarians. The Persians, who fused with the Blacks of Persia, the Elamites, were a branch of these Aryan language groups. According to Chancellor Williams, in his book The Destruction of Black Civilization, "There is evidence that the earliest Aryan chiefs were Black."(33) That should be no great surprise to any Black person and is just as ironic as the American Indians having fed the Plymoth colonies, yet having their lands stolen from them and exterminated, or of the Zulus and other South Africans helping the Dutch, German and French settlers, teaching them Zulu and other African languages (which developed, mixed with Dutch, German and French into Afrikaans), yet being subjected to racist apartheid for more than thirty years and having much of their lands stolen.

The Indus Valley civilizations of Harappa and Mohenjo-Daro which were founded by Blacks of the Kushitic-Ethiopic as well as Australoid-Negritic branch of the Black race, experienced some difficulties as time went by. A number of factors led to the disintegration of some of the major urban centers, although Black Indian civilization endures till this very day. According to Stanley Wolpert, the Harappan civilization experienced some drastic changes by 1750 B.C. which brought about rapid disintegration and the deterioration of the major centers. It appears that the environment was abused, and the area made bare, then the beauty and style of ancient times such as the high quality craftsmanship applied to pottery, architectural buildings, and the drainage system, regressed in style.

Wolpert points out that two small villages near the town of Chandu-daro called Jhukar and Jhangar have had their names used to describe the time periods of deterioriation which took place in Mohenjodaro and Harappa. Wolpert writes, "It appears that the highly efficient wealthy and powerful empire of Harappa sustained some cataclysmic blows which left its great cities and towns to the occupancy of squatters from neighboring villages and from more remote regions; people whose level of culture was more primitive than their predecessors. Their buffware was much cruder, their seals simpler and totally different in design from those of Mohenjo-daro in its heyday." (34)

Two major factors contributed to this destruction, with the first being nature, and the second being invasions and destruction by the barbarians from Eurasia, who spoke languages in the Aryan group, and who though mainly Caucasoid included other conquered groups, who may have been captured during the barbarian sweep into India. The possibility that natural disaster such as flooding caused the destruction of the Indus Valley civilization's magnificent cities, is very real. Yet, this flooding could have been deliberately caused by the invaders. According to Wolpert, archeological studies by George Dales and Robert Raikes has brought a new light to the evidence that flooding or earthquake may have caused destruction of Mohenjo-daro and Harappa. This catastrophie may have been caused when the Indus River flooded and overrun the area, including the agricultural regions. The large amount of jewelry and other precious and valuable items found in piles that had been made in order to carry away, as well as tools of copper found in the higher levels of excavated earth in the affected areas show that perhaps those who kept these items were about to flee from some disaster, such as a rising flood.

The inhabitants abandoned their homes and their cooking utencils were found in positions which suggested that they could have been thrown about by some force. Evidence of burned straw and a roof that had caved in and fallen was not found. In the area people had been trapped as they tried to escape for the remains of five people found, show that they were trying to escape. Wolpert states that, "at least thirty skeletons have been found at Mohenjo-daro alone, not buried but trapped, killed by some terrible disaster. They were assumed until recently to have been massacred by an invading army, though now it seems more likely they were fleeing combined earthquake and flood." (35)

The disaster and natural calamity that destroyed the Indus Valley civilization, though causing much destruction was nothing compared to the fact that these floods could have been induced by the barbarians, who opened the floodgates and allowed the Indus Valley to flood, so that conquest and settlement would be much easier. Their establishment of a cultural and racial domination was even more devastating than the supposed floding of the region.

The barbarians lived on their cattle and other animals, which they grazed on the stepps of Eurasia before their move to the South. They worshipped their ancestors and burnt their dead, since it was part of their religion. Marriages among the barbarians was based on the patrilineal system. Women were expected to bring the dowry. The wife lost legal status and inheritance was passed on the father's side to his sons. The wife had no rights and could not devorce. Property such as land was not held by the community but by the individual. The individual was taught that he was first, and not the community, as was taught in Black societies.

The most profound habit of culture of these barbarians was a love for making war and causing destruction. This type of mentality contributed to the invasions of the lands of the established, peaceful Black civilizations of India, Khemet, Nubia-Kush and of the Chinese civilization, which is why the Chinese and Khemites both built walls to keep them out.

The barbarian invaders of India held an artificial sense of supereority over the Blacks of India, who were culturally, intellectually and in many ways physically superior to them. This feeling of superiority by the barbarians was possibly the reaction to an innate inferiority complex. This form of reverse psychology has been the case not only for the invaders of India, but for those who invaded Egypt, Semite invaders who used their religion and their "one God," idea, which was copied from the

Black Egyptians, as a means of holding themselves superior over the Blacks of Egypt.

The sight of the greatness of Black civilizations with their well established societies, where the rule of law prevailed, their organized workforce (this aspect was trashed by the Aryans who used it as a means of forming the caste system, however, this division of labor system, still exists throughout Africa ), massive monuments, beautiful cities and other aspects of civilization shocked these barbarians who reacted out of envy and jealousy, as some people react when they want something that others have.

The barbarians brought little material culture to the Indus Valley civilizations except perhaps the horse, which is doubtful. They were also supposed to have brought stronger weapons of war, however, the Blacks of India also had strong weapons, fast chariots and fierce warriors. All the advanced aspects of Black culture were already established in the Indus valley by the time the barbarians invaded, and among these aspects may have been the chariot which may have come by way of Africa, where it had been used in the Sahara since prehistoric times, as Henri Lhote's work clearly shows.

The barbarians brought the original and earliest forms of organized racism based primarily on the color of skin. From the beginning, the barbarians believed that they were superior to the Blacks of India. This artificial sense of superiority was fortified and incorporated into the barbarians' religion. The invaders' religion, which became the backbone of some practices to this very day, created as part of its philosophy a strict division of races and classes according of the complexion of skin, with black skin being the lowest and pale skin being the highest. That philosophy was the exact opposite of the religious beliefs of ancient Africans such as the Khemites and Nubian-Kushites, that the blacker the skin, or being of "The Chosen People of the Sun," the Black race, was a blessing, since the sun was the ultimate representation of God, and moreover, gave them the Blacks the ingenuity to create civilization when the rest of the world was in barbarism, as well as making them the Blacks, the autochonous or original people of the earth.

However, the philosophy of the religion came from a long oral tradition that was later transferred on written texts called, "Books of Knowledge" or Vedas. These were kept by oral storytellers who studied them for recitation. The Rig Veda also called, "Verses of Knowledge" contains about 1,017 Sanskrit poems to different Aryan Gods asking for favors. These poems are among the earliest Indo-European literary works still available. The Rig Veddas were probably written down after 600 B.C., which makes one wonder whether the racial and class codes were not established after the barbarians invaded India. Similarly, in modern times, the racist apartheid system was established in South Africa after the European invaders encroached on the lands of the African Bantu and Kong-San peoples. In the U.S., slavery and segregation was imposed on the Blacks from Africa, as well as the original Black inhabitants of the U.S., who have lived in North America for more than 30,000 years, according to current findings.

In all three cases; ancient India, South Africa, the U.S., the racist invader, despite his myth of his racial superiority, forced themselves on the women of the so-called "inferiors," creating a "mongrel" race to act as a buffer between themselves and the pure Blacks. This mixed race of Black and white invader was used to further oppress the Blacks. These racial concepts were put into effect against the original Black inhabitants of the Indus Valley, and were enforced through a sophisticated racial and color code.

Stanley Wolpert gives a description of the lifestyle of the barbarians. "The term "Aryan" while primarily a linguistic family designation, had also the secondary meaning of "highborn" or "noble." The Aryan "commoners" or Vish (the word later used to designate the largest class in Aryan society, Vaishyas), were most broadly devided into tribes or "jana." Though united by language and religion, as well as warfare against their common non-Aryan 'dark' enemies, the Dasas (blacks), these tribes appear generally to have been at war with one another." (36)

The roots of today's racism and classism on a diabolical scale was planted by the barbarians, who also spread it wherever

206

they invaded. Moreover, it was held down with rigid race, class or religiously sanctified and disguised racism. The history of barbarian racism in India and elswhere against Blacks, who were in all cases more advanced than these fair-skinned, blue eyed barbarians is important to know. It was the same people who invaded Europe and other parts of the world during the modern age, and further spread this odious form of racism around, also disguising it under Chrisitanity and other Semetic religions, based on fairy tales about the so-called, "curse of Ham," which was used as a justification for slavery, racism and discrimination in the U.S., Europe and Latin America against Blacks, and apartheid in South Africa, and the continued rape, enslavement and theft of African lands in Sudan and parts of North Africa and South East Asia.

Wolpert continues, "The distinct separation between martial, royal and priestly classes found among the Aryans appears to have diminished over time, if indeed, the priest-kings had ruled pre-Aryan Harappa, it may be that the Aryan Rajas learned from their (Black) slaves to rely more heavily upon the council of their own bramans. At any rate, the hymn of the "Sacrifice of the Cosmic Man," (purusha-sukta) which appears in the tenth and final "book" the Rig Veda, explains that the four great "classes" (Varna) of Aryan society emerged from different parts of the original cosmic man's anatomy, the Bramans issuing forth first, from the mouth; the Kshatriyas second, from the arms; the Vaishyas third, from the thighs; and the Shudras last, from the feet. This "revelation" according to which all rajas who were Kshatriyas by birth, fell below all Bramans who alone were associated with the cosmic "head," may well have roused ancient royal wrath, though not enough to delete the sacred hymn or alter a word of it." (37)

Inspite of the way the barbarians regarded themselves after they had adopted Black Indian civilization and lifted themselves to a position of power while looking down on the same Blacks who made them civilized, much of the evidence proves that they the barbarians who invaded India from the northern wilderness, were both intellectually and culturally inferior when compared to the Blacks of India.

Drusilla Dunjee Houston points out that the Aryan invasion occurred ages later in the history of India, after Indian civilization was well established by the Blacks, and much earlier than the period when the Indian epics were written. She also states that the ancient records state that the Indi, or non-Aryan princes ruled India. They were of the Cushite Black, the same race that civilized a circular region around the world in the tropical and subtropical zone.

As for the Bramin, she states that they have mixed up over the ages, causing them to have a similarity in cranial features to the Sudra. The period of rule of the Bramin type belonging to the Turanian or Caucasian race in the Christian era. She points out that, "The Tamils, Telegu, Malayalam, and Kanarese," are all remnants of the ancient Cushite race. She makes it clear that according to the authorities, the Black Rajputs were not of the same race as the invading barbarians, and the ancient Vedas record the deadly conflict between the Bramins and Kshattriyas who were Black. She regards the Vedas as being the blueprint for the racial and class social system that later developed to benefit the invaders. These books claim that the wars did not end until the Bramins were not able to take political control, yet, they were able to take custody of the ancient books, and control the priesthood. These people later mixed with the original Black population to create some of today's Indian population.

The maniacal racist and "class consciousness," of the barbarian invader of India is difficult to understand. Such racism is so profound among the descendants of these barbarians in Europe and other nations today, that a deep sense of subconscious inferiory may be the real reasons for projecting a feeling of superiority on other people, particularly Black people. The racist legacy passed on by the barbarians to all their descendants is something that every Black person must fully understand in order for us to crush it mercilessly and retake our position as the world's greatest people. We will never be able to confront and destroy racism and those who practice it unless we know why it exists in the first place, why it was invented, and do all in our power to vehemently reject religions and ideologies that put Blacks in an inferior position, talk about curses on

Blacks, or push the false doctrine of some God who looks like the same people practicing racism and barbarism against Blacks worldwide.

It boggles the mind to think that people who were nothing but savage, nomadic barbarians who followed a pastoral culture had such a low selfesteem, that they had to create a system to uplift themselves in order to feel superior, while at the same time, putting down, enslaving and treating the Blacks into artificial inferiors by establishing a rigid race and class hierachal system.

The comparison between the two peoples and their level of cultural advancement would have to have been like comparing the culture cowboys with those of city dwellers and suburbanites in places such as Los Angeles, New York or Lagos, Nigeria. It is similar to comparing the culture and lifestyle of the Masai, who are pastoral, with that of the citydweller of Nairobi, Kenya. The barbarians had no advanced civilization that could have been compared with that of the Australoid-Negritic Blacks who built the Indus Valley civilization. These barbarians were in no way racially, culturally or intellectually superior to the Blacks of India or any place they invaded.

Wolpert describes the material culture of the invaders:

"Unlike the (Black) peoples of Harappa and Mohenjo-daro who lived in some of the most beautiful cities, and most well organized urban centers in the ancient world, the barbarians lived in tribal villages with their migrant herds. Their houses, fashioned of bamboo or light wood have not survived the ravages of time; they baked no bricks, built no elaborate baths or sewer systems, created no magnificent statues or even modest figurines; they had no seals or writing, no faience art, no splendid homes." (38) On the other hand, these qualities were exactly what the Blacks of India, specifically today's Black Dalits and Tribals, the direct descendants of the Blacks who built India's first civilization had as part of their day to day material culture.

Houston makes clear that by about 3,000 B.C., no branch of the Aryan race produced the Rig Veda, and no white nation had "blacksmiths, chariots, or the civilization shown by these books.

These books, she points out appear to be the writings of Hindu Kush (Black) colonists who came from the region of Hindu Kush, or Nubia-Kush and migrated downward on the Indian plains. The Black Kushites then took Dravidian women who were also Black.

Between 3,000 B.C. to 4,500 B.C., the society was led by fathers who were the family priests, and conductors of sacrifice of horses. Women were not distroyed and had a high position in Black society in pre-barbarian India. According to the Rig Veda, houston tells us, the Cushites were the workers of metals such as copper, they cut hair, worked gold, worked and built with wood and were husbandmen. The chariot was the vehicle of war in ancient India, as was in other Kushite or Black nations of the ancient world. The Blacks loved agriculture and ate beef. Their Gods were similar to those of Khem, Kush and Mesopotamia. By 4500 B.C., they had towns and were building ships. Neither the Semites or Aryans had any of these arts during the same period, Houston states.

In comparing the races of the later period of history who descended from the "Aryan or Japethic race," Houston makes it clear that even after the Hebrews left Khemet, they could not weld iron. The Persians who are supposed to be the heirs of the barbarian Aryans, did not know of carpentry and hired Khemites to do such work in Persia. The Romans and Greeks, two peoples who were in part originally of Indo-European origins (the Dorians and Latins were part of the Aryan invasions to Southern Europe about 1700 to 1500 B.C.), were still cave dwellers who used stone impliments. As for the Goths, ancient and early Middle Ages barbarians (ca. 300-400's A.D.),who may be the closest resemblance to the ancient Aryans who roamed and plundered parts of Europe and later destroyed Rome, they had no metal-working skills, they took no interest in making images and worshipped the Nordic Gods, Thor and Odin. They were a branch of the nomadic peoples of Europe who did not know agricultural skills, and like white Americans of the pioneer days, individualism was a cherished vertue (except when uniting to stay in control and oppress other peoples)

Similar invasions to what occurred in India against the Black civilizations there, also occurred in Khemet about the same period and by the same people, the barbarians who originated in Eurasia. In Egypt they were called Hiksos or Hik Shasu, which translates to, "Shepherd Kings," in the Khemetic language. The Hiksos invaded Khemet about 1645 B.C. During their rule of the land, the contributed nothing culturally to the Khemite empire except devastation. They built no temples, monuments, pyramids, canals, cities or classic works of art. They contributed nothing to the culture of Khemet and left it in shambles, after they were driven out by the Khemites. These Hyksos were Semites, who during that period were similar in hue and racial composition to the Assyrians, a mixture of Caucasian and Negritic tribes who migrated from the Arabian peninsula.

The Hyksos had not been able to control the religious life and philosophy which developed based on the workship of the sun and Black Godliness, established by the Khemetic religion, which was based on beliefs they regarded as factual. Among these beliefs was the value of having black skin and of being Black. To the ancient Khemites, Nubians and Kushites, as well as other Ancient Africans, having black complexion (or dark complexion) was a sacred blessing from Aten, the Sun God. It was the highest honor bestowed upon any human, after being born. The Khemite priesthood promoted this ideology, which to them, was based on thousands of years of observation.

The Khemite priesthood was so strong, that no foreign influence was allowed to contaminate its ancient philosophical structure. Otherwise, the religion of the Khemites could have been similar to that of the barbarians, who invaded India, with its racist caste and "varna" (color) hierachy, with the Black Khemites being oppressed to the lowest level. The real power in ancient Khemet was the Khemite priesthood based in Woset (Thebes) who controlled the foreigners and barbarians who sat on the Khemite throne, through force of arms. The Hiksos were eventually driven out of Khemet after a period of armed struggle and warfare. In like manner, a similar period of armed struggle occurred in India, when the Black Indian (Kushite) inhabitants and kings, fought with much ferocity against the barbarians.

211

There is some doubt about whether the Aryans carried out the destruction of Harappa, Mohenjo-Daro and other regions of the Indus Valley Civilization through force of arms, or whether other means were used in the application of this destruction. Stanley Wolpert asks this question:

"Were the Aryans, a relatively primitive tribal peoples, in fact capable of storming and conquering fortified Indus Cities? Perhaps. They had harnessed their horses to chariots (a method first used by Africans in the Sahara in prehistoric times, P.A.B.),and they seem to have wielded hafted bronze axes (a few of which were found in the highest strata of Indus cities), as well as bows and arrows. They had been toughened by their trek, had endured blistering sun and crossed high passes deluged with sleet and snow. The Rig Veda itself however is unconscious of that journey and of the Aryan "invasion" of India. Yet, it does mention Aryan victories against "fortified places," (pur) within which dark-skinned people (dasas) had sought in vain to defend themselves against the fairer (wheat colored) Aryans. (The sanskrit word "dasa" later came to mean 'Slave')." (40)

No attempt will be made to dispute what may be historical fact yet, has to wonder whether the invasion of the Indus Valley by the barbarians was a simple matter. The primitive backward state of the barbarians and their backwardness in technology compared to the Blacks, may have not hampered their ability to make war. Still, the Blacks of India were also militarily advanced. Houston points out that the Blacks of India, despite the attempt of the barbarians to conquer and repress them, were great warriors who fought fiercely. Houston writes in her book, Wonderful Ethiopians of the Ancient Cushite Empire (1985), "One non-Aryan chief described this race (the Blacks) as having a fearful swiftness, unyielding in battle, in color like a dark blue cloud."(41) This statement clearly indicates that the Blacks

212

resisted the invasion of the barbarians. The barbarians' victory may have not been through conquest by war, but by religion.

# CHAPTER SEVENTEEN

# AFRICAN TRADE WITH CHINA AND THE FAR EAST

African trade with China goes back to prehistory, perhaps to a period in time when the Mongoloid type was not the dominant race in China and when Blacks were the overwhelming number of the inhabitants in parts of China. The influence and settlement of Blacks in parts of China, Japan, S.E. Asia and the Pacific Islands are more ancient than that of the Mongoloids. In fact, the Black presence in China and the Far East, predates the development of the Mongoloid race by tens of thousands of years. James Brunson explains:

"Anthropological finds dating from the Upper Paleolithic through the Mesolithic periods (20,000 B.C. 8,000 B.C.) substantiate the existence of "Negroid" types in China. At Chou-Koutien, in a cave near Peking, skeletal remains of an old man (Negroid Neanderthal), a woman (Eskimo or Mongolian), and a young female (modern day Melanesian), were found. Even earlier fossil remains of the Negroid type have been found in the Upper Pleistocene period (50,000 B.C. to 10,000 B.C.). From southern China, the provinces of Szechwan and Kiangsi, two human skulls, the Tzu-yang Man (Mongoloid) and Liu-chiang (Negroid type) man, have been unearthed."(1)

During the historical period, perhaps between 8,000 B.C. to 1000 B.C., Blacks migrated from ancient nations of Africa and the Middle East such as Khemet, Nubia-Kush, Sumer, Elam, Punt, India and even the drying Sahara, to settle in China and parts of the far East. Trade with China may have occurred about 3000 B.C. to 2600 B.C. By then, Africans were sailing about 8000 miles or more to the legendary land of Punt, down the East coast of Africa, and possibly around it and further still. Journies to China and the Far East would have been much closer.

Ancient Khemetic civilization as well as that of Nubia-Kush and may have sent their merchant ships, merchants and even culture bringers to Neolithic China. Trade and commerce may have occurred and even this early in Chinese pre history, the Chinese may have been facinated by African products, in the same way they were facinated by African animals sold to them during the Middle Ages. Between 8000 B.C. to 1000 B.C., the Africans of Nubia-Kush, Khemet, Negau (Somalia), Ethiopia (Abbyssinia) made frequent trips to the Far East on missions of trade and commerce.

The establishment of cultural transfer from Nubia-Kush, Khemet (Egypt), and Mesopotamia began about 3000 B.C. to 2000 B.C. Trade would have followed naturally during this period when Pharaohs such as Sneferu, Senwosret and Sahure, know for sending their ships to far-away lands, would have also established routes to the far East, and sent expeditions to the region. Pharaohs such as Senwosret are known to have sailed to Elam (Mesopotamia) and the Black Sea region, with thousands of Khemite and Nubian-Kushite soldiers. These Black soldiers settled in the region. According to R.A. Jairazbhoy, Herodotus described the descendents of these Black soldiers, who settled around the Black Sea area around his time. "There can be no doubt that the Colchians are an Egyptian race. Before I heard of any mention of the fact from others, I remarked on it myself." (2) Jairazbhoy writes:

"Herodotus goes on to say that he investigated the matter on both sides, and found that the Colchians had a more distinct recollection of the Egyptians than the Egyptians had of them. According to him the latter believed that the Colchians were descended from the army of Sesostris (Senwosret). Herodotus says that his own conjectures were "founded first on the fact that they are black-skinned and have wolly hair."And he offers two more evidences to his claim the practice of circumcision, and the art of linen weaving, both of

216

which he elaborates." (Edt. I. V. Sertima, African Presence in EarlyAsia, 1995, p.59).(2)

The fact that these Blacks were in the Black Sea area during the 1900's B.C. opens the possibility that they could have sailed as far as China and Japan during that period and earlier on. African trade with China is probably older than Chinese civilization itself. The era of African control of the Mediterranean and the Ethiopian Sea (the Indian Ocean) goes back to 3000 B.C. to 4000 B.C., when African ships sailed the waters of the Indian Ocean, the Pacific and the China Seas. In fact, during this very period, African ships were sailing to Byblos, in the Levant to search for papyrus, pulp and wood. These journeys occurred more than 800 years before China's first Dynasty, the Black Xia Dynasty, and 2000 years before the certainly Black Dynasty, the Shang. During this period, Africans were masters of the seas.

The Africans of Khemet, Nubia-Kush, Negau, Punt and other Black kingdoms in northern Africa sailed to lands such as Lebanon for timber. The Khemites sailed about 8,000 miles to Punt and southern Africa for various precious commodities. They went to Cyprus for copper, the Indus Valley for trade with the Black Kushites living there, and to parts of Europe for various goods and metals. Journeys to the Americas during this early period were also possible. If one takes into account that the distance between Kush, Khem and the farthest point of Punt which is around southern part of Mozambique, is about 8000 miles which is about the same distance between Egypt and mexico, and less than half the distance between West Africa and Brazil. Sailing to these places would have taken about the same amount of time it takes to travel from Punt to Khemet.

So, the ancient Africans could have easily sailed to and from China in about four months or less than the amount of time it took to sail to and from Punt. Apart from the journeys of the ancient Khemite and Kushite ships to China and the Far East, there is at present a Negroid presence in the Far East that may be more recent than the Mesolithic and Paleolithic Africans, who were the first modern human inhabitants of the East, from the

217

South Arabia to Southern Japan, the Pacific Islands and Australia, and Hawaii. This Black element in East Asia may be the descendents of ancient migrants, traders, and settlers, who remained in the region, where the Black presence was overwhelming at one time.

Jacques Gernet examines the racial types portrayed by the Chinese during the Shang Dynasty in his book, Ancient China, From the Beginnings to the Empire. "From the south came at least some of the tin necessary for bronze casting, in the shape of ignots. Certain Shang bronzes on which were represented Melanesian (South Pacific Negroids) or Negroid human types (large, round faces with flattened noses) also confirm the existence between Shang China and the countries of south-east Asia." (3 )

The Black traders referred to in this chapter who were also aboriginal as well as prehistoric Black migrants from Africa and the Mesopotamian region, may have introduced bronze working to China, as well as the chariot and other aspects of Chinese civilization. In fact, Chinese civilization itself was brought about by the first two Chinese Dynasties, which were composed of Black emperors and founders.

According to Wayne B. Chandler (African Presence in Early America, edt. I. V. Sertima, 1992, p. 245), the founders of the Shang Dynasty were described as having, "black and oily skin," by the Chou, who invaded and took over their kingdom. Chandler quotes H. Hardclett, author of China, A History in Art (1968, p.12; Brown and Brown Pub.) "The Chou after overthrowing the Shang Dynasty were found to be no more than barbarians with no philosophy or culture of their own. They therefore willingly adopted the Shang culture and way of life."(4)

James Brunson gives a thorough description of the Black Shang Dynasty's contribution to the creation of Chinese civilization:

"The Shang (Chiang of Chi'ang) (1766 to 1100 B.C.), is recognized as putting China on its history proper. This royal house is considered an offshoot of the

Neolithic Langshanoid culture,giving it a long unbroken tradition. Many Chinese archeologists are convinced that the Shang settlement at Erhlztou, (in southern Shansi, and northwestern Honan), is the earliest evidence of their existence. Traditionally, the territory of the Hsia dynasty, Erhlitou, is believed to be the site of Po; capital of King T'ang of Ta, founder of the Shang Dynasty. As mentioned, these people were initially matrilinear in culture, worshipped a mother goddess, and practicing agriculture. They had a priesthood, and practiced religious ceremonies that included a form of sati burial (ritual sacrifice). Aquainted with metal-working in bronze, the making of a form of porcelain ware, and silk weaving (an invention of southern China), the Shang people are credited with bringing together the elements of China's earliest known civilization."(5)

It is rather heartening to know, as Brunson states, that much of what has been described as "Chinese," culture and inventions were actually the inventions and cultural contributions of the Black Shang Dynasty and the Blacks who lived in China before the Mongoloid invasions. One invention credited to the Chinese was gunpowder. Yet, gunpowder was used thousands of years before the Chinese. The ancient Egyptians and Nubian Kushite priests used gunpowder, during their religious ceremonies. In fact, gunpowder was among the products which came out of the chemical experiments performed by the ancient Egyptians and Nubian-Kushites. Even the "English" word, "chemistry," is a combination of "Khem," in reference to ancient Egypt and the word "black," and "mystry," which refers to the sciences taught by the Khemite mystry schools. Since the ancient Khemites established a network of scientific institutions called, "Mystry Schools," the name 'chemistry," may have been used by invaders such as the Greeks (in their own language, not English), to refer to these institutions and their scientific, technical, religious and magical works and teachings.

According to Dun J. Li, in his book, The Ageless Chinese, the use of gunpowder appeared during the tenth century A.D.

"Mention of sulpher and nitrates, two of the materials used to make gunpowder, appeared in written records as early as the Han Dynasty. However, they were then used by alchemists to make elixirs, and it was not until the tenth century that they were mixed with carbon to make military explosives. The words "fire cannon," rocket, "missle," and "fire ball," appear time and again in the official Sung history as well as two other books written during the same period. The first detailed description of using "fire cannon," in warfare was in connection with a battle fought in 1126 when the Sung army used it against the invading Nuchens. The so-called fire cannon was a tube made of bamboo (reminds one, particularly in the Caribbean and in Africa of the cannons made of bamboo, and fired up to go off with kerosine used around the Christmas season, P.A.B.) filled with gunpowder which, when fired, threw a flaming missle towards the enemy.(6)

The use of the horse and chariot began in the Sahara. There, it was used by Africans between 2,000 B.C. to 7,000 B.C. The Hyksos are said to have brought the horse and chariot to Khem during their invasion of the Khemite Empire about 1645 B.C. The use of the horse and chariot in the Sahara seems to go back to about two to three thousand years before that period, to about 5,000 B.C., when the paintings made at Tassili may have been in progress. The horse and chariot may have been a gift from Africa to the rest of the world, and may have reached China during later periods in history. In fact, the horse and chariot was in use in China about 1766 B.C., during the Shang Dynasty, a period when it is believed Blacks ruled and lived in China in large numbers.

Iron was being used in Khem much longer than it was being used in China. By 1500 B.C., the Khemites were using iron on a small scale. By that same period, the West Africans may have developed their iron industries to a more sophisticated level compared to the late Stone Age experimental period. In fact, the high development of iron by the Mende speaking people of West Africa between 6000 B.C. to 1500 B.C., made the use of bronze as a metal for making weapons and other heavy tools and weapons, quite obsolete. In fact, very little of it was used for weapons. It is highly possible that West African iron goods may have been carried to Olmec Mexico about 1500 B.C. to 1100 B.C. The Kushites, like the Khemites made use of iron but did not use it in the development of their weapons until their enemies the Assyrians almost defeated them during the 600's B.C. The Chinese also began using iron sometime around or after 600 B.C.

Ironworking began in Africa about 2600 B.C. in West Africa, according to Nigerian archeologists. This was a steady progression from working with iron during the Late Stone Age. From West Africa and the Sudan, ironworking spread to the Middle East, Asia and Europe. The spreaders of iron and iron implements could have been traders, merchants 282 or warriors. African traders in search of amber, percious stones, lapis lazuli and tin, may have followed a land route through Central Asia to China, where they traded iron for the local goods. African trading ships had done so for ages, by taking the sea routes. In fact, African trade with China involved a large number of products. Gold, live animals, manufactured goods, bronze utencils, ivory products, copper and bronze products, and a number of other products such as iron farming tools, left ports such as the Red Sea port of Adulis on Nubian, Khemite and Abbyssinian (Ethiopian) ships to China. They returned with cargo such as silk and many other products unique to China.

This early trade with Africa also included the entire coastline of East Africa, from Somalia southward to Zimbabwe, which was one of the regions where trade was carried out on a grand scale as early as 2600 B.C., between the Khemites and Nubian-Kushites with the Puntites. Trade with China in this area may have begun before 3000 years. Trade between the Puntites and the prehistoric Chinese (which included Blacks) may have been among the very first trade carried out between an African region with the Chinese, during the time of their early formation as a civilization. Although very ancient trading occurred, particularly during the time of the migrations from the drying Sahara, and the movement of Blacks across the Indian Ocean to the South Pacific and Asia, it was between 3000 to 2000 B.C., that established patterns and frequent excursions occurred. Ships

221

from Punt and the rest of Africa could have easily sailed to China and East Asia in their own ships, as they did later in history, during the early to late Middle Ages.

From what is known about Punt, the land the Egyptians called "The Land of the Gods," it included the entire coastline of Eastern Africa, down to South Africa, and possibly around the Cape of Good Hope to West Africa. Punt, in other words, was the rest of Africa and lands in the vincinity. Zimbabwe could also have been an are where the Khemites and Nubians visited, for there, massive temples, stone structures and a history of ironmaking, agriculture, cloth weaving and producing implements jewelry and tools of iron, gold and silver, was part of the culture.

Along the east coast of Africa a number of cities were built from the early Christian era, to about the 1600's. These cities stretched from northern Somalia to southern Mozambique, and were among the most magnificent cities in the ancient world. A village or small town shown in a painting at Hatshepsut's tomb at Dier al Bahri, may have been one of the ancient ports, where goods were bought and sold by the Khemites and Nubian-Kushites. These Puntite ports may have very well been used to load Puntite goods to China and India, and to unload goods from the Far East to the Puntites.

Both Africans and Chinese encountered other nations who traded with them, during their long histories, while these nations passed near their territories. Traders from India took part in a heavy amount of shipping activities between the two regions when shipps stopped in their ports either on the way to China, or back on their way to Africa. According to the Greek historian, Strabo, who lived about 63 B.C., "As many as 120 ships sailed from the port of Myus Homus, on the Red Sea to India and China at any given period."(7)

Trade between Khem, Kush and China was also strong during the time of the Ptolemic userpers and invaders of Khem during their occupation of the land and control of the Khemite throne. This trade was being carried out about 400 B.C., and was already in full effect long before they invaded Khemet. During that period, till after the Christian Era, most of the cultural flowering and maritime activity occurred in the eastern part of the Mediterranean and East Africa, which had become the cultural hub of the region. Most trade and shipping from Khemet, Nubia-Kush, Ethiopia (Abbysinia) and Punt, occurred on the Red Sea Ports, and along the coast of East Africa. During this period, most trade to China was carried out by African ships going eastward.

# CHAPTER EIGHTEEN

# AFRICAN TRADE WITH CHINA DURING THE MIDDLE AGES: THE SWAHILI CIVILIZATION

Trade and commerce between Africa and China reached a high level before the Middle Ages, (500 A.D. to 1500 A.D.) Trade between the Far East, particular China, flourished between 300 B.C. to about 1500 A.D. This trade included an area from the Horn of Africa, to Zimbabwe, where remains of Chinese pocelain dating to this period have been found in the world famous Zimbabwe ruins, which werespread over an area about the size of France. During the mid part of the Middle Ages, the African trade with China by way of the sea, was infiltrated by the Persians.

Robert W. July describes the Persian infiltrators, in his book A History of the African People as, "seafarers who monopolized the carrying of trade bringing ever popular African ivory to India and farthest east where it was variously in demand for palanquin litters and incense in China, as dagger handles, sword scabbards, jewelry, and ornaments in India. By the tenth century, the East African entrepots had added gold and iron to their exports, (that trade may go back to the time of Sahure, about 2600 B.C.), the iron coming from coastal deposits in the Mombasa-Malindi area, the gold brought down from the far interior to the southern ports along the Mozambique coast. Leopard skins were another popular export, and far-away China was so facinated by Africa's exotic animals as to send an expedition during the fifteenth century in search of giraffes which was thought to be related to in some fashion to the elusive unicorn." (1) This giraffe was a gift from the Emperor of the Swahili kingdoms to the Chinese Emperor.

Africa's trade with China and India flourished before the increase of the Arab traders into the region, after 700 A.D. This period was hundreds of years before the Arabs invaded Khem (Egypt). The Africans had thousands of years in advance of the

Arabs and in fact ventured into the Far East before the existence of the Caucasians, Chinese or Arabs. Arab accounts of East Africa after 700 A.D., gives a better idea of what trade and commerce was like when they came on the scene, as well as after.

The insatiable appetite for African slaves, led the invaders into African territory. African women were kidnapped and used as domestic slaves and harem women for the pleasure of the invaders. As for gold, it also led to the infiltration of northern peoples into the Swahili region, although this lust for gold was much stronger among the Europeans who infiltrated the region centuries later, beginning with the Portugese. Thus, the motivation of the early Middle Easterners for opening trade with the East coast of Africa and stepping on the toes of the Chinese and East Indians, who had been involved in trade with this area from the earliest times, was based on the desire by the invaders to dominate the area, controle its resourses and enslave the Africans. This infiltration of the Middle Easterners in the region, may have led to the Chinese cancellation of any future trips of their ships along the coast of East Africa, for reasons of exploration, or establishing trade, after the trip by Cheng Ho's massive fleet about 1440 A.D.

Yet, ships from China continued to trade with Africa continuously into the present period. The trade and commerce which existed before Cheng Ho's massive fleet sailed to East Africa, and down to the southern part about 1440 A.D., was of great significance. According to Paul Bohannan, in his book, Africa and Africans, "There are several Arab writers from the seventh to the tenth centuries A.D., who gave us good records of the African areas of this time. But it is not until our own era that we begin to know the extent of the trade and the contact with India and China. Sir Mortimer Wheeler, the British archeologist, said that the history of Tanganyika can be written in Chinese Porcelain, undoubtedly Chinese and Indian cloth were also brought in extensively in this period. The Chinese by the forteenth century all had four to seven mast sailing ships of at least 2,000 tons that plied from Java across to eastern Africa. Some of the Arabic records earlier than this indicated that

226

Javanese ships could carry as many as two hundred people and there is one recorded occasion when as many as twenty seven thousand Chinese landed in East Africa." (2)

Most of the trade which took place during the Middle Ages between Africa and China, Japan and other Far Eastern countries as well as India and South East Asia, was not limited to the ships if these nations mentioned above, as the passage by Bohannon seems to indicate. From the very beginning, African trade with these nations from Khemet, Kush, Nubia, Abbyssinia, Sumer, Elam and other Black civilizations on or near the African continent, was carried out in African sailing ships and galleys. During the Middle .

During the Middle Ages, the East Africans had developed a versatile, sea-going ship, called the dualamtipi. It sailed to India, China and and other places east, from ports such as Mogadishu (which was totally devastated during the time of this writing due to warfare between Somali factions, which resulted in the occupation by U.S. and U.N. troops), Kilwa, Sofala, and others on their way to India and China.

The dualamtipi was a versatile ocean-going ship, used by the Swahili people to travel up and down the East African coast, to Arabia, the Persian Gulf, India, China, Indonesia and other nations of the Far East. Basil Davidson describes this type of ship in his text, The African Genius. "East African trading vessels were of a design common to the Lamu archipelago and Bajun Islands. Of great antiquity, the "mtepe" was used for many centuries. Held together not by nails or other metal clinches but by palm fibre lashings, these ships could be as large as seventy tons." (3)

Davidson not only recognizes that the dualamtipi was of very ancient origins, but he comments on the sailing skills of the East Africans, who can be said were among the worlds first sailors. "The East African Bantu people were accomplished sailors, and their boats helped to keep each group in touch with the others. The result was the gradual development of the Swahili civilization which gave the Bantu peoples over an immensly long territory a common language, a common religion, continuing contact with each other and a common culture." (4)

The Swahili were a collection of African people who lived on the coast and spoke a common language, related to the Bantu language system, but with a small mixture of Arabic words.

The Swahili civilization was the general culture from Somalia, to the coast of southern Mozambique, an area much more expansive than the coastal areas controlled by large nations like India and China. The Swahili could have been regarded as a single giant nation which included Somalia, Kenya, Tanzania and Mozambique. Their culture and influence also spread west into the interior as far as Zaire (Congo). The overall history of the Swahili civilization goes as far back as the time of Sahure, about 2600 B.C. when Khemite ships traded with the region.

Of course, the Arabs brought their religion and some of the words of their language became part of the Swahili vocabulary, yet their linguistic influence was only a small part of the Swahili language, neither was it dominant. Their cultural influence did not go into the inland areas, where the Africans rejected them. The purpose of the Arabs and others among the Bantus of East Africa was in the beginning of trade. Soon, however, they managed to spread their religion in the area, which was fortified by the Arab policy of forcing Africans to convert or be slaves, particularly those of the interior. The Arabs' influence on the culture of East Africa was not as profound as some have pointed out before, except for religion, and a few other aspects of culture, changed among a few people who were coastal dwellers. The general culture changed slightly after 700 A.D., only to adapt to the changes that were occuring where ever the Arabs went such as Northern Africa, Spain, South Europe in the Balkans, North Eastern Africa, Central Asia, S.W. China, India, Indonesia and other areas in S.E. Asia. All these areas had to adapt to the Arab domination of the seas, and some joined rather than fought. In the case of the Swahili, that move was a strategic one designed for their benefit. Most of the basic and complex African culture remained intact, including the better treatment of woman by the Africans.

The Swahili cultures and civilizations of East Africa may not have been quite different from that of the empires of Ghana,

Mali, Songhay, Bornu and Kanem, and others who began thousands of years before the Christian era but adopted Islam during the Middle Ages as a way to break the Arab monopoly on trade in the Mediterranean, and other places. Nations such as Mali, Ghana, Songhay and outlets to the Atlantic Ocean, but others like Kanem-Bornu, and the Mossi and Hausa States of the Sudan were landlocked and needed the caravan trade routes between themselves and northern Africa and the Mediterranean.

In all these societies, except the Mossi Empire, who vehemently rejected any type of foreign influence for a long time, including religious influence, remained solidly African but adopted the religion of the Arabs which gave them some influence and led to the destruction of these great empires, as soon as they lost touch with thieir own African culture and ancient heritage. (It is time for Africans worldwide to get to their senses and realize the role of other people's religious beliefs in destroying African culture, reject these foreign religions and beliefs, and return the religions of our ancestors, before the invasion). The foreign traders who lived in separate areas of the major cities of the Swahili States and the West African empires, built mosques and temples in foreign quarters such as in the city of Kumbi-Saleh of Ghana, and Mogadishu of Somalia.

The above observation was the case in the Swahili coasts where the same suspicious attitude the Arabs remained even hundreds of years after the Kushites were driven out of their former kingdom, Khemet (Egypt) by the Assyrians, or the Arabs invaded parts of Egypt, Somalia, and Ethiopia. There is no doubt that the descendants of the same people whose empire, the Nubian-Kushite Empire, was destroyed by the Assyrians, and of Kush which was later distroyed by the Axumite occupier of Ethiopia (Axum) Ezana, fused with the Bantus to create the Swahili culture. These, along with people who had been there since the time of Sahure (2600 B.C.) formed the Swahili civilization before the coming of the Arabs around the 700's to 1000's A.D. To further fortify the culture, the descendents of the same people who traded with the ancient Egyptians still traded in the region.

One of the Arab writers who visited the Swahili coasts during the Middle Ages was called Ibn Buttuta, who was also a scholar and traveler from Morocco. He was born in 1311 and may have begun his travels during his years as a young man. By 1311 Buttuta visited the Swahili states, including the large cities of Kilwa, in Tanzania. He describes the first city on his itenerary, Mogadishu as, "a very large town, "with people who had, 'many camels,' and with wealthy merchants and leather tanners and workers. "The merchants," he wrote, "are wealthy, and manufacture a material (probably fine leather) which takes its name from the town and which is exported to Egypt and elsewhere." (5)

Ibn Buttata describes the food of Mogadiscio's people which was typical of the diet of most of the coastal areas, as "rice cooked with butter, served on a large wooden dish with it the same side dishes and vegetables." (6) The basic foods were accompanied at each meal by pickles and spices "(cooked) unripe bananas in fresh milk...as a sauce," and curdled milk with peppercorns, vinegar, and saffron, green ginger and mangoes." Mogadiscio, like all the East African towns and cities, was ruled by a sultan whom the local people called Sheikh, and its peoples whom the local people called Sheikh, and its peoples whom Buttuta noted were Black, and were muslims." (7)

"Ibn Battuta found Mogadiscio to be a pleasant civilized city with a dignified system of government and law and a teeming economy. He was even more impressed by Kilwa, however, which was the southern most city of consequences on the East African coast. Kilwa was built on an island which was only a few hundred yards off the coast of southern Tanzania. Battuta noted that it was, "in the land of the Swahili...in the land of Zanj." He described it as a principal town on the coast, the greater part of whose inhabitants are Zanj of very black complexion. It was, he found, "One of the most beautiful and well constructed towns in the world. The whole of it is elegantly built. The roofs are built with mangrove poles. There is much rain. The people are engaged in holy war, for their country lies besides that of the pagan Zanj. Their chief qualities are devotion and piety..."

"Kilwa's importance was due to its command of the flow of African goods out of Central and Southern Africa into the Indian Ocean commercial system. Although Sofala, which Battuta placed at half a month's march from Kilwa," was the point at which the goods arrived at the seacoast, they were then shipped up to Kilwa for sale to the fleets of large ships that came from Arabia, India and China. It is only likely that there was a steady flow of African goods from the inland country around Lakes Tanganyika and Malawi to Kilwa, but little is known of the routes of which inland peoples brought them to the coast." (8)

According to Jefferson E. Murphy in his book, The Bantu Civilization of Southern Africa, the products from the central and southern part of Africa passed through Kilwa making it a center for trade into the interior and across the Indian Ocean and elsewhere. To the north and the east and south were also included in the areas of trade. Goods first arrived at the Sofala city on the coast and it took about half a mongh of walking, from Kilwa to reach and trade with ships from China, Arabia and other places.

Sofala had a great port and ships from all over the world and around Africa received and exchanged goods. In the ruins of Kilwa, many thousands of pottery pieces from China, India and South Arabia, and other lands have been found. Fleets of Chinese ships also visited the cities of Mogadicio and Malindi around the early 1400's and may have taken such journies earlier than the 800's A.D. By then the Chinese ships were huge compared to that of others of the day. These ships were not only huge, but averaged about 300 feet long. They had three masts and five layers of decks. One such group of ships visited East Africa about 1417 and in 1431 with over 20,000 men and was comandered by a Chinese Admiral called Cheng Po (or Cheng Ho)

The author states that in the 1200's coins were being minted in Kilwa and these coins were used in trade all along the Swahili coasts. Swahili civilization attained a high level of cultural and economic development by 1300 through 1500 A.D., July observes. By that time, there were about sixty large towns and cities along the East African coast inhabited by the Swahili people, including ports of call for large trading ships. July gives these cities as the most important to the international commercial trade in the region, and far off to the north and east. "Brava, Kismayu and Mogadicio in Somalia; Lamu, Pate, Malindi, Mombasa and Vumbu Kuu in Kenya; Bagmayo, Zanzibar, Mafia, and Kilwa in Tanzania." (10)

Basil Davidson gives the Portugese assessment of the Swahili Coasts after they, the Portugese ravaged the area during the latter part of the fifteenth century. The account is how they saw it before this act of barbarism. He states that the Portug;ese destroyed the Swahili cities but made records of what was there before they carried out their acts of barbarity, beginning with Vasco da Gama, who was shocked to find high civilization and maritime trade in the area, and where the Swahili ships were many times bigger than their own caravels. Reports by other Portugese invaders who followed Vasco de Gama soon afterwards state that Kilwa had, "many fair houses of stone and mortar very well arranged in streets...with doors of wood, well carved with excellent joinery." Mombasa was described as being, "very fair place with lofty stone and mortar houses, well aligned in streets after the fashion of Kilwa." (11)

Swahili was the primary language spoken in the region although foreign traders and a few settlers from the Arabian peninsula and the Near and Middle East spoke their own languages, as well as those Blacks who learned the language. A form of written Swahili was present and Swahili literature and books developed with writings by the Swahili people on subjects such as poetry, history, government, philosophy, theology, moral behavior, and principles of science.

The Swahili cities were swamped at various historical intervals by Arabs and other northerners who brought their warships with them well armed, and ready to take over. After a period, they were able to establish themselves over the cities of the Swahili and like invaders in other parts of Africa, they were absorbed into the culture, although the religion they brought, remained with the Africans to this very day.

The previous paragraph brings to light, what was a typical example of what happened to African civilizations, some

232

established thousands of years before the seventh and eighth century. Civilizations as ancient as Khemet (Egypt), Nubia-Kush and Punt (the Swahili Coasts), have all been invaded by the same people who established their culture and religion by force or otherwise. The mistake made by Western writers is to give credit to the Arabs for Swahili civilization or any other civilization in Africa. This racist mentality, is of course, the same old system of thinking used as a means of trying to denigh Africans the capability of creating their own civilizations, while granting the honor to people who were vertually barbaric and uncivilized, when the Black Africans were the greatest contributors to technology and classical civilization.

In the case of the Swahili, their civilization was a continuation of the ancient maritime civilization of Punt which existed before Sahure who was Pharaoh in 2600 B.C. Paintings of a seacoast town or village somewhere along the eastern, south-eastern, or western coasts of Africa, clearly shows that during the time of Hatshepsut (1400-1500's B.C.), there were seaports and maritime activity from Somalia to the coast of Mozambique and further south into Swaziland, Zimbabwe, South Africa towards West Africa and elsewhere.

The people of East Africa had trade contacts with the Khemites Nubians, Kushites, Ethiopians, Phoenicians, Sabeans, Elamites, Sumerians, East Indians and other Black kingdoms and empires earlier than 2600 B.C., when Sahure sailed down the Red Sea from Thebes, on his journey to Punt or southern Africa. At that same time period, trade with Black nations in the far East, such as Xia and Shang China, and Indonesia was being carried out. In fact, between 2600 B.C. to 2000 B.C., waves of Blacks from Africa, were partaking in a very ancient migration route (which began as early as 100,000 years ago) towards parts of Melanesia and the South Pacific. According to Ianoke Raikadroka, President of the Fijian Community of Los Angeles, in an advertisement in Shekere, the official newspaper of the African Marketplace and Cultural Faire, held in Los Angeles, California the weekends of August (last three weekends), the Fijians and other Melanesians migrated from Melanesia over four thousand years ago.

There was also significant trade between the East African Swahili Coasts and the interior of Africa, thousands of years before the Swahili emerged as a distinct ethnic group in East Africa, and hundreds of years before the birth of Christ. In fact, many of the products the Puntites, and later the Swahili traded or bartered, came from the interior regions. This reality was one of the reasons for the spread of Swahili into parts of Eastern Zaire, during the early Christian period and through the Middle Ages. The trading and commercial networks established by the Swahili (or rather the Bantu and Kushite people who occupied the East African coasts), were in place before the Arabs emerged as a world power after the 700's A.D., and began their invasions of North Africa and elsewhere.

The accounts given by the Khemites and Nubian-Kushite sailors who visited Punt, which should be the collective name for all the Eastern as well as South-Western and Western parts of Africa, was of a place rich in natural beauty and resources, and where trading towns and cities were already established. The shipwrecked sailor in the book, The Shipwrecked Sailor, gave an account of Punt as a vast land with a king, and a civilization of its own. Even the island of Zanzibar, where the sailor in the ancient story may have been shipwrecked, may have had settlements, towns and cities. In fact, one particular island on the East African coast contained an ancient port, called Suakin, was constructed from blocks of coral. Many of the Swahili cities contained buildings constructed with this material.

Although the cities, towns or villages along the coast of Eastern Africa during the time of Sahure and Hatshepsut were not as sophisticated as those of the Middle ages (their sophistication is unknown due only to insufficient historical records at this time) what matters is that they existed, were used as ports and trade centers, as well as commercial centers. Eyewitnesses gave accounts of them. One example of what these towns may have looked like was expressed in a painting on the wall of Hatshepsut's Temple, at Dier al Bahri, Egypt. These ancient towns may have become the eighty-five Swahili cities which dotted the coast of East Africa from Somalia to Southern Mozambique.

These towns and villages existed before the time of Abraham and before he left the town of Ur. The African culture and civilization brought these trading cities about was begun by the Africans who lived in the region along the coasts and the interior. This maritime culture never diminished and continued into the Middle Ages.

The Arabs, Persians and Omanis were late comers to the Swahili Coasts and they were attracted to the area because of its high level of culture, its wealth, and the easiness of its people who were already quite cosmopolitan due to their trading and commercial contacts with the ancient civilizations of Khemet, Nubia-Kush, China, India, Ethiopia and interior Africa. When the first Arab ships landed on the shores of East Africa, they established themselves in the ancient trading towns, living in their own 'quarters' in these towns. Their religion was then spread among the Kushite-Bantu inhabitants and due to that, it was easy to spread other aspects of Arab culture such as language and religion. These were not totally accepted and the African quickly absorbed these aspects, making them more African. Some control by the invaders was accomplished by masive immigration, which included soldiers from the Middle East, as well as marines.

The occupation of African lands from 600 A.D. till the present time is one that will have to be delt with by Africans. The idea of indigenous African religion and its replacement of religions that make Blacks turn to the Gods of conquerors, is one that has to be seriously considered because religion of invaders has led to the misery we face as African people today. If the followers of one religion had not considered Blacks as 'infidels' worthy of slavery if they did not convert, the total destruction of African culture and civilizations which occurred during the slave trade would not have occurred. Furthermore, the position of Black people would not have been lowered to such a low level among the earth's people.

It is with the establishment of a genuine religion that puts Black and African interests and culture high above, that Black people worldwide will be able to see the beginning of a world created by themselves, for themselves. However, mistakes made in the past, atrocities carried out in the name of religion, and customs which takes away from the God given rights of our people must be abolished. We have seen how religion has been used by the invaders of African land to take control over the minds of the invaded, declare by decree and based on religious falcity and superstition that the Black race was supposedly 'cursed' due to the blackness of our skin, and use it as a justification to enslave millions of our people.

The time has indeed arrived for Black people worldwide to bow to their own ancient Gods, to establish their own religious philosophy, architectural temple building styles, religious lore and rites, and in fact return to the religion of the ancestors, with modications to adapt to this modern era. A religion which applies the scientific principles as used in Voodoo, Shango and Macumba, where forces of nature, ancestral and other metaphysical sciences are used, seems more appropriate to the improvement of the lives of Blacks worldwide. Yet, a few changes would have to be made.

No foreign religion which has Black people worshipping the images of the invaders' racial group or type, will ever contribute to the rising of Black people, out of our current lowly position as a people. The invaders' religions has not merely contributed to the spiritual confusion of Blacks worldwide, it has helped keep the Black race world wide in the political, religious, psychological and physical domination of the invader, while we continue to worship them and accept their false theories about their superiority and godliness.

The return to the worship of the Sun, nature and the ancestors as living, functioning elements and forces whose presence and memory as well as bloodline (our ancestors) has a direct influence on our everyday lives, should be the primary composition, would give Blacks a strong direction. The very fact of being Black, created by God and the rays of the sun, should be part of Black religion. A theology based on science and on factual truth, concerning the spiritual and psychological superiority of blackness, should be brought about. Should we return to the time when Black people were the Chosen People of the Sun ( God ) and should that belief manifest itself in our religion and day to day life, we will return to a position of superiority, for it will be a time when being Black will be synonymous with being Godly and better in many ways. It is left to us to change the lowly position we presently occupy among the peoples of the world.

The occupation of African lands from the 600's A.D., and afterwards and the forcing of religious beliefs that were changed to spread the superiority of the invader, while changing the African aspects, and characters, as well as the occupation of African lands and the brainwashing of African people, must be resolved. While the Europeans have left Africa, there are still colonialists who occupy parts of northern Africa, where the Black people who have refused to bow are presently being exterminated through warfare and planned starvation and diseases. One has to wonder whether the massive starvations in Africa that has killed millions since the ninteen-seventies, as well as the appearance of mysterious diseases such as AIDS (Acquired Immune Defficiency Syndrome), are not part of a conspiracy to depopulate the African continent in order to make invasions and massive immigrations by those with their exploding populations in the Mediterranean and northward, to focibly occupy African land, as the Semites have been doing, without much resistance by Africans.

Africans will have to start planning for the improvement of the continent, the increase of the Black population in order to retake and reoccupy the lands of our ancestors stolen by the Semites in North Africa, and the bringing about of a world Black renaissance in science, agriculture, technology and commerce. We Africans worldwide will have to begin seeing these possibilities particularly when nations such as England, Spain, Germany, France and the U.S., with their own large populations, which they encourage to have more children, tell Blacks worldwide to control the Black population. No Black nation should encourage any population control. In fact, they should use their large populations to help make the lands more productive, the nation more technologically and financially powerful.

## East Africa As The Invaders Saw It

The East Africans of the coastal Swahili city-states accepted the Arabic religion and opened the way to some Arab influence on the culture and language. Still, this influence was not overwhelming in comparison to the overall African culture itself. Slave trading, and foreign invasions after the Arab invasions contributed to the downfall of the Swahili civilizations. According to Jefferson Murphy, in his book, The Bantu Civilizations of Southern Africa, "The early visit by Al-Masudi and the later visit by Ibn Buttuta provide clear and valuable first hand accounts of life in the developing cities of the Swahili civilization. Archeologists have begun excavation in a number of ruined sites, and have found the crumbling remains of once beautiful buildings, along with the myriad pieces of debris that were left by civilized people over a period of a thousand years. Yet for the past few centuries, the great cities of the Swahili have been nearly dead. Some were abandoned, gradually to disappear under the attacks of weather and pillagers. Others declined to sleepy towns populated by fishermen and petty traders. The decline of this once-great civilization is a story in its right. And once again, it was the impact of the portugese which created conditions under which the Swahili civilization found it impossible to mentain its former greatness." (1)

The impression of travelers and some Europeans who visited the Swahili coasts was far from praiseworthy. During the 1800's the entire region was ravaged by Arab and European, and local slave trading and the population was devastated, or killed off. One observer, James Prior made this observation in 1812:

"The remains of the wall that formerly encircled the town are still partially visible, though overgrown with weeds. We traced it to some distance; it has been two feet thick, and seems to have enclosed a considerable space." He continues by pointing out, "that Kilwa was important during the days of Vasco de Gama but "as from present appearances, to be scarcely worthy of credit. The people were said to be numerous." (African

Civilization Revisited, by Basil Davidson, from James Pryor, Voyage Along the Eastern Coasts of Africa, ect...London, 1819).(2)

Captain W.F.W. Owen, a British Navy officer made this comment in 1821 or 1826 and pointed at slavery as one of the causes of the destruction and retrogressioon of the ancient maritime civilization of the Swahili. He states that the Quilimane which was and is on the coast of Mozambique, "is now the greatest market for slaves on the east coast. They are purchased with the blue dangerees (blue jeans) colored cloths, arms, gunpowder, brass, and pewter, red colored beads, an imitation of coral, cutlery and various other articles." (3) He continues, "the riches of Quilimane consisted in a trifling degree gold and silver, but principally of grain which was produced in such quantities as to supply Mozambique." He blames the introduction of slavery for the erosion of the industrial and agricultural economy which was replaced by war and violence in order to supply slaves to the Portugese.

He observed that because of the slave trade in the area of Quilimane was not able to grow a sufficient amount of corn to feed its people. (Its a shame the process is taking place in the region today, brought about by similar circumstances.) He regarded Kilwa as a miserable village with wretched Arab hovels among the ruins of the formerly great and wealthy city. Semitic and European enslavement of Africans was the primary reason for the destruction of most African civilizations and cultures which were present during the Middle Ages and afterwards. Still, many African civilizations were strong enough to remain free of Arab or European infiltration. Ethiopia and the Mossi States are two examples.

# CHAPTER NINETEEN

# TRADE AND COMMERCE BETWEEN ANCIENT ZIMBABWE AND OTHER REGIONS

From the ancient accounts given by the chroniclers of Pharaohs such as Hatshepsut and Sahure, or officials like Hennu, all who sailed to Punt or sent ships to the Puntite region between 2500 B.C. to 1493 and afterwards, Punt may have included an area from Cape Guadafui on the Horn of Africa to South Africa, and beyond towards West Africa. Journies to Punt may have also included the Americas, including parts of Central America, Mexico, Peru and North America. These areas were obviously not the Punt the Egyptians talked about, however they were included on trips which took about three years to complete.

Punt was situated on the Continent of Africa, for certain. Trade between the Khemites (ancient Egyptians), Nubians, Kushites, and other ancient African civilizations took place. During their visits to Punt, the merchants of these kingdoms and empires passed through Zimbabwe, where the culture and an organized society was already in progress. Although some historians agree that the roots of Zimbabwean civilization began about 300 B.C., others such as Dr. Khalid Al Mansur point out in his book, Seven African-Arab Wonders (1992), that the Zimbabwe Ruins with its massive constructions of uncemented stone slabs, massive fortifications and temples which dot an entire area larger than France, is about 6000 years old. J.A. Rogers describes the southern part of the Great Wall of Zimbabwe as being built about 2000 B.C. (Africa's Gift to America, 1968, Helga Rogers Publishers, Saint Petersburg, Florida). By looking at the size and extended area these monuments cover (some are as larger than three football arenas, and dot an area larger than France), then it is quite possible that they were built continuously over a period of six thousand years, beginning perhaps, about 4000 years Before Christ.

241

Present dating of a portion of these magnificient stone cities spread from Zimbabwe to South Africa's transvall region, point to the beginning of construction about 300 years Before Christ. By then iron was being used and made. Ironically, the use of iron ore and red ocre in Swaziland and the region goes back to 40,000 years Before the Present! Human culture and development, including the discovery of making fire goes back to about 500,000 to 1,000,000 years. Infact, apart from Ethiopia and parts of East Africa, Southern Africa is one of the cradles of the original Black Homo sapien race, which gave birth to all other so-called "races."

Two Iron Age cultures developed in Zimbabwe and the surrounding area continued a new phase of development about 300 B.C. One of the cultures which developed during this period is called the Machili Forest Station and the other is called the Gokomere Culture, whose people were agriculturists and herders of cattle who grew a variety of crops. These people were speakers of Bantu languages who migrated to the area and joined with the people who were already there. One migrant group, the Shona were in control of a vast area of Southern Africa.

By 1000 A.D., the Shona people controlled the area and improved on the culture. They had a tradition of building in stone, which included building settlements surrounded by high stone walls. The Karanga, a group which belonged to the larger Shona Nation who had began moving into the area by 400 A.D., also contributed to the further development of the culture.

In the book, The Destruction of Black Civilization: Great Issues of a Race From 4500 B.C. to 2000 A.D. (1976), explains:

"The states which were to form the Empire of Monomotapa (Mwenemutapa) were engaged in a number of diversified industries by 300 B.C., which led to interstate trade and foreign commerce over the Indian Ocean as well. The archeological evidence garthered all over this vast territory made it clear that iron technology and allied crafts were well advanced long before the Christian Era. The spread of the economic revolution over Africa by the Iron Age may have come from the

242

southern center as well as from Meroe in the north east."(1)

Chancellor Willams states that the level of economic progress and civilization was connected, and were maintained by a very industrious and artistic people who performed their work to their utmost best. They made gigantic storage jars for grain and glazed them with the best of skill, making them attractive in appearance. Like most of Africa, the workers of that civilization held the philosophy that their work was a reflection of themselves, so they did their best performance, and put out their best work.

The previous description of the Empire of Monomotapa (Zimbabwe) from about 300 B.C. gives an idea of the attitude of the Africans in the region of Southern Africa, where Khemites, Nubians, Kushites, and other Black civilizations of Africa, Mesopotamia and the Far East had trading contacts as early as 2500 B.C. The Zimbabwe Empire also conducted trade and commerce with China, India, Indonesia, and the Black nations of Melanesia and the South Pacific, Black Thailand, Kambudjia (Cambodia), and other lands of the East, after 300 B.C., into the late Middle Ages.

The Gold, iron, ironware, weapons of steel, iron hoes, tin, copper "X" bars, foodstuffs, leather and animal skins, and animals were all part of the commodities traded. Ivory, precious stones, carved ivory, ebony and other manufactured wood products, ostrich feathers, spices were transported on ships. These ships were African ships or the longboats used to carry goods and products from one are to the other. The Swahili used their own ships, the duala-tipi to carry goods from the East African coast to other areas of the Indian and Pacific Oceans, the Mediterranean, the Persian Gulf, the Red Sea and the Arabian Sea.

Arabs and others such as Persians and Omanis arrived in trickles during the early Middle Ages, then increased in number by the 1200's A.D. Their objectives were the acquiring of gold and definitely the enslavement of Africans. The Europeans arrived about 300 years later, beginning with the Portugese. Before then, the main export of Zimbabwe to outsiders was gold, but iron and steel utencils were also being produced in Zimbabwe and exported to India, China and other nations in the East as well as the Mediterannean. Africans had already developed the most advanced iron smelting process and were the first people on earth to produce steel of high grade and quality, as early as 300 B.C., and earlier. By 1200 A.D., the Africans of East Africa were still producing the most advanced steel for swords, spears, cooking utensils and tools for craftsmanship and working the mines.

Workers of gold, copper, iron and tin were also part of the industrial makeup of ancient Zimbabwe. These workers belonged to secret societies and crafts guilds who contributed to and were part of the metal working industrial class. The use of iron and steel was so widespread in Zimbabwe and the rest of the Southern African region, that iron was being used in Natal, South Africa about 1000 years Before Christ. The use of bronze was primarily for ornaments and in the case of some societies, bronze was used for surgical instruments.

Chancellor Williams points out in his book, The Destruction of Black Civilization, that pottery-making was done with the utmost skill and beauty. It was aesthetically pleasant to the eye. Craftspeople, artisans and other professionals existed and contributed to the greatness of the society. Miners worked the thousands of places where iron, gold, tin and copper were mined. Architects built some of the most magnificent structures on earth out of evenly cut slabs of rock, held together without cement. Some of these enclosures which protected settlements made of stone, were about the size of three American football fields, with their walls over thirty feet high and eighteen feet thick.

Zimbabwe means "House of Stone," which refers to the many massive stone fortifications built throughout the nation of Zimbabwe and the surrounding area, beginning in ancient times, till the 1400's. However, according to Dr. Khalid al Mansoor, author of Betrayal by Any Other Name, and Seven Arab-African Wonders, the Zimbabwe ruins were built about six thousand years ago. According to J.A. Rogers, in his book Africa's Gift to

America (1968) (2), parts of the walls of the Zimbabwe ruins were built about 2000 B.C. Thus, there may have been a continuous process of building from prehistoric times.

Zimbabwe was also called the Empire of Mwenemutapa. It included a vast area, and a large number of sites over Zimbabwe and parts of South Africa, an area larger than France. The origins of Zimbabwe may have been both Central Africa, the Sudan, and Southern Africa itself. There is no doubt that there were people in southern Africa of the Bantu speaking group, who had began migrating to the area from Western Nigeria and Cameroon before 1000 B.C. In fact, Zimbabwe and South Africa may have been portions of the lands of Punt, visited by many Khemite Pharaohs since Sahure about 2 500 B.C.

It is said that the Bantu people migrated out of their original homeland in Cameroon, West Central Africa, and spread out to the area throughout the southern half of the continent. The dates for this migration however is not as accurate as it should be for it is usually given as being somewhere about 100 B.C. But that may not be exactly correct, if the migrations occurred at least one or two thousand years before and continued through the early Christian era.

The most probable time of the Bantu migrations may be sometime during the period when iron was put to use as an agricultural implement and helped increase the food supply, build better weapons, and do a variety of things that helped the people in their migrations. Iron was used in West Africa as early as 2600 B.C. to 1100 B.C. by cultures similar to that of the Nok culture of Nigeria which occurred about 500 B.C. During the period of 1500 B.C. to about 700 B.C., and even earlier from Nubia-Kush, migrated into West Africa and they could have displaced the people who were living there before. These first inhabitants may have decided to move to new areas after the arrival of the Nubians and Kushites. Thus, the Bantu migrations to the southern half of Africa from West Africa may go back as early as 2730 B.C., when Sneferu conquered the northern part of Nubia-Kush.

Some historians claim that the Bantu speakers moved south only after the discovery of iron and the introduction of new agricultural crops such as yams and bananas from Indonesia. But iron was being used in West Africa long before the so-called introduction of the banana which occurred about the middle part of the Middle Ages. In fact, based on evidence garthered in West Africa as well as in Olmec Mexico, a conclusion can be made that iron was being used during the Late Stone Age in West Africa, and as early as 1100 B.C., in Mexico, where iron beads were found in a bag, next to a gigantic Olmec head with distinctly Negritic West African facial features. Furthermore, it is quite possible that iron itself was in use by 1500 B.C. Furthermore, it is quite possible that iron itself was first used in the area before the beginning of the Bronze Age, when all other peoples were using copper or stone. The amount of iron in West Africa and the ancient mining traditions of the West Africans helped push Africans towards the use of iron from an early period.

The claim that bananas, yams and other crops came from Indonesia or Asia around the 1000's A.D., may or may not be accurate. Both iron and the practice of agriculture developed independantly in West Africa, free from any so-called outside influence. In fact, by 7,000 to 5000 B.C., the Mende People of West Africa had developed advanced agricultural techniques. By the Late Stone Age, they were using iron along with stone tools. By 10,000 B.C., the Niger-Congo language family from which the Bantu languages originated, were being spoken in West Africa. Thus, a very ancient period of culture had developed long before the migrations of the Bantu from their base in the Cameroons and Eastern Nigeria. Unless the Kushites also brought ironworking techniques to southern Africa, its spread was from West Africa. The bananas and yams may have also spread from West Africa to the eastern and southern part, before it was reintroduced into West Africa through trade. In fact, it is just as likely that the bananas and tropical yams were introduced from Africa to Melanesia, Indonesia and the South Pacific by the great wave of Blacks who sailed from Africa to Asia and the South Pacific about 20,000 years B.C., and

246

according to Ianoke Raikadroka, President of the Fijian Community of Los Angeles, about 2000 B.C.

If the banana and yams came from Asia and the Bantu spread it from West Africa, where they originally migrated from, then the Bantu would have had to spread the banana and yam, along with ironworking from eastern Africa, when they were first introduced to these crops by Melanesians or Indonesians trading with or migrating to Madagascar or East Africa. Ironworking as spread by the Bantu speakers along with the cultivation of bananas and yams, which are supposed to have been increased due to the use of iron tools, spread from West Africa with the Bantu Speakers, to Eastern and Southern Africa. The Kushitic speakers could also have spread these crops as well as working with iron to Southern Africa. After all, it was Kushites from Nubia-Kush who may have spread iron working technology to Han China about the 600's B.C.

Unless the Bantus, who had already settled much of Eastern Africa long before the supposed introduction of the bananas into East Africa about 1000 A.D. had remigrated into. West Africa with the banana and tropical yams, then there is no way either the banana or iron spread to West Africa with the Bantus. In fact, it was the other way around.

In retrospect, the ancient people of Zimbabwe, before the Shona, Karanga and Matabele, were a mixture of Bantus from Western Africa and Kushite migrants from the Nubian Kushite Empire, who left their areas due to upheavals such as Senefru's 'scorched earth' policy against the Nubians about 2000 to 3000 B.C., or migrations of Saharan groups escaping the drying farmlands, into West Africa, who displaced earlier established groups, who moved further to the southern part of Africa.

Trade between the ancient people of Zimbabwe and the coast of East Africa, and with nations far away such as China and India, as well as Central, Western and North-Eastern Africa, goes back to Hatshepsut and others before 1493 B.C., and afterwards until the Middle Ages. By 900 A.D., the Bantu speakers had established a large empire based on trade. Products such as iron, iron tools and implements, gold and gold jewelry, copper, animal skins, ivory and ivory carvings, and a wide range

247

of other products left the interior for the Swahili coasts, where they were shipped on boats such as the dualamtipi and on foreign vessels, to the Arabian peninsula and the Far East and India. The Africans imported goods such as silk, chinaware, glass items and other products.

The importation of cloth or ironware into Southern Africa and particularly Zimbabwe, where both the manufacture of cloth and the making of iron products were highly technical skills, was merely another aspect of the trading process. African steel and iron products such as hoes, tools, weapons and cooking utencils were famous on the world market, therefore, their importation of iron products from outside of their territories does not mean that they were unable to manufacture these items themselves. They merely desired a wider variety of products and an open avenue to the markets of those they desired to import from The working of iron into steel, the manufacture of ironware and cotton cloth were very ancient arts and sciences among the Bantu speakers and other Africans. In Southern Africa, the manufacture of steel weapons, iron utencils and other implements and tools was very important to the overall trade. These products were spread all over Eastern Africa, where steel was being produced earlier than 300 B.C. through the Middle Ages, to this very day.

The Africans of East Africa in the area of Kenya invented the world's first blast furnace. They built tall cones of brick about six or more feet high, and about four feet wide at the bottom and two feet wide at the top, where smoke and other gasses vented out. These fernaces were kept hot by clay pipes and hand pushed bellows, which surrounded the cones and pushed air into the burning charcoal in order to heat and melt the iron ore. The art of making steel was kept secret by the Africans. So secret was the process, which was closely guarded by the secret societies and iron-workers guilds, that steel comparable to what the Africans had been making since between 200 B.C. to 400 B.C., was not manufactured by Europeans until the mid 1800's. Africans had also developed the forced-draught furnace wih bellows to smelt their iron ore before any other people.

The working of iron and steel in Africa had gone to a level unequaled anywhere on earth. So creative were the Africans in the making of tools, weapons, kitchen utencils and other objects that the artistic level reached a height unequalled by any one during the Middle Ages. While others were using iron weapons and utencils, the Africans were using both iron and steel, and had by then developed various types and grades of steel. This steel was exported to places like Arabia, India, Persia, Syria and China, as well as Europe. Goods such as cotton cloth, gold ornaments and a number of manufactured products were also sold through the Swahili to other nations.

Jefferson E. Murphy examines the quality of the artifacts found in Zimbabwe in his book, The Bantu Civilization of Southern Africa.

"The most illustrative evidence comes from an archeological site at Ingombe Illede just north of the plateau near the great Kariba Gorge of the Zambizi Valley, a number of richly ornamented skeletons have been recovered from graves in a spot which seems to have been a center for elephant hunters. The Ingombe Illede skeletons were buried clothed in fine cloth, some of which was spun locally; a number of clay spindle whorles for spinning cotton cloth have been found at the same site. Their arms and legs were sheathed in bangles of copper and gold, and a number of iron tools have been found nearby. Necklaces and belts of shells and gold, very artistically made, were strung around the necks and waists of several skeletons."

"The Ingombe Illede artifacts date roughly to the period of A.D. 900 1200. The wealth of the people, and the numerous imported goods buried in the graves, show that they were involved in a lucrative trade system."(3)

The Zimbabwe people had created a trading system, which gave them access to the world's markets during the period of 900 A.D. to 1200 A.D., however, this was merely a continuation of a very ancient process. During this period, the Shona people of

Zimbabwe, controlled the area and brought some greatness to the culture by making it better than it was. The started by building massive settlements surrounded by thick stone walls all over the region. One branch of the Shona, called the Karanga had begun moving into the area from West Central Africa about 300 to 400 A.D., and had settled in other areas to the west of Zimbabwe, before moving into the Zimbabwe Kingdom.

The culture of Zimbabwe went through a renaissance. They built larger homes with adobe-type mud, perhaps similar in style to that of the Ndabele, with their square to rectangular roofs, courtyards, painted geometric designs, smooth walls of clay, well woven straw roofs and painted designs on the houses and wall fanses. The Karanga houses contained stone platforms and varrandas. They created better products for export. As time went by, they were able to elevate themselves to a position of dominance and took control of the trade routes used by the Swahili to trade with the nations of the interior of Africa.

The Karanga established a monophysite religion in Zimbabwe with a highly organized priestly class, who established a system of religious beliefs, which enabled them to strengthen their political power. What the Karanga did in using religion to maintain and gain political power among their own people, was similar to what the Christians and Semites did in their aim to dominate and control Africa. However, the difference was the Semites and Christians used tricks, deception, biblical falcities and myths such as "The Curse of Ham," and other lies, in order to gain control and to destroy the self esteem and pride of Africans. They were successful in their attempt to twist the minds of Blacks, who began to worship images of the enslaver, kidnapper, raptist and slave trader, believing that the images given by the invader, was of some supreme "God," and not realizing that the invader was playing a deceitful trick. The Karanga used religion to unify the Zimbabweans and to maintain the ancient religious practices of the adoration of ancestors and the ability to use elemental and spiritual forces for the common good.

Africans worldwide need to look to the past and find examples where Africans rejected foreign religions and

250

developed their own, after realizing that these foreign religions of the invaders were designed to pacify the Africans and to conquer their minds in the process. Today, as in the past, an indeginous African religion must be established in order for Africans to become independent of the religions of others.

Unless we reject the religious beliefs of others, we Africans will always remain the mental slaves and religious colonies of the peoples whose religions we continue to follow. They will continue to blind us to the point that even when they occupy our lands or declare religious wars against people of our own nationality of race, or use their religion as a way of making us look at them as superior peoples, we will still not be able to realize we are being tricked.

The establishment of pure African religion based on the Africans' philosophy and way of looking at life is essential in rebuilding the African mind, soul and spirit. There are religious practices that must be reformed such as the idea that we must make the descendants of people who commited crimes, pay for these crimes, by making 'slaves' of the descendants. This practice is also done in India, where the original religion was Animism which came originally from Africa, as well as the aboriginal inhabitants of India, who are of the African race.

The religious beliefs of the enemies and enslavers of Black people should be rejected and abandoned, and a new system of African religion, religious lore, written religious works, temples and other essentials of religion must be established. The building of temples to Christianity or other non-African religions is foolhardy. Where are the African temples gracing the skylines of African cities, towns and villages? Where are there classical examples of African architecture beautifying the streets and suburbs of African cities? Where are the massive temples to Ogun, Shango, Gu, Montu, Amon, Apendemak, Isis, Ra (the God of the Sun, of Blackness) or Osirus. We Africans, like other peoples have not developped an architectural style associated with the traditional religion of Africa while the styles of other peoples are worshipped.

The use of religion by invaders, slave raiders and traders, and colonizers who destroyed the souls of some Africans, while they commited the most horrible holocaust known to humans, the African slave trade, should not be allowed to continue. The religious beliefs of enemies who want Blacks to bow to them or to their Gods, cannot continue. We are intelligent enough to realize that the slave master's tool of brainwashing and conquest has been used to keep us down, for while some send their missionaries and churches to Africa, the Caribbean and other nations to "Christianize" Blacks, they send the teachers, scientists, technologists and money to the Japanese, Taiwanese, Europeans and others who have committed the most horrible crimes against humanity, and who really need Christianizing, yet based on the racist, patronizing policies of both religious organizations and their governments, they pretend to have the interests of Africans and Blacks at heart, while what they really want is to spread their religion worldwide.

The Karanga religion was purely African and it helped unify the people and their leaders against the Arab and Portugese invaders. The Karanga kings were regarded both as priests and rulers, whom the people saw as a conduit to the supreme God. The building of massive temples and structures for worship took place. Those built on the hills were used as places of worship as well as the habitations of the priests. The Karanga developed stonework and build into a high art by building more massive fortresses and temples.

The Rozwi, a branch of the Shona, not politically connected with the Karanga, elevated themselves to a position of power above the Karanga by establishinig a well organized military organization which protected their trade with the east coast of Africa and made them rich and powerful. The army also became better in its martial skills, which helped the Rozwi take control over the kingdom. The Rozwi built a powerful empire in the area they controlled. During that period of 1200 A.D. and afterwards, the Zimbabwe kingdom led by the Karanga increased the military and established a powerful central government.

A Rozwi king called Mutota 1, tried to unite the Karangas with his kingdom sometime in the 1440's. Mutota wanted to expand his territory to the Indian Ocean in order to have access to the trade on the Swahili coasts, as well as the Indian Ocean. Mutota's military campaign caused an increase in the wealth of his kingdom by collecting tribute from vassal states. Such tribute was paid in copper, gold, salt, ivory, livestock and other products. A network of river and road highways were maintained to move goods from the kingdom to the coastal cities.

The commodities brought in by the army an by tribute also attracted trade goods which made the kings wealthier. Works of precious metal and other products were traded with coastal traders for a variety of products. The Rozwi's wealth and power increased after the death of Mutota about 1450, due to the improvement of artistic styles, and trade. During this period, artistic works such as goldsmithing, stone carving (for which Zimbabwe is very famous today, where such work continues) and metalworking.

> Jefferson E. Murphy states: "In the homes and courts of the Rozwi rulers, wealth abounded. Plaques and ornaments sheathed in gold were common, as were numerous chests of beads, bracelets, bangles, belts and other objects made from shells and gold. Even utilitarian articles such as combs were beautifully made, sometimes of gold. Karanga artisans made fine points for swords, arrows, axes, hoes, and other tools and weapons of iron. Houses were built of stone and daga and those of the nobility were quite large." (4)

The Zimbabwe civilization was destroyed, beginning with the Portugese after the late 1450's and ending with the various military campaigns from the southern and Central African militarists. The Semite slave traders also played a part, due to their hunger for African slaves. This slave kidnapping and trading helped depopulate the region and make it much weaker. These forces contributed to the destruction of a civilization that began its flowering about 300 B.C., and continued to prosper until the 1840's.

A lot of lessons can be learned from the experiences of the Zimbabwe civilization, as it relates to trade. The following must be borne in mind. The Zimbabwe people established a highly skilled industrial complex, which made their products attractive to other nations. They established an organized religion based on traditional African religious beliefs. That prevented outsiders from influencing the behavior and minds of the African people and helped unite them with their leaders and their own ancient cultural traditions.

The ancient Zimbabweans greatly improved on their ability to produce food and their agricultural industries were among the most developed and advanced anywhere. Some of these ancient techniques such as terracing and hillside irrigation may help in today's agriculture. The ancient people of Zimbabwe were among the worlds large exporters of rice. They built a strong military and improved on their weaponry by creating new and better designed weapons. They united and incorporated other nations into the empire, which enabled them to fight and win against invaders.

The ancient Zimbabweans pushed for the establishment of trade with others and found access to the sea, where their products were shipped to other regions. To maintain access to the sea, kings like Mutota made his army extend its influence over the region and exact tribute on vassals and foreign agents who wanted to trade. The Zimbabwe people and their kings encouraged arts and crafts which helped keep the manufacturing industries blooming. They expanded their markets to nations as far as China and they carried out trade with Africans on the coasts as well as the interior of Africa. All the above factors helped maintain Zimbabwe civilization from 300 B.C. and before, to the 1840's, and till this very day, when aspects of the culture continues to exist, or has been rejuvinated. Zimbabwe remained resilient despite outside pressures and its people are still very culturally and spiritually strong despite a century of British settler racism and colonialism. The Zimbabwe civilization begun more than four thousand years ago, and was uninterrupted as a civilization until the 1840's. Their achievements should be an inspiration to Black people worldwide. Furthermore, if Zimbabwe's temples were built between 7000 to 6000 years Before Christ, then Zimbabwe civilization may be the oldest civilization on earth ranging to about 9000 years, and having among the most ancient building complexes on earth.

# CHAPTER TWENTY

# WEST AFRICAN TRADE AND COMMERCE: THE EMPIRE OF MALI: TRADE AND INDUSTRY

After the destruction of Ghana by the Almoravids about 1067 and again in 1203 A.D. by the Malians, a new empire rose in Ghana's place. It was much larger than Ghana and was called The Empire of Mali. Mali stretched from the Atlantic Ocean in the west, pass the city of Gao in the east. From north to south it occupied an area from the Tropic of Cancer in the north, to the Senegal River in the south. Mali, like Ghana before it, was an African empire with some ot its people, primarily the elite, being of the Muslim religion.

Daniel Chu and Elliott Skinner describes Mali in their book, A Glorious Age in Africa:

"Mali was a land of plenty plenty of everything. On the fertile soil of Mali, farmers grew sorghum, rice, taro, yams, beans and onions. They raised poultry, cattle, sheep and plenty of game meat. Cotton was also grown in many parts of Mali and great quantities of cotton cloth were available for clothing. The industrious people of Mali skillfully put their country's resources to use. Every large city or middle sized village had its own craftsmen, woodcarvers, silversmiths, goldsmiths, coppersmiths, blacksmiths, weavers, tanners and dyers."

"But the greatest source of income for the government of Mali was neither agricultural nor manufacturing. It was trade. Having replaced Ghana as the greatest power of the western Sudan, Mali also took over the trans-Saharan gold-salt trade. To protect the important trade routes between the Maghreb and the Western Sudan, Mansa Musa, Mali's Emperor established friendly commercial relations with the Sultan of Fez in Morocco. By this time the Empire of Mali, and Morocco were practically next door neighbors. Mali's boundaries had pushed far enough northward to include the Taghaza salt mines (which were well outside the borders of the old Ghanian Empire.)" (1)

"In the gold-producing regions of the south, however, Mali had the same difficulties as Ghana in trying to gain complete control over the Wangara gold miners. The people of Wangara were apparantly expert jungle fighters. In addition, the tsetse flies in the forest belt were disasterous for the horses of the Malian cavalry. The result was that nobody could tell the Wangara people what to do or not to do."

"Mali like Ghana, controled Wangara's gold output. By the time of Mansa Musa, the western source of gold for Europe. And these Sudanese (West African) gold mines would remain Europe's major source of the precious metal until the 'discovery' of the 'New World' across the Atlantic Ocean. In a very significant way, Mali's external trade (trade with other countries) differed from that of Ghana. In Ghana's time, gold and other trade goods from the Western Sudan moved northward through there to the countries in Europe on the other side of the Mediterranean Sea."

"In the days of Mali, a second major trading route was established. This one pushed off north and east, across the Sahara to Tunis and Cairo, Egypt. Gradually, the north east trade route became the main one. This development started a new era in which the influence of Egypt began to play an important role in the Western Sudan." (1)

Mali's trade was not restricted to the north of Africa. They also traded with the southern part, Central Africa, the forest kingdoms of the Yorubas, Akan-Ashantis, Bini, Guineans and others, just as they had been doing for the gold of the Wangaras. Many of their goods came from the kingdoms and lands south of the location of their empire.

## The Empire Of Songhai And Trade

Highly organized trade continued after the fall of Mali. Before the second invasion of Mali by the Moroccans in 1203 A.D., Songhai was on its way to become the new empire that would replace Mali. After the fall of Mali, Songhai became the most powerful empire in Western Africa. This new empire called Songhay was like Mali, a continuation of a previous empire, which was Mali. Songhai had in its middle, running lengthwise, the largest commercial waterway in West Africa, the Niger River. The boundaries of the Songhai began miles east of Takeda in the east and stretched to the Atlantic Ocean. From the north, it began at Taghaza in northern Mali to the northern border of the Ivory Coast, and Burkina Faso. This empire was about half the size of all Europe, or larger.

Trade flourished along the Niger River which ran along the southern curve of Songhai. The river was the main artery of trade and commerce throughout the empire, and it ran the length of it. Traders from all over Africa and other parts of the world, came to cities such as Gao, Timbuktu, Jenne and other ancient cities, to trade goods and products. Like Mali before, the people of Songhai were Muslims who had been converted in part, by the invaders from the northern Sahara and Morocco. The rest of the culture, and trade pattern of Songhai were purely African. The ancient trade in gold and salt continued and it was still one of the most important reasons for trade in the area. But manufactured goods and other products were also quite important and were carried along the river to the Bight of Benin in the south east, and to the Guinea Highlands in the south-west. Coastal kingdoms such as Benin, the Yorubas, Ashanti and others benefitted from the regional Songhai trade networks.

The ancient tradition of manufacturing products for export and local consumption continued in Songhai. The Songhais continued to make cotton cloth, iron and steel weapons, cooking utencils, farming tools, cartwheels and wagon wheels and other items. Jewelry, leather products and clothing, sandals, shoes, horse accessories and a wide variety of products were manufactured giving rise to profitable enterprises. The products of Songhay, like those of Mali and Ghana before, became part of the commodity trade between Europe, North Africa and Asia.

The Songhai, like the Zimbabwe Empire of Southern Africa, produced manufactured goods and products that other nations became famous for. The Songhais like the Malians, produced the best leather products on earth, but the Morrocans got the credit. The Zimbabwean Empire produced the highest quality steel during the Middle Ages, yet that steel was called Damascus steel. This same attrocity continues today with the calling of Ghanian chocolate, "German chocolate," or coffee from the Caribbean or Africa, "French," or "Swiss" coffee.

Chu and Skinner describes the Songhai as farmers, fishermen, hunters, craftsmen and women, traders, and warriors who came together and became the most important group of people in the area. From a city called Dendi, they moved upriver and settled in a place called Kukya, (a city described by Chancellor Williams as being in existence during the time of the Khemite (Egyptian) Pharaohs, approx. before 700 B.C.), near northwest Nigeria. That settlement prospered and became a great city and their capital.

By the ninth century, Berbers, wanderers from the northern deserts swept down on Kukya, occupied it and installed their own king against the will of the Songhai people, who resented the intrusion. The Berbers, like the Arab invaders before them were attracted to the wealth of the Songhai Empire, which was even greater in political influence and wealth than Ghana or Mali before them.

One notices the same pattern of invasions by the same type of people since the Hyksos invaded Khemet about 1720 B.C. Groups of pastoralists or semi-barbaric peoples always invade, destroy, or cause disturbances in highly organized and advanced African civilizations. However, these groups are only successful when African nations began infighting, or become militarily or economically weak. The Berbers were remnants of an Asiatic people who invaded Northern Africa in ancient times. These Asiatics mixed with the Africans, who are the aboriginal inhabitants of the Sahara, and who still consist of a large majority of the population in the region today. Thus, Berbers can be as Black as any African from West Africa, or a fair as any Caucasian.

The Songhai, like the Malians did not reject the religious teachings of these Berbers and other alien invaders, but instead, they converted to the religions of the invaders, attracting more invaders who entered as religious teachers and missionaries. As for the invaders, it did not matter that the African elite followed the same religion as themselves (as it still does not matter today), invasions of African lands, and enslavement of its peoples continued all the same.

One has to conclude that the spread of the religion of the invaders into the great ancient civilizations of Africa, was not because the invaders were concerned about the salvation of the African soul. It was merely a way to gain control of the African mind and a foothold in these great, rich empires, began and built by the West Africans. It is ironic that soon after the Africans accepted the religions of the invaders, or the so-called traders and travelers, the armies of these traders and travellers followed, causing havoc and destruction wherever they went, and also being defeated and wiped out by the African armies.

They Songai people soon found out the true nature of the invaders after the invaders had held power for a short time. Skinner and Chu explains the feelings of the Songais and explains that becasue of the resentment felt by the Songais towards the Berber invaders, the Songhais moved further upriver and created another town called Gao. The Dias continued to follow in their attempt to spread their control in the area occupied by the Songhais. Later on, Gao was also occupied by the Dias.

These Berbers consolidated their hold on Gao and other cities of the Songhai people, but this hold was soon smashed by the true inheritor of the Songhai throne, a prince called Ali Colon and another called Sulayman Nar who had been held captive by the Malian Emperor Mansa Musa. These two princes were sons of Dia Assabai. Ali Colon founded a new dynasty called the Sunni.

The importance of Songhai grew as an empire with the coming to the throne of Sunni Ali Ber in 1464. Its capital Timbuktu was re-captured around 1468 from the alien rulers who had held it. Timbuktu had been a Songhay trading city from the earliest times and a center of learning. Chu and Skinner remarks. "It had a great university, Sankore, which attracted

261

many students from distant parts of Africa. Scholarship and commerce were the glories of Timbuktu."

Another group of nomads called the Tuareg, a misture of Black Africans and Asiatic peoples, invaded Timbuktu in 1433. They too were defeated and expelled by Sunni Ali Ber. Sunni Ali also tried to take over another city called Jenne. During the 1200's A.D., the Soninke built a city called Jenne, which was situated in a remote area along the Beni River, a branch of the Niger. The city was located about 300 miles south-west of the city of Timbuktu. Jenne was difficult to invade due to the swamps in the area which surrounded it. The only way to enter in and out was through a maze of waterways and streams.

The importance of Jenne as a center for scientific and schorlarly advancement must never be downplayed or forgotten. Jenne's value was not high only because it was a university city, but because in Jenne, the ancient tradition of education as begun by the Khemites and Nubian Kushites, reached a new and improved level. In comparison to what the ancestors of the same Africans in Songhay and West Africabegan in Khem, Nubia, Kush, Ethiopia (Abbyssinia), Negau (Somalia) and Ghana, before 600 B.C., these Mideaval universities were the highest level of education during their period.

Jenne is a testament to the achievements of Africans, as early as the development of the neolithic civilizations along the Nile Valley about 17,000 years ago. Moreover, Jenne's protected position in the swamps of the Niger, kept it safe from invaders and helped its inhabitants to carry on with their medical, scientific, scholarly and commercial persuits.

Chu and Skinner observes. "Jenne was also a match for Timbuktu as a commercial center. One reason for Timbuktu's commercial success was that caravans carrying goods had to pass through Timbuktu to get to Jenne." (2) Sunni Ali put Jenne under seige for almost eight years before he decided to give up, due to the hardships suffered by the town. Sunni Ali, amazed by the courage of the King of Jenne who came to his camp, took over Jenne but did not destroy it. He later married the mother of the King whose city he had captured.

During the reign of Sunni Ali, the city of Gao was the home of about 10,000 people. It was a valuable trading city and was one of the important cities along the trade routes across the Sahara. Another important city was Takedda, a place where copper was mined during the time of Sunni Ali as well as Mansa Musa. Sunni Ali's rule came to an end after twenty-five yers when he drowned trying to cross a river about 1492.

Among the kings of Songhay who followed Sunni Ali was Askia Muhammed, who took over after beating the army of the former king, and son of Sunni Ali. In 1493, Askia's troops and that of the king engaged in a fight in which the king lost. Askia Muhammed was a devout Muslim and after his return from Mecca on a pilgrimage, he engaged in wars against those who refused the religion of the Arabs and Berbers. By then he had expanded the length and breadth of his empire. Among Askia's enemies were the Tuareg, who are alledged by some to still be involved in the enslavement of Africans in Mauritania and parts of West Africa today. Sunni Ali's rule came to an end after twenty five years, when he drowned trying to cross a river about 1492.

During Askia's pilgrimage to Mecca, he "had an audience with the Caliph of Egypt, who solemnly appointed the Askia his religious lieutenant in Songahi country. "The appointment was sealed by placing a bonnet and a turban on Askia's head." (3) This act by the Caliph of Egypt may seem flattering, but there seems to have been a religious and political motivation behind it. It appears that the old trick of trying to make Africans believe that they were respected or on an equal footing, was at play, even though by appointing the emperor of an empire greater than occupied Egypt (now occupied by the Arabs) as a "leiutenant" of a foreign nation seemed so much like appointing a vassal, and therefore can be construed as an insult to the African Emperor. The mentality of the Caliph of Egypt was the same carried by those who have used these same types of tricks to spread their influence, and to take total control later.

The Tuarag nomads launched raids along the north-east against Askia who decided to put a final end to their raiding activities, for good. He attacked them from a base in the country of the Hausa, in a place called Air and captured it. He then drove out the Tuaregs. A permanent settlement was then founded probably as a garrison to stop any more Tuaregs from raiding Songhai territory. The town of Air still exists and is still occupied by Songais.

Songhay became powerful and wealthy as an empire. By the early 1500's, the empire wasdivided into provinces ruled by governors appointed by the Askia. The elimination of the ancient religious practices rooted in the African philosophy, psyche, and philosophy of life was also carried out in Songhay, and the religion of the invaders were given prominence. Inspite of the Askia being a Muslim, that did not stop the invaders who were also of the same religion, from trying to destroy Songhai or launching raids against her.

After the death of Askia Muhammed in the 1538's, his sons took over the throne. The empire soon began to disintegrate due to despotism. A Moorish invasion from Morocco followed. They seized the salt mines, and attacked the Songhai Empire. This Moorish army was armed with the latest European guns and perhaps cannons. They won against the Songhi, despite taking heavy losses themselves. These particular Moors were unable to rule the Songai and brought more ruination to the area. The Moroccans invaded and left about the 1880's.

## The Effects Of Invasions And Alien Religious Concepts On Black Culture

The sad demise of the great empires of West Africa, as well as other parts of Africa, and of civilizations which go past 8,000 B.C., was caused by many factors. The trick of converting Africans to foreign religions was perhaps the most harmful aspect of the colonializing and brainwashing process, for even a conquered nation can retain its self respect and dignity as long as its culture, religion and self worth is left intact. However, when religions and ideologies which promote the worship of images of the enemies, colonizers and enslavers as the image of "God," and they are accepted by Blacks, then we have already lost our very souls and thoughts. We have become slaves in the same manner

264

that the Black Dalits, were made "untouchables," or slaves by the religion imposed by the invaders of India over three thousand years ago, which continue to be practiced to this very day!

The scheme of converting Africans to foreign religious beliefs while occupying their land was a major problem faced by these African empires, for it turned strong, proud people into subjects of certain religious empires. This forced conversion of Africans, whether it was in the religion of the Semites, or that of the Christians destroyed the ability of Africans to expand their indigenous and ancient religious beliefs of African monophyism, worship of the sun and nature, and ancestor worship. These religious concepts are the religions developed by Africans themselves, free of alien ideas. These religious beliefs were African belief in a supreme being, or monphyism, with the sun as a representative of the supreme God, nature as being connected to the God head, spiritual and elemental forces and the importance of ancestors.

These religious concepts are the system of beliefs that Africans have had for hundreds of thousands of years. These beliefs have sustained Africans and have contributed to them being the first people to develop and invent world civilization. As soon as we begun to reject our own beliefs and philosophy for that of the slave master and slave kidnapper, we lost our very soul and longed for the soul of the people whose religions we were fooled into believing will lead us to salvation. We found out later that that we Black people became the most wretched, most brutalized, and most hated people on earth, because like sheep, we accepted anything an any religious ideas thrown in our faces, without question. All that had to be done was for the thrower to be of a pale hue.

The problems mentioned above is particularly true in this era. For example, a certain religious group which declared that Blacks or the "Children of Ham" were cursed by Noah, and thus not worthy of being priests in that religion, continues to convert Africans and other Black people who blindly accept this religion which helped in perpetrating racism against Black people. This so-called "Christian" religion may disband if they realize that Christ himself may have been a Black Jew and that the description of God in Revelation, is of one with feet of burnished bronze, and hair like sheep's wool.

This foolish acceptance of religious beliefs that we Africans did not invent is the utmost in stupidity. Why would anyone accept a religion that sanctifies racism, or wants to make slaves out of them, particularly if they are not of that religion. Why would anyone want to accept any religion that declared Blacks have no souls, are cursed and therefore should not be priests of that particular religion. These beliefs are not merely blatant lies and defamation of the character of the Black race, it makes the entire religion of these charlatans one big lie. Only one who has no pride in himself or in his own people, and who does not understand the power of religion in making the propogators of a particular religion hold unto their control and domination of the rest of the world through brain washing, will continue to follow these religions.

The solution to this problem is for all Africans and Blacks to return to the religion of our ancestors before the contamination of the invaders and colonialists. The solution is to return to the worship of one supreme God represented by the sun and nature, observation of elemental and spiritual forces, the establishment of written lore, books the building of magnificient temples and so on. In fact, the return of ancient African religion, would focus on using the natural metaphysical powers to apply to everyday use.

The following factors contributed to the destruction of African civilizations:

Barbarians, pastoralists and nomads from lesser cultures of the plains or deserts invade the settled, advanced civilizations of the south. These invaders are usually successful mostly when the civilizations are in a state of weakness. The invaders all have one thing in common, whether it was the barbarian Indo Europeans who invaded India about 1700 B.C. or the Hyksos and Hebrews who invaded or infiltrated into Egypt, or the Arabs and later Christians who invaded Africa. They used religion to put themselves in a position of superiority, discover that Africans are a very spiritual people and fill their minds with falsities. Their techniques of control were as follows:

(1) Forced conversion and turning the attention of the converted To worship a God in the image of the invader, or teaching falsities about accepting poverty, discrimination and the evil treatment of the invader, for an afterlife of happiness.

(2) Having among the religious writings of these religions that some "curse," was placed on the Black race, therefore, slavery was to be their lot, if they do not accept certain Religions. The sad irony is that no matter how much some of these religions insult the intelligence of Black people, we still follow them, or convert as if there is no time to think, or research the background of teachings of these religions.

(3) Having all the sacred religious sites in the country of the invader and having Blacks look to these countries such as the country where the head of the church or religion resides.

(4) Twisting the minds of Black people to the extent that some Blacks will start believing they are people whom they are not. For example, certain religious groups require converts to emerse themselves in their religion, forget their racial and ethnic group and regard themselves as "brothers" to the converter. Yet, these same converters continue to carry racist policies against Blacks disguised under the cover of religion. They use the converts to carry their racist, colonialist policies against their own Black people, declare religious wars against them, and contribute to the cultural destruction. Slavery is a prime example, where Black brothers took each other as slaves for the benefit of someone else.

The following observation was made concerning the invaders' use religion to gain control and domination over the Africans.

(1) Race before religion:

Despite the fact that the Sudanic Black empired were of the same religion as the invaders, these invaders still destroyed the Black civilizations. Their primary motivation seemed to have been the enforcement of racial domination and hegemony as well as religious control over the Africans. Based on this historical experience, Blacks should put race before religion. To be Black is a direct result of God's choosing of the Black race, by blessing the race with the sun's rays. Thus, being Black is in itself a religious symbol of much sacredness. Thus, no matter what is said of propogated by religious converters, to reject their teachings is not to reject God, but to prevent others from pushing their own racial and political agenda on Black people. After all, is it not these same religious converters who flood into Africa and the rest of the Black world, who have declared Blacks are cursed and should be made slaves, about five hundred years ago, and continue to believe these falcities?

(2) The establishment of the indeginoous religion of Africans as was done in Zimbabwe before the Semites, Portugese and others destroyed it, was essential in the keeping of unity and strength among the people. We see that religious lore, temples, codes of moral and ethical conduct, and various facets of religious belief developed from the traditional African philosophy of living. African culture was made richer by keeping the traditional African religion and rejecting all others.

# CHAPTER TWENTY-ONE

# THE FOREST KINGDOMS OF WEST AFRICA THEIR WEALTH AND COMMERCE 1500 B.C. to 1500 A.D.

The ancient kingdoms of West Africa which occupied the Coastal Forest Belt, from Guinea in the west, to Cameroon in the east, had trading relationships with other nations of the region, across and within the Sahara, and even westward across the Atlantic Ocean to the Americas. Trade between various parts of West Africa and other regions within the continent has been documented to extend as far back as the period between 20,000 to 10,000 B.C. According to Wayne Chandler, the Sahara, East and West Africa was covered by an inland sea. On this massive body of water, Africans used sailing ships to conduct trade and commerce with one another. He mentions in African Presence in Early Asia (1995, p.376), that the aquatic peoples were Negroid who were also master ship builders.(1) They transported an African cotton to the Americas as early as about 4000 to 5000 B.C., according to Ivan Van Sertima, in his book, They Came Before Columbus, (Random House, 1976)(2). Furthermore, current evidence points to an even more remote period for Africans of the "b" group blood type, who seems to have crossed from West Africa about 12,000 to 6000 years ago, according to James Grundy, in an article to Ancient American (May/June, 1997, p. 18).(3) Even this date is a more recent date, for the earliest evidence for an Africoid Black presence in the Americas is before 75,000 B.C., according to James Gladwin, of The Gladwin Thesis, (McGraw-Hill, Men Out of Asia, 1947).(4)

However, between 3000 B.C. to 1500 A.D., what became the great kingdoms of West Africa such as the Ashantis, Beni, Yoruba, IgboIkwu, and others were either settling in from the drying Sahara, or building their own indigenous civilizations in the forest areas, independent of outside influence. The kingdoms which came to be known by the Arabs and Europeans during the

Middle Ages, did not spring from the earth with the coming of these peoples. These ancient kingdoms were well established by 1500 B.C., and continued an unbroken line of civilization until the arrival of the Arabs and Europeans during the 1500's A.D. During theis three thousand year period, Europe was in the Dark Ages, and earlier still, between 400 A.D. to 1500 B.C., a number of barbarian tribes existed in Europe, from the naked, blue painted Celts during the Greek period (400 to 800 B.C.), to the savage and barbaric Vandals of the 400's A.D.

Between 400 to 600 B.C., the Carthaginians, Egyptians and Phoenicians had sent their ships and merchants to West Africa for purposes of trade and commerce. During that period, iron had been in use in West Africa as early as the Late Stone Age through a period around 2500 B.C. The emergence of the Nok Culture, in which the inhabitants of the region produced naturalistic figurines of humans out of terracotta, classical artwork, efficient agriculture, and well organized towns and villages, occurred and expanded throughout West Africa. This period began about 3000 B.C. and merged into the period of the Great West African Kingdoms and Empires beginning about 1200 B.C. to the 1600's B.C. Stone was being carved with naturalistic perfection, and later on, bronze was being carved with naturalistic perfection.

The area where these ancient forest kingdoms occupied in an area covered by forests, and high mountainous country, from which rivers flow into the savannah areas about two hundred miles north, or flow into the Bight of Benin, to the sea. The forest area covers terrain from Senegal to Cameroon, and from the Niger Delta to Sokoto in the north. This distance averages about 300 miles from the lush, green and rainy coastal areas to the savannah lands to the north. Large rivers such as the Pra River, the Niger, the Volta and the Benue drain southward into the Bight of Benin.

The forest kingdoms of West Africa was one of the primary trading places from as early as 1500 B.C., this date can be said to be in the middle of a period which may have intensified about 3000 B.C., when migrants from the Sahara and the drying regions of West Africa began moving into the forest areas in order to find new lands. It was about 1500 B.C., that Africans whose origins are partly in West Africa may have established a physical presence in ancient Olmec Mexico, and contributed to the development of the Olmec civilization.

There was extensive trade between West Africa from before 1100 B.C., till the Europeans began kidnapping Africans along the coastal lands about 1500 A.D. The issue of trade between the Americas and Africa has been touched upon before, yet it must be included in those periods in history, or in those regional areas where it most likely occurred. It also is more likely that the earliest trade between Africa and the Americas took place on the West Coast of Africa, where the proximity is the closest, and where sea currents can deposit ships on the shores of South America, the Caribbean, and the United States.

The history of West Africa has never been fully researched, therefore, who knows whether West Africa was not a center of civilization on the same or similar level with Khemet, Nubia, Negau, Kush, Abbyssinia, Sabea, Sumer, Elam, India or any of the Black civilizations of eastern Africa or Asia. In fact, West Africa's civilization can be compared to some of these in their highly skilled craftsmanship, governing, customs, sophistication of language, building ability, use of metals, agriculture and other criteria, including the invention of writing.

Pyramids and massive buildings and temples were also built in West Africa, although many of these have been destroyed or covered up by sand. The lack of many massive temples and other architectural works in the forest kingdoms in comparable to Egypt or Nubia-Kush, may have to do with the lack of materials such as stone suitable for building on a massive scale, although clay and other materials such as wood were used. Pests such as the tsetse fly, which makes extensive outdoor labor unhealthy for some people and the lack of draught animals to help due to the mosquito borne diseases and malaria, may have all contributed to the lack of building on a massive scale in West Africa, as had occurred in other parts of the Black world.

That building program may have been carried over to Mexico, where a frenzy of architectural activity, pyramid

271

building and structures occurred between 1200 B.C. till about 400 A.D. During that period, iron may have been brough, sent or traded to those who lived in ancient Mexico. This conclusion was made based on the fact that iron beads were discovered next to a collosal Olmec stone head, with distinict Negroid features.

During the early years of West African trade with the Americas, till the late 1400's when the Portugese began trading in slaves along the coast of West Africa, Africans from West Africa made frequent voyages across the Atlantic Ocean in boats similar to the ones which were used to sail up and down, along the Niger and other rivers of West Africa today. Rafts, double canoes and larger boats may have also been used. If we refer to Columbus' account that one of his colleagues encountered Africans on the Cape Verde region, who told him that they load their long-boats with goods to sail across the Atlantic towards the Americas, than it is very likely that these trips were occurring thousands of years previously.

Knowledge of nautical and astronomical sciences was advanced in Africa and Africans had no fear of the ocean, neither did they believe that the world was flat. The astronomical sciences in West Africa and the rest of Africa was so advanced that certain readers of the stars could predict drought, rainfall or various aspects of the weather by observing the position of the stars. Nations such as the Dogon People of Mali were so advanced, that their astronomical observations, recordings and skill in mapping out and following the course of stars such as the Syrius (Dog Star worshipped by the ancient Khemites) star system, and the accuracy of their calculations have baffled modern scientists. These astronomers have only rediscovered the movements of the Syrius star system with the modern, highly sophisticated instruments. This tells quite a bit about why things invented Africans, such as religion and culture must be kept intact and free of outside permeation or influence.

West African trade with the Americas is one of the most important aspects of African history, yet that era which lasted for more than three thousand years has not been researched by many. It is important to know about this period, because it shows that while Africans on the West Coast of Africa were blocked from trade with the Mediterranean, they found trading partners across the Atlantic, in the same way that Africans on the east coast of Africa found trade with China, India and the various nations and kingdoms of the Indian Ocean Basin as well as the Pacific and Asia, after the Mediterranean became dominated by barbarians and Euro Asiatic powers.

A journey across the Atlantic to the Americas on a good current during clement weather, would have been an easier task and may have taken about the same time as sending goods back and forth from northern and northeastern Africa, across the Sahara with its hot, dusty environment and thousands of miles of sand, across the Sahel and other semiarid region, across the savannah and across the mountains and highlands, down the great rivers, before they reached the capitals of the West African kingdoms, which were situated along the coasts.

This distance would have made trading across the Atlantic Ocean by ship seem rather easy. Moreover, draught animals carrying goods to West Africa would not have lasted in that environment with its dangerous tsetse fly which kills horses, cows and other beasts of burden, as well as outsiders and those who lived in the region.

A journey by ship around the northern port of Byblos about 1500 B.C., to the Bight of Benin in West Africa, is about two to three times less from the Guinea coast of West Africa to Brazil. West Africans may have looked to the Atlantic for trade due to the various conflicts that were occuring during the period, with barbarians such as the Sea Peoples, the Greeks, Jews, Assyrians, Persians and others who were at one period or another in control of the shipping routes in the Mediterranean. During these occurrances, the West Africans would have avoided this area where the northern peoples were at conflict with each other. Furthermore, the gold, metals and wealth of these West African kingdoms would have made them targets of interest and invasion had the Africans extended a strong presence in the Mediterranean. In fact, during the early part of the Christian era, this is exactly what occurred when Roman and Carthaginians crossed the Sahara to West Africa and described the West African kings as being bedecked in gold and jewels and riding on chariots. Trade across the Atlantic between the Africans and Native Americans was much safer and became very profitable.

Access was another reason why West Africans decided to strengthen their trade with the Americas, while their ships were hardly found in the Mediterranean. During that period (1500 B.C. to 400 B.C.) Ships from nations like Khemet, Kush, Nubia, Negau, Mauri (Carthage), and other Black kingdoms in the Mediterannean and North Africa had easy access to the trade routes and trade goods from places such as Byblos, Cyprus, Europe and Asia. West African traders did not because they were much further away and preferred to trade across the Atlantic, where a West African ship or longboat could sail all the way to and from Mexico, the Caribbean, South America and the United States without having to be harrassed or to pay tribute to other nations along the way, before they reached their own territory.

It was from this very ancient trading systems and trade routes to the Americas began by the Africans, that Christopher Columbus heard that there was land across the Atlantic, to the west. He found out on a journey to West Africa, that Africans were taking frequent trips back and forth with longboats and ships loaded with various types of goods for trading with the inhabitants across the Atlantic, to the west. Before going into the known or suspected aspects of West African trade with the Americas, the evidence for West African trade and contact must be examined.

Apart from Khemet (Egypt), civilizations like that of the Nubians and Kushites who controlled the empire immediately south of Khemet all the way to the south-central part of Sudan, as well as the ancient civilizations of Ghana, Mauri (from which the term "Moor" originated) and some of the forest kingdoms along the coast of West Africa, were all trading civilizations who sailed from part of Africa to the next, and into foreign areas such as pre-Celtic Spain.

Africans from West Africa, as well as North Eastern Africa are the ones who crossed the Atlantic during the period of the peak of Black civilization and the second renaissance, between 1500 B.C. to 1500 A.D. Much of the evidence is based on the massive collosal stone heads of people with distinctly Negroid features, as well as hundreds of terracotta works of people with Negroid characteristics, and a number of clues which connect them with the people of an area from West Africa to Sudan. African helmets fastened with rope, leather ear flaps, cornrow hairstyles, braids with beads at the back of the head, war helmets identical to that worn by the ancient Nubians and Kushites, and kinky hair common among Negroid people. Some of these heads have been termed "Olmec" since they were found in the part of Mexico called "Olli" or "The Land of Rubber," by the Maya Indians of Mexico.

Hundreds of pottery figurines, terracotta heads and other artifacts which represent distinctly Negroid features have also been found over the past one hundred years in Mexico, the South-east U.S.,(where an existing Black nation of prehistoric Black origins, the Ouachita, still exist and are still distinctly Black). Other evidence have also been found in Texas, Costa Richa and through parts of Central and South America. Various cultural clues and traces unique to Africa can be seen in the faces of these statuettes, and terracotta heads. The African hairline is clearly visible in a fine stone head from Veracruz. It was carved during the classic period of the Olmec civilization, a period of about 600 to 400 B.C.. It is about seventeen centimeters from the head to the chin.

Another head of about 12 centimeters does not only possess Negroid features, but the hairstyle is of African design. This terracotta head from the Totonac culture is on display in the National Museum of Mexico City. There are ear plugs or enlarged errings in both ears, a style common throughout Africa. One of the most impressive types of evidence shown on that terracotta head and other such works is the application of scarification marks, which identifies the nationality of this head and continues to be applied in Africa to this very day, to serve the same purpose of identification. The style of scarifaction tatoos show that whoever was the model for the terracotta head had to have come from West Africa or the Nile region, perticularly Sudan. These exact patterns still exist today among the Nuer and other tribes of Sudan.

275

Some of the heads of terracotta or stone are so distinctly African that when compared to West African terracotta or stone heads of the same or a latter period, there is no doubt that they are identical in many respects, from the black painted faces, to the exact representation of Negroid racial characteristics and features. Two terracotta heads made from the period of 1000 B.C. to 500 B.C., when compared, are almost exactly alike in the style of creation and the facial features. These heads came from different countries. One terracotta head, shows the realistic portrayal of a Black African male and comes from the ancient city of Ife, West Africa. The second head is a terracotta with racial and facial features similar to the one from Ife, with the face painted black, yet, this one was found in the Mexican high plateau among Aztec artwork. It is now in a storeroom of the National Museum of Mexico City and is 14 centemeters high.

Other heads of collosal stone found in Mexico are similar to heads made in the same fashion in Tanis, Egypt and parts of Kush and Nubia. The connection between West Africa, Nubia, Kush and Egypt is quite ancient. Some of the people who live in West Africa today, their places of origin include Egypt and Nubia-Kush, as well as the Sahara. Migrations may have occurred during the alien invasions of Egypt and Nubia, or the drying of the Sahara. These occurances took place between 3000 B.C. when migrants from the drying Sahara moved into West Africa, to about 500 B.C., when a number of peoples left Egypt and Kush for West Africa. Events such as the invasion of Nubia by Seneferu about 2592 to 2568 B.C., invasions by the Hyksos about 1700's B.C., the freeing of the Hebrews from Egypt by Pharaoh Merneptah between 1295 to 1187 B.C., the invasion by the Persians during reign of Darius during the 500's B.C., all contributed to the movement of people from Egypt to Sudan as well as West Africa.

Thousands of Nubians, Egyptians and other Africans migrated west ward, past Lake Chad, towards West Africa, during the periods mentioned. Others went directly southward into Kenya and further into Southern Africa and Central Africa. Still others remained along the Nile river valley, and are today among the peoples called the Nuba, Nuer, Dinka, Shilluk,

Massai, and other so-called Nilotes. Various Nubian and Khemetic cultural traits are still to be found among these groups, as well as the peoples of West Africa such as the Wolof, Yoruba, and others. These practices include circumcision of males, kingship rituals, matrilineal succession and other traits.

The question of boats have been used to deny Africans the credit for sailing back and forth across the Atlantic. African boats are usually judged by the European standard, which is either a caravelle, or Greek galley. Because the boats Africans used during their journeys of trade with the Native Americans were not of the exact design as European ships during the Greek and Roman period, such as galleys, some skeptics have said that they could not possibly have crossed the Atlantic in smaller boats and if they did, they were merely "slaves," of people such as the Phoenicians.

Various experiments concerning boats made from reed to tree trunks to animal skin, have been used to prove that people could have and did cross from the nations of West Africa to the Americas. In 1969, on the sands behind the Great Pyramids of Egypt, shipwrights from Lake Chad in West Africa, helped Thor Heyerdhal build a reed boat. (5) His boat was designed after the ones used by the ancient Khemites before the era of building boats in Lebanon cedar, before 3000 B.C.

Thor Hayerdahl made a great miscalculation. The ship was built by West Africans in the styles they have used for thousands of years, but Thor Hayerdhal did not begin the journey in West Africa, where the builders of the ship came from, but at Safi, Morocco, more than one thousand miles further from West Africa to Barbadose. Also, he did not reinforce the ship as had been done in ancient times. The second ship Ra 11 reached Barbadose after 57 days at sea. This time he decided to build Ra 11, like the ships of ancient Egypt, and today's West Africa and Lake Titicaca thousands of miles away in the Andes Mountains of South America. In the case of South America, the shipwrights were Aymara Indians.

The reed boat is a common type of watercraft used in West Africa and other parts of the world, yet these were not the only types of boats used by the Africans of Egypt, Nubia and West Africa. The boats which crossed the Atlantic between 4000 B.C. to 1000 B.C., were most likely the same or of a type similar to the ones shown on Nubian rock drawings of about 3000 to 4000 B.C. This is so because West Africans brought the same boatbuilding techniques with them from the areas of Africa they migrated from, which includes the Sahara, where boats with sails were being used between 10,000 to 20,000 B.C., and cave paintings dating back about 7000 B.C., exists.

In some of the drawings of prehistoric boats found in Nubia, curved hulls driven by paddlers and sails are clear. Egyptologists like Sir Flinders Petrie believe that all these drawings represent papyrus boats. Naval architecture historian Bjorn Landstrom, thinks that some of the curved hulls shown on the rocks and on Nagadeh 11 pottery suggest either a basic three-plank vessel or even larger boats that are variations on the three-plank concept. The planks would have been sewn togehter with rope. The larger version must have boasted some interior framing in order to hold them together. Some of the hulls show vertical vertical extensions of bow and stern. Without exception, all the hulls showing sails either have this vertical extension fronr and back or a deeply curved profile.

This style of boating is still used in West Africa today, particularly along the Niger River, where river trading by boat takes place. Such boats are usually carved out of a massive tropical tree, fitted with planks to enlarge them, and covered with a ten or cabin over the top. Such boats were usually six to eight feet across, four feet deep and forty to fifty feet long. Tents and cabins of woven straw mats were used to cover them. Sails of straw are used to direct these ships when convinient, along with paddles. There is no doubt that these types of ships were used in ancient times during the period of trade between West Africa and the Americas.

Apart from these, the Nubians, Kushites, Khemites, Ethiopians and other African civilizations were known traders in the Mediterranean as well as the Atlantic. Apart from the Phoenicians who circumnavigated Africa about 600 B.C., the Nubians who had been in control of Egypt and the

Mediterannean region were traders who had gone as far north as England to mine tin for their bronze weapons, before they switched to Iron about 600 B.C. The Nubians used Phoenician sailors from the time they gained influence about 1100 B.C., over the Egyptian military and political establishment, under the Ramsid Pharaohs to about the mid 600's B.C., when they retreated from Egypt back to Nubia-Kush after the Assyrians invaded Egypt. During this period, the Phoenicians were vassals of the Nubians, who were their overlords.

This close relationship between the Phoenician vassal states with the Nubians have caused some to speculate that the collosal stone "Olmec" heads of ancient Mexico, which show distinctly Negroid features were nothing but "slaves" or "servants" of the Phoenicians. Thus the response is, whywere so-called "slaves" and "servants" given prominence among the Native Americans, dwarfing their so-called masters? (6)

Skeletons described as Negroid have also been found in preColumbian layers in the valley of the Pecos River, which flows through Texas and New Mexico, empties via the Rio Grande into the Gulf of Mexico. Also, in February 1975, a Smithsonian Institution team reported the find of two Negroid skeletons in a grave in the U.S. Virgin Islands abandoned by the Mongoloid Caribs (there are Negroid Caribs of pre Columbian origins called Black Carib, Garifuna, or Califunami) long before the coming of Christopher Columbus to the New World. According to Ivan Van Sertima (1976), soil from the earth layers where the skeletons were found was dated to A.D. 1250. A study of the teeth showed a type of dental mutilation characteristic of African cultures. (7)

These skeletons were found after doubt continued to remain about the actual physical appearance of Africans in the Americas from pre-historic times, to the Middle Ages. During the international congress of American anthropologists said the only thing missing in connection with the Negroid terracotta of ancient America as final proof of an African presence were Negroid skeletons. Because of these finds and various types of evidence, most anthropologists now agree that indeed there was a permanent African Negroid presence in the Americas. Some of the greatest proponents are those who live in the country of Mexico, where fields with Negroid carvings, statues, collosal stone heads and other artefacts representing Africans and African features are spread over a vast area of the landscape.

The conclusion has to be made that Africans established a wide network of trade between West Africa and the Americas. That conclusion is made because of the evidence available and because the West Africans who inhabited the coastal forest region of West Africa were at a better advantage and closer to the Americas in miles, than the Khemites and Nubian-Kushites, although they too visited the Americas. Trade between the coast of West Africa, and the nations of the Mediterranean may have been more difficult than trade from West Africa to the Americas. Africans had no fear of sailing, nor of the Atlantic, and the knew that the world was round and not flat. And so, there was no fear on their part of sailing across the Atlantic any time between 4000 B.C. to 1500 A.D., and much earlier. The arrival of the Portugese during the late 1400's A.D. along with other Europeans who cruised the coast of West Africa looking for slaves may have brought a slow but sure end to the long period of transatlantic trade between the Americas and West Africa.

It is only logical that no Ashanti, Yoruba, Igbo, or Mandinka would dare venture on an expedition across the Atlantic to the Americas if he knew that slave traders would kidnap him and his crew. At that period in history, certain churches had given their political the so-called devine "authority" to enslave the Children of Ham, or any Negroid, or black-skinned people, anywhere on earth. During this period, African kings were also being influenced by slave traders who brought in a new evil to the region from both Europe and the lands north and north-east of the Sahara. These slave traders and kidnappers of Black people contributed to the rapid disintegration of some of the Black civilizations of the forest regions along the coast. Due to this, a period of warfare began which brought about more destruction and degradation to the area and its peoples.

Trade between West Africa and the Americas came to an abrupt end just as the slave trade was beginning. In fact, when Columbus and other Spanish explorers ventured into parts of the

Caribbean and Central America, they were told of Africans from "Ethiopia" who had built towns and settlements in areas such as Columbia and Panama long ago, but who came in conflict with the Native Americans. By the late 1400's the Europeans were making trade contacts with Africans. At first gold was sought. Soon afterwards, slaves were exchanged for European guns, tobacco, run and the same deadly products peddled to Africans in Africa today, and those in the ghettos of America, Brazil, the Caribbean, and other lands with large Black populations. The results are today worse than they've ever been. Today, the demons mind altering drugs, alcahol, and invented diseases are causing the same devastation to Blacks worldwide that the "edict" which encouraged the enslavements of Blacks worldwide caused beginning about the 1400's.

The hunger by Africans for European goods, instead of making their own products, like the Japanese did during the latter part of the nineteenth century, led to the underdevelopment of Africa. It changed Africa from the world's most wealthy and industrious region, to the least developed, in a few years. Many Africans continued to remain in this position today when we should be doing something to regain a superior position in the world of trade and commerce. The lust for things European led to the later enslavement, occupation and colonialism never before seen in human history and a traffic in humans that caused the deaths of about 50 to 100 million killed and enslaved by the enemies of Black people.

This fact is one of the reasons why people who constantly call for the control of the African or Black population anywhere on earth are preaching genocide and should be challenged. It is why every Black man and Black woman must regard bringing more Black children into this world and raising them to stand tall, proud and contribute to the greatness of the Black race. That should be a sacred duty, as well as an act of respect and homage to the millions of our ancestors who died during the slave trade, bringing about a great decrease in our numbers all over the world, and making us much easier to oppress and conquer. The fifty to one hundred million of our great ancestors killed during the slave trade must be replaced. We Black people do not need the enslaver or the conqueror's religion to turn us into mental slaves, while they send their scientists, technologists and industrialists to Japan and to Europe. What is needed is to bring about scientific and technological advancement throughout the Black world.

West Africa's trade with the American Indians did not include any inferior-superior position. They traded on equal terms and exchanged goods and products of great quality such as the ones described by the Aztecs themselves. The Aztecs described these Africans' merchandise as, "vivid colored mantles of cotton cloth, the cloaks so richly dyed they seem to copy the iridescent plumage of the birds, ear pendants, smoking pipes; the unique appearance of their wares, luxuries,"(7) all describe products of high quality brought by the West Africans to Mexico.

The mention of 'guanin,' an alloy of gold, silver and tin, used by the West Africans as a trade item and called 'kanin' by them, is another testament to the type of goods and products traded by the forest kingdoms of West Africa. Metals were traded with the American Indians and there is evidence that iron was among them, or was used by Africans during their building in Mexico. The possibility of iron being used during the Middle Ages, as it was surely used during the period of 1500 B.C. 4000 B.C. to 500 B.C. is highly likely even though no iron tools or weapons have been discovered in the ancient Olmec sites as yet, except the bag of iron beads, found buried next to one of the giant, collosal, stone heads.

It is well known that West Africa has a high level of iron and iron was being used there as early as the Late Stone Age. Africans from West Africa could have traded iron tools, weapons and other utencils to the American Indians or Africoids who lived in the Americas before 1492 A.D. The 'colored mantles of cloth' mentioned by the Aztecs has been discusssed before, yet because we are dealing with the Middle Ages, needs further examination. The cloth mentioned by the Aztecs are reminiscent of the multicolored head cloths worn by the Kran people Liberia. The designs mentioned such as, "radial wheels of the sun,

282

feathers and stylized shells, the skins of tigers (probably lepoard or chitah skins), the form of rabbits, snakes, fishes, and butterflies, mingled in the myriad of motifs with triangles, polygons, crosses, squares and crescents," (7) resembles to a great degree, the cloth and designs manufactured and painted by the Ashanti, Yoruba, Mandinka and other nationalities of West Africa.

Apart from these goods, jewelry, gold, silver, and other ornaments, foodstuffs, colanuts, crowie shells such s the ones the 'pochteca' may have worn around their ankles, leopard skins, ivory, copper "X" bars, alloys of gold, silver and tin in the form of spear heads, colored glass beads, baskets and many other products found their way on West African longboats or ships which crossed the Atlantic to Mexico and the rest of the Americas.

# CHAPTER TWENTY-TWO

# WEST AFRICA FROM 600 A.D. TO 1500 A.D.: THE FOREST KINGDOMS

Kingdoms rose up in the coastal regions of West Africa during the Middle Ages and had been developing thousands of years earlier. Some of these kingdoms, like those who continued from the prehistoric Mende speaking cultures aboriginal to West Africa and the Southern Sahara, which led to the Nok culture, were organized earlier than 3000 B.C. Others, such as the kingdoms of the Wolof, Ashanti and Songhai were partly migrants who came to West Africa from Sudan and Egypt and mingled with their already established indigenous Black borthers and sisters of West Africa. In fact, linguistic affinities with ancient Egypt and Nubia-Kush (Sudan) as well as oral history and customs, place the Wolof, Songhai, Yoruba and others in the Khemite-Nubian-Kushite region earlier than 2000 B.C. and as late as the 350's A.D., when Nubia was invaded by the Askumites. Moreover, according to the oral history of the Songhai people, they left Egypt about the time of Moses departure from that land.

The West African coastal kingdoms were engaged in the most lucrative trading system ever devised and one of the oldest and longest lasting. The fact of trade and commerce between 20,000 to 10,000 B.C. has already been discussed in this text. Extensive trade was carried over a region covered with large bodies of water on large ships. The West Africans of the coastal regions were engaged in agriculture. The Ishongo people who inhabited the Kongo forest regions of West Africa. By 3000 B.C. through 500 B.C., trade between the coastal regions of West Africa and other regions had become well established.

The coastal dwellers were master traders and boat builders, and their boats sailed along the great rivers of West Africa such as the Niger, and south along the Kongo river. They also sailed along the sea coasts, and accross the Atlantic which made up for their not having easy access to the Mediterranean region. Their gold was transported by traders and through shipping from the seaports of West Africa to the markets of the Mediterranean, Europe and Asia. This trade in gold goes back to at least 600 B.C., when the Phoenicians landed in West Africa, after they were ordered to circumnavigate Africa from east to west, beginning in Egypt.

The African ability to trade effectively and their love for trade and commerce was among the most important abilities and among the most ancient. The coastal forest region of West Africa contians some of the most fertile land on earth. In this area, a wide variety of crops were sold to other parts of Africa, to Europe, Asia and across the Atlantic to America. This trade ended during the 1500's and may have begun as early as 30,000 years ago.

The average West African family of the ancient and Middle Ages period of West African history, cultivated about nine acres of land. They planted yams, taros, kola nuts, bananas, sweet potatoes, okras and other vegetables such as peanuts, plantains, cocoa and rubber. Some of these crops such as the plantain and peanut, as well as rubber, were shipped to the Americas, particularly Mexico and Peru, from West Africa, or had been reshipped, or reexported after coming from the Americas in prehistoric times.

The culture and societies of the West Africans originated in West Africa, the Sahara, Sudan and Egypt. Others may have places of origin as far as Southern Arabia. Yet, all these cultures were Black cultures. These cultures were brought to West Africa by the ancestors of the very same Africans who exist in West Africa and the Americas today. The practice of Susu, the economic system which makes use of collective resources for the purchase of commodities and the building of wealth (collective capitalism), developed faster in the forest regions and the coastal regions of West Africa.

Robert W. July gives a thorough analysis of the culture and environment that gave rise to the susu economic system from its early stages. He states that in the forests, people were protected in their small homesteads. There, they worked toward having

286

everything they needed and communities lived in an atmosphere of peace. Every individual had a place in the social order and no one, including the ruler, was able to enrich himself or become more powerful than those around him.(8) In this type of society, new ways of doing things were not readily accepted and religion played a part in contributing to nonconformity. This attitude was common in the isolated communities or villages.

The majority of the inhabitants of West Africa lived in larger, more developed states such as Benin, Ife, Igbo-Ikwu, Oyo and Ashanti. The states and kingdoms of the Ashanti and Dahomey (Benin) were strong and had widespread political and economic control and an advanced culture. It was such cultures which produced and created masterpieces in terracotta, stone, iron, gold and bronze between 3000 B.C. to 1000 A.D. In particular, the bronzes created a few hundred years before the Christian Era, represented a number of styles and topics, while others represented the features of kings, nobles, soldiers and asssistants. These bronzes are equal in quality and style to the world's best and may have been an artistic tradition handed down from the Nok period of about 3000 B.C. to 300 A.D.

Trade between the forest kingdoms of the Ashanti, Yoruba, Mende, Fon, Igbo and others with the nations of the Sudan region and the Mediterranean, Kush, Nubia, Khemet and North Africa, as well as Southern and East Africa occurred, creating widespread trading and commercial activities in all directions. July observes that contacts in the forests were not as easy as that of the people who lived in the savanna lands, who were able to maintain trading contact s with North Africa and other areas. Still, trade was an essential part of the existence of the forest and centers were available where local goods were sold to places further away along trade rouotes that were quite ancient. Among the products exchanged was sea salt from the coasts, for the iron or gold from the lands further inland. Each economic group, for example the pastoralists who lived in the grasslands, sent their goods to the forest regions to the South where they were exchanged for goods such as textiles.

The major occupation in the forest region was agriculture, yet specialized skills such as working metals, producing cloth, or mining became the specialities of others. Trade was carried out by women in markets and buying and selling became the main way of earning a living for larger population groups, such as the Dyula who placed their traders in areas where caravans crossed so that they would be able to engage in buying and selling of products. Urban centers developed from smaller trading posts where goods had been bartered. Commodities such as gold and gold dust, cloth, kola nuts, shea butter, salt, fruits and vegetables and a wide variety of products were to be found in these market centers. July describes the towns as places for cultural and personal exchange, relaxation and where information was passed on by the people who came from places far and near.

## The Kingdom Of Oyo

The kingdoms of the Yorubas, Ashanti and Benin were composed of a number of city states which developed in the foest region and coastal areas out of small villages built between 3000 to 1000 B.C. These citystates flourished during the period of trade with the Phoenicians, Egyptians and Carthaginians. Herodotus mentions the voyages of Hanno about 450 B.C. to West Africa, as well as Pharaoh Nikau's ordering of Phoenician ships to circumnavigate Africa about 600 B.C. During that period, the kingdoms of West Africa were very ancient and existed as organized, agricultural and manufacturing civilizations who carried out trade with people both near and afar.

The Kingdom of Oyo was made up of a number of states and a centralized center, with its major part being the urban area of Oyo, where the monarchy ruled. The central ruling class were allied with the surrounding provinces, as well as those who controlled their own local affairs. States or provinces who had been captured and paid tribute to the center were of the least in political rank.

The state leader of the Oyo was called the Alafin, a powerful king and ruler. He had a well organized court, with officials who performed state and palace functions. The king was controlled

288

in part by representatives of the people in the same way that the U.S. president is checked by Congress. July calls these officials the Oyo Mesi, an aristocratic group of leaders who controlled the seven wards of the city of Oyo, and who were also members of the counsil of state, and the ones who chose a new king. The Oyo Mesi had the power to judge Kings who could not perform and forced them to commit suicide. This act prevented tyrannical rule. The checking of the power of the king was also done by the Ogboni Secret Society (which is very much needed to be revived among Blacks in the U.S., the Caribbean, South and Central America, Europe, India and Sri-Lanka, Melanesia and the Black South Pacific, and Australia to build a military and economic strength and defend the interests of Blacks in all these regions), a powerful organization that approved or disapproved the decisions of the king. Obas or princes of royal blood from the provinces were allowed to rule in their areas, as long as they paid tribute to the king.

## The Kingdom Of Benin

Benin was another of the Yoruba city-states that had an extensive trade network which included its neighbors, the rest of Africa, the Americas, Europe and the Middle East. The origins of Benin is similar to that of the rest of the coastal and forest kingdoms as well as the savannah empires of ancient West Africa. Like the others, its origins goes back to a period in history before 3000 B.C. Benin was part of the great Iron Age civilizations of West Africa. By 1200 B.C., Benin was well established. In fact, according to the book, General History of Africa, (p. 301, 1990), the Iron Age in Nigeria began during the Late Stone Age, sometime before 7000 B.C.

During the Middle Ages, princely people from the ancient kingdom of Ife brought Benin back to glory during the thirteenth century and added to its cultural vigor. Robert W. July adds. The migration of royalty to Benin from Ife, brought about a new period of greatness to Benin and made it one of the most magnificent kingdoms in West Africa. A power struggle between the king and the noblemen, was one of the factors which helped make the change. After it was over, the political system became more organized and the royal ceremonies more elaborate. The new political stability gave way to the development of greater art, urban living and trade. It brought about a more stable king and kingdom.

The Benin Kingdom was one of those against the slave trade which began as soon as the Portugese landed on the West coast of Africa on the shores of the West African kingdoms. The Portugese who tried to open the trade soon abandoned their efforts. The traditional religion of the Benin people was kept and foreign religious ideas were rejected, due to the hypocracy noticed by the people of Benin and the connection of these religions with the slave trade. Moreover, the Portugese were selective in their trade and tried to keep firearms out of the hands of the Benin kingdom.

Benin was one of the great kingdoms along the West African coast. Robert W. July describes it as being, "a virile society. During its sixteenth century apogee," he continues, "Benin City was a stronghold twenty five miles in circumference, protected by walls and natural defenses, containing an elaborate royal palace and neatly laid out houses with verandas and balustrades, and devided by broad avenues and smaller intersecting streets. The power of the Oba was apparent in his wealth, his divinity, his domination over commercial transaction and his large and lavish court. In this prosperous society, the wealthier classes dressed and dined very well. Beef, mutton, chicken, and yams were staples, while the less well-off made do with yams, dried fish, beans and bananas. No beggars existed in Benin, where those unable to keep themselves were normally surported by the king and lesser officials." (9)

Benin declined during the nineteenth century. This decline began before that period, due to a number of factors. Slave trading was one of t he major reasons for its decline. Rivalry among the chiefs and king, pressure from European traders and their armies, and pressure from the pastoralists of the north.

Basil Davidson gives some insights into what the economic reasons for Benin's decline may have been. He states that the kings had a monopoly on trade with foreign nations and thus prevented the growth of private enterprise so that the entire state would benefit from the trade. This economic policy continued when new kings took over until the 1800's.

Inspite of their economic problems, the kings of Benin were a powerful and wealthy lot. During the king's palace included galleries "as big as those on the Exchange at Amsterdam, with wooden pillars encased with copper where their victories are depicted," a Dutchman who visited the king in 1702 said. Benin City had "many wide streets and large houses."(9)

Benin's decline as a great kingdom occurred during the 1600's and apart from their participation in the slave trade, the concentration of power in the hands of the king who could not be checked by a council was a major factor. The royal art made out of brass declined in artistic quality quality and became cruder and a lack of feeling compared to their art during the 1400's and before.

## Dahomey

Dahomey was one of the most notorious kingdoms before the 1900's A.D., due to its trade in slaves, which began with the arrival of the Portugese during the late 1400's. Before that period, Dahomey was similar in its culture to the other city-states and kingdoms of West Africa. Dahomey did not reach its peak until after it was no longer a vassal of the kingdom of Oyo. Dahomey's main source of trade goods was its neighbors, and later, the European enslavers who encouraged slavery and the kidnapping of Africans in the northern part of the kingdom.

Dahomey was a well organized society with a strong government and military apparatus. Robert W. July states in his book, A History of the African People, that Dahomey's monarchy had its capital at Abomey and followed a form of kingship that was not of the customary traditional form due to the way they ruled. The government was based on the rule of the king, and instead of bing paid, civil servants were given gifts for their work. The king supported the army from his own personal wealth and did not allow the secret societies known for their

291

checking of the king's power, to exist. Dahomey's army was composed of a regiment of woman soldiers, or amazons.(10)

Dahomey's demise came quickly as soon as they began to establish trade with the slave-hungry Portugese and other Europeans. The slave trade turned the culture from one of strict security and high organization, to one where making war for the capture of slaves, executions sponsered by the state and other forms of human rights violations and degredations led to the lack of moral conscience by those in power and the quick destruction of the kingdom. The lack of sympathy for the lives of some of the inhabitants, by its leaders and officials, led to a lack of sympathy for them and their quick destruction.

## The Ashanti

The Ashanti Migrated from the savanna areas of West Africa about the 11th to 13th century A.D. However, according to Goddy Wichendu's Historical Map of Great Afrikan Empires and Kingdoms, [(The African Magazine, 1994-1995, African Publishers, Jamaica, New York, (back page)], the Ashanti Empire was in existence from about 1600 B.C. to 1823 A.D.(11) It is very likely that other groups joined the already established Ashanti Kingdom over a period of hundreds of years since its founding. Later on, groups such as the ancient Ghanians, Malians, Songhais, Kushites and Khemites fleeing termoil in their own lands joined with the original Ashantis and expanded the empire's territory and population. Such was the case with the Yoruba, who are composed or Africans who began the ancient Kingdom of Ife, Oyo and others about the same time as the founding of ancient Ashanti. Some of the ancient Yoruba may have migrated from Egypt, South Arabia (Sabea) and parts of ancient Nubia-Kush.

Robert W. July concentrates on the more recent kingdoms of the Ashanti. According to him, by the early 1600's, Akan the parent or larger group from which came the Ashanti. The Akan controlled a number of trading states who conducted commercial activities among each other and with their neighbors on the southern coast of West Africa. International trade also developed and it contributed to the historical path the Ashanti was to take. They had been trading with the northern empires and kingdoms, such as Mali, Ghana, Songhai, Kanem-Bornu, across the Sahara to North Africa, Egypt, Nubia, Kush and the vincinity Ethiopia and other areas of East Africa, during the early 1400's. The primary exports of the Ashanti were salt, gold, kola nuts, cloth, food products, precious stones and a variety of other products. These products were quite famous in the northern regions of Africa.

After the Portugese landed on the shores of the Ashanti Empire, the slave trade and trade from the north by way of the Atlantic Ocean came into being. It lasted for over 150 years. The Portugese also sold guns and manufactured goods for gold. By the latter part of the 1600's the areas where gold was mined grew in importance and expanded their commercial activities. Older trade routes to the north were reestablished and Europeans such as the Dutch, British, Danes, Portugese and French built trading posts and forts on the shores, while Portugese and French ships traded in the region.

By the late 1700's, the population of the Ashanti Kingdom was over five million people who occupied a land area of one hundred and fifty thousand square miles of forest and savannah land. For two hundred years, the Ashanti people prospered, beginning from a group of Twispeaking people who migrated from the south and others who migrated from the north-east to form a powerful kingdom ruled by a king called Osei Tutu, and held by a powerful symbol called "The Golden Stool," a stool made of gold and said to hold the soul of the Ashanti Nation.

Osei Tutu died in old age somewhere about 1712, after he had brought about the various groups and formed the Ashanti Nation. The Kingdom became more powerful when a new king called Opoko Ware ruled between 1720 to 1750. They continued their trade with the grass lands empires to the north and the Europeans who were establishing forts and trading posts on the coastal areas.

The Ashanti conducted a series of wars against the Fante people who belonged to the same Akan group as the Ashanti and subdued them further. The Ashanti attacked the British and defeated them, but were lated defeated and made a colony of the British. The Ashanti established a city called Kumasi before 1816 for the purpose of trading. This city expanded after 1817. A European official called Bowdich said in 1817 that the inhabitants of Kumasi burnt their rubbish every morning at the "back of their streets," and that they "were as nice and cleanly in their dwellings as in their persons." ( )

Merchants came to trade in Kumasi as far as Arabia and a few Mulim traders were allowed to conduct business and commercial activities. The king of the Ashanti had a large civil service, composed of local people as well as Muslims from Mali and other lands. By the time of Osei Kwadwo, who ruled from 1764 to 1777, the office of the king80 became more powerful. He appointed men to political, commercial and financial high positions based on merit. He enlarged his army and created a personal army to keep hold of his power. The capital which was by then about 40,000 people had its own army called the Ankobia.

Trading developed to a high level and a centralized trading organization run by the king, competed with the private sector for trade and mining of metals, chiefly gold. By 1873, Ashanti traders journied back and forth from the coast to their territory to buy and sell goods. The king's officials were paid and in their old age, they were given a pension. Those who saw over his trade were allowed to keep some of the profits. Both the foreign and trade business was controlled by the king and his officials, and communication was carried out by messengers (most likely talking drummers as well) who traveled over an extensive series of highways. According to Bonnat, the Ashanti king knew what occurred throughout his empire.

The Ashanti empire was subdued by the British only because the British had more guns and cannons. They also applied the cunning practice of 'devide and conquer.' Descent from various parts of the empire and a lack of unity (as Blacks we must take note) led to its weak ness and final defeat by the British. The Ashanti became involved in a series of regional conflicts, particularly with the Fante. British intervention led to the Ashanti's defeat and the exile of their king.

# End of Part One

Part Two is Susu and Susunomics: The Theory and Practice of Pan-African Economic, Racial and Cultural Self-Preservation.

# REFERENCES

## CHAPTER ONE

1. Chandler, Wayne "The Principle of Polarity,"African Presence in Early Asia, edt. Ivan Van Sertima, Transaction Publishers, New Bruinswick, NJ: 1995, p.376.

2. Pearlman, D. San Francisco Chronicle, San Francisco: April 28, 1995

3. Rogers, J.A. Sex and Race, Volume 1: 1957, p.56.

4. Diop, C.A. Civilization or Barbarism, Lawrence Hill Books, Brooklyn: 1991, p.14.

5. Diop, C.A. Civilization or Barbarism, Lawrence Hill Books, Brooklyn: 1991, p.15.

6. Chandler, W. "The Principle of Polarity," African Presence in Early Asia, edt. Runoko Rashidi and Ivan Van Sertima, Transaction Publishers, New Bruinswick, NJ: 1995, pp. 376-377.

7. Diop, C.A. Civilization or Barbarism, Lawrence Hill Books, Brooklyn 1991, p. 23.

8. Runoko Rashidi, James Brunson and Wallace Magsby, African Presence in Early Asia; edt. Ivan Van Sertima, Transaction Publishers, New Bruinswick, NJ: 1995, pp. 316-317.

9. Beasley, Leontine L. Negro Trailblazers of California, Bancroft Library, L.A., Calif.: 1919, pp. 17-18.

10. Rogers, J.A. Africa's Gift to America, Helga Rogers Publishing Co., Saint Petersburg, FL: 1967, p. 23.

11. Discovery Magazine, December 1997,

12. Van Sertima, I. They Came Before Columbus, Random House,New York.

13. Chandler, W.B. "Trait Influences in Meso-America: The African-Asian Connection," Edt. Runoko Rashidi and Ivan Van Sertima, African Presence in Early Asia, Transaction Publishers, New BruinsWick, NJ: 1992, P.241.]

14. Burenhult, G. Traditional Peoples Today, W. Owen Ltd., Australia: 1994, pp. 77-97, 92-122.


## CHAPTER TWO

1. Diop, C.A. Civilization or Barbarism, Lawrence Hill Books, Brooklyn, NY: 1991, pp. 46-49.


## CHAPTER THREE

1. Rogers, J.A. Africa's Gift to America, Helga Rogers Publishing Co., Saint Petersburg, FL: 1967.

2. Pearlman, D. San Francisco Chronicle, San Francisco: April 25, 1995.

3. Mobetter News, OMNI-U, P.O. Box 1447, South Holland, IL: Vol.VIII #3.

4. Camerson, I. Into the Unknown, National Geographic Society, Washington, D.C.: 1987, pp. 10-11.

5 Pearlman, D. San Francisco Chronicle, San Francisco: April 25, 1995.

6    Posansky, M.  "Introduction to the Later Prehistory of Sub-Saharan Africa," edtrs.    James Curry and G. Mokhtar; General History of Africa, UNESCO, Paris: 1990, p.39.


## CHAPTER FOUR

1.   Diamond, J.  Discover Magazine, February 1994, pp. 74-75.

2.   Stavrianos, L.S.  A Global History, Third Edition; Prentis-Hall, Inc., Englewood Cliffs, N.J.: 1983, p.232.

3.   Mokhtar, G.  and James Curry, "The Peopling of Ancient Egypt and the Deciphering of the Meroitic Script," General History of Africa, UNESCO, Paris: 1990, p.39.

4.   Diop, C.A.  Civilization or Barbarism, Lawrence Hill Books, Brooklyn: 1991, p. 52.

5.   Rogers, J.A.    Africa's Gift to America, Helga Rogers Publishing Co., 3 Saint Petersburg, Fl.: 1973.


## CHAPTER FIVE

1.   Diop, C.A.    Civilization or Barbarism: An authentic Anthropology; Lawrence Hill Books, Brooklyn: 1991, pp. 116-117.

2.   Diop, C.A.....pp. 112-113. 3. Williams, C. The Destruction of Black Civilization, Third World Press, Chicago, IL: 1974.


## CHAPTER SIX

1.   Breasted, James; 1909.

2. Bakr, A. Abu; General History of Africa, edt. By G. Mokhtar and J. Curry UNESCO, Paris: 1990, p. 62.

3.Diop, C.A. Civilization or Barbarism, Lawrence Hill Books, Brooklyn: 1990, p. 17.

4. Yoyotte, J. (Libyan origins according to Egyptian documents of ancient Times), France: 1958, C-RGLCS, 8,4.

5. Rashidi, R. "A Working Chronology of the Royal Kemetic Dynasties,' edtrs. J.E. Brunson and Ivan Van Sertima, Egypt Revisited; Transaction Publishers, New Bruinswick, NJ: 1989, p. 106.

6. Bradley, M. The Black Discovery of America, Personal Library Publishers, Toronto, Canada: 1981, p. 137.

7. Williams, C. The Destruction of Black Civilization: Great Issues of a Race From 4500 B.C. to 2000 A.D., Third World Press, Chicago, IL.: 1974.

## CHAPTER SEVEN

1. Hibben, F.C.; Thomas Y. Crowell Company, New York: 1945, p. 172.

2. Wellard, J. The Great Sahara: 1965, pp.33-35.

3. Holy Bible, Genesis, Chapter Six, verses 3-7.

4. Wellard, J. The Great Sahara: 1965, pp. 33-35.

## CHAPTER EIGHT

1. Burenhult, G. Traditional Peoples Today, W. Owen Ltd.,

Australia: 1994, pp. 24-25.

2. Hancock, G. Fingerprints of the Gods, Crown Publishers Inc., New York: 1995, pp.411-416.

3. Assimov, I. The Egyptians, Houghton Mifflin Co., Boston: 1967, p. 38.

4. Van Sertima, I. Egypt Revisited, Transaction Publishers, New Bruinswick: 1993, p. 215-218.

5. Bernal, M. Black Athena, Rutgers University Press, New Bruinswick, NJ: 1987.

6. Mc Leod, Time Magazine, New York: 1997(Sept 15), p. 103.

7. Sewell, B. Egypt Under the Pharaohs.

8. Mokhtar, G. and James Curry; General History of Africa, Vol. II UNESCO: Paris., p.68

9. Gordon, Cyrus; Before Columbus, Crown Publishers Inc., New York: p. 63

10. Mokhtar, G. and Curry, J. (edtrs.), A. Abu Bakr, General History of Africa, UNESCO, Paris: 1990, p. 68.

11. Caroli, K. Ancient America, Issue #8, January/February, 1995, p.6

12. Williams, C. Destruction of Black Civilization, Third World Press,
Chicago: 1976, p.136

13. Williams, C.......1976, p. 136

14. Williams, C.........1976, p. 136.

15. Asimov, I.  The Egyptians, Houghton Mifflin Co., Boston: 1967, p. 38.

16. Diop, C.A.  Civilization or Barbarism; An Authentic Anthropology; Lawrence Hill Books, Brooklyn, NY: 1991, p. 92-95.


CHAPTER NINE

1. Diop, Cheikh A.  Civilization or Barbarism, Lawrence Hill Books, Brooklyn, New York: 1991, pp. 103-108.

2. Snow, P.  The Star Raft: China's Encounter With Africa, Widenfeld and Nicholson, New York: 1988, p.2

3. Van Sertima, I.  African Presence in Early America, Transaction Publishers, New Bruinswick, NJ: 1992, pp.240-308.

4  De Quatrefages; The Pygmies, D. Appleton Co., New York: 1885, p. 51.

5. Williams, C.  The Destruction of Black Civilization, Third World Press, Chicago, IL: 1976.


CHAPTER TEN

1. Tarharka, Phoan G.  "The Nubian Renaissance," edt. Ivan Van Sertima, Egypt Revisited, Transaction Publishers, New Bruinswick, NJ: 1995, p. 261-270.

2. Hereen, Arnold H.  Historical Research Into the Politics, Intercourse and Trade of the Carthaginians et al...Oxford: 1832, p. 411.

3. Von Wuthenau, A. "Unexpected African Faces in Ancient America," edt. Ivan Van Sertima, African Presence in Early America, Transaction Publishers, New Bruinswick, NJ: 1992, p. 92.

4. Hareen, Arnold H. Historical Research Into the Politics, Intercourse and Trade of the Carthaginians, Ethiopians and Egyptians; (D.A. Talboys, Oxford: 1832, p.411)

## CHAPTER TWELVE

1. Van Sertima, I. They Came Before Columbus, Random HouseNew York: 1976.

2. Egwuonwu, Chief Ani D. Afrikan Publishing Co., Jamaica, New York: 1996 (The African Magazine).

3. Bradley, M. The Black Discovery of America, Personal Library Publishers, Toronto, Canada: 1981, pp. 26-27, 33.

4. Bradley, M...1981, pp. 19-20.

5. Posansky, M. General History of Africa, Vol. II; UNESCO, Paris: 1990, pp. 297-298.

6. Diop, C.A. The African Origin of Civilization; Lawrence Hill Books, Brooklyn, NY: 1974, pp. 157-158.

7. Burenhult, G. Traditional Peoples Today, W. Owen Ltd., Australia: 1994, p. 133.

8. Van Sertima, I. African Presence in Early America, Transaction Publishers, New Bruinswick, NJ: 1992, p. 90.

9.  Posansky, M. "Introduction to the Later Prehistory of Africa," edt. G. Mokhtar and James Curry, General History of Africa, UNESCO, Paris: 1990, p. 301.

## CHAPTER THIRTEEN

1.  Wai-Andah, B. "Prehistoric Trade and the Earliest States of West Africa," General History of Africa, Vol. II, edtrs. G. Mokhtar and J. Curry, UNESCO, Paris: 1990, pp. 337-338.

2.  Warmington, B.H., "The Carthaginian Period," edtrs. G. Mokhtar and James Curry; General History of Africa, Vol. II; UNESCO, Paris: 1990, p. 247.

3   National Geographic Magazine, Vol. 142, #2; p. 2.

4.  Herm, G. The Phoenicians, The Purple Empire of the Ancient World, William Morrow & Co. Ltd., New York: 1975.

5   Diodorus of Scicily, Book II, Chapter 21.

6   Diop, C.A. (edt. G. Mokhtar) A General History of Africa, UNESCO, Paris: 1990, p. 251.

7   Herodotus, The Histories, Book II;

8.  Williams, C. The Destruction of Black Civilization, Third World Press, Chicago, IL.: 1976.

9.  Warmington, General History of Africa, Vol. II; edt. G. Mokhtar and James Curry, UNESCO, Paris: 1990, p. 251.

10. Bohannan, P. Africa and Africans; The National History Press, New York, NY: 1964, p.43.

11. Bradley, M. The Black Discovery of America, Personal Library Publishers, Toronto, Canada: 1981, p. 26, 28.

12. Bohannan, P. Africa and Africans, The Natural History Press, New York: 1964, p. 43.

13. Bradley, M. The Black Discovery of America, Personal Library Publishers, Toronto, Canada: 1981

14. Van Wuthenau, A. Unexpected Faces in Ancient America, Crown Books, New York:

15. Mack, Bill Fate Magazine, "Ancient Phoenicians Visited America," Vol. #9, Issue 48; Llewellyn Worldwide Ltd., Saint Paul, Mn: 1990, pp. 51,52.

16. Chandler, W. "The Principle of Polarity," African Presence in Early Asia, edt. Ivan Van Sertima, Transaction Publishers, New Bruinswick: 1995, pp. 360-370.

## CHAPTER FOURTEEN

1   Gordon, Cyrus H. Before Columbus, Crown Publishers Inc., New York: pp. 56, 58-60, 62-64.

2.  Cameron, I. Into the Unknown: The Story of Exploration; National Geographic Society, Washington, DC: 1987, pp. 9-15.

3.  Cameron, I. Into the Unknown: The Story of Exploration, National Geographic Society, Washington, DC: 1987, pp. 9-15.

# CHAPTER FIFTEEN

1. Roux, G.    Ancient Iraq; The World Publishing Co., Cleveland, Ohio.

2. Cox, G.A.    African Empires and Civilizations, African Heritage Studies; 1994, p. 106

3. Massey, G.  Book of Beginnings, Vol. 1; University Books; University Books, London: 1881, p. 27.

4. Houston, D.D. Wonderful Ethiopians of the Ancient Cushite Empire, Black Classics Press, Baltimore, Maryland: 1985.

5. Cox, G.A.    African Empires and Civilizations; African Heritage Studies: 994, p. 106

6. Roebuck, C.    The World in Ancient Times; Charles Schribner's Sons, New York, NY: 1966, p. 40

7. Rashidi, Runoko; Journal of African Civilizations, edt. Ivan Van Sertima, Transaction Periodicals Consortium, Rutgers Univ., New Bruinswick, NJ: 1982, pp. 137-138.

8. Rawlison, G.  Five Great Monarchs of the Ancient World, Vol. III; White Slone & Allen, New York: p. 500.

9. Williams, C.  The Destruction of Black Civilization, Third World Press, Chicago: 1976.

10. Time Magazine, New York.

11. Chandler, W.  African Presence in Early Asia, edt. Ivan Van Sertima, Transaction Publishers, New Bruinswick, NJ: 1995.

12. Wolpert, S.  A New History of India, Oxford University Press, New York, NY: 1997

13. Chandler, W.B. African Presence in Early Asia, edt. Ivan Van Sertima, Transaction Publishers, New Bruinswick, NJ: 1995.

14. Houston, D.D. Wonderful Ethiopians of the Ancient Cushite Empire, Black Classics Press, Baltimore, MD: 1985.

15. Rashidi, R. Journal of African Civilization, edt. I. Van Sertima, Transaction Publishers, New Bruinswick, NJ: 1982, pp.84-85.

16. Wolpert, S. A New History of India, Oxford University Press, New York, NY:1977, pp.6-8.

17. Wolpert, S. A New History of India, Oxford University Press, New York, NY: 1977, p.21.

18. Rajshekar, V.T. The Black Untouchables of India, Clarity Press, Atlanta: 1987, p.43.

19. Chandler, W. African Presence In Early Asia, edt. Ivan Van Sertima, Transaction Publishers, New Bruinswick, NJ: 1995, p. 363-365.

20. Wolpert, S. A New History of India, Oxford University Press, New York, NY: 1977, p.19.

21. Wolpert, S. A New History of India, Oxford University Press, New York, NY: 1977, p. 20

22. Wolpert, S. A New History of India

23. Wolpert, S. A New History of India.

24. Wolpert, S. A New History of India.

25. Bradley, M. The Black Discovery of America, Personal Library Publishers, Toronto, Canada: 1981, p.137

26. July, R.W. A History of the African People, Charles Schribner's Sons, New York: 1974, p. 20.

27. Stavrianos, L.S. A Global History, Third Edition, Prentis-Hall, Inc., Englewood Cliffs, N.J.: 1983, p. 36.

28. Wolpert, S. A New History of India, Oxford Univerity Press, New York: 1977, p. 20.

29. Bradley, M. The Black Discovery of America, Personal Library Publishers, Toronto, Canada: 1981, p. 21.

30. Brunson, James E. "Unexpected Faces in Early Asia," A Photo Essay," edt. I. Van Sertima, African Presence in Early Asia, Transaction Publishers, New Bruinswick, NJ: 1995, p. 205.

31. Williams, C. The Destruction of Black Civilization, Third World Press, Chicago, IL: 1976, p. 21.

32. Wolpert, S. A New History of India, Oxford Univ. Press, New York: 1977, pp. 21, 22.

33. Wolpert, S....pp. 22, 23...

34. Wolpert, S....pp. 24, 26...

35. Wolpert, S....pp. 29, 30...

36. Wolpert, S....pp. 29, 30...

37. Houston, D.D. Wonderful Ethiopians of the Ancient Kushite Empire, Black Classics Press, Baltimore, Maryland: 1985, p. 215.

38. Wolpert, S. A New History of India, Oxford University Press, New York: 1977, p. 25.

39. Houston, D. Wonderful Ethiopians of the Ancient Cushite Empire, Black Classics Press, Baltimore MD: 1985, p. 221.


## CHAPTER SIXTEEN

1. Brunson, J. African Presence in Early Asia, edt. Ivan Van Sertima, Transaction Publishers, New Bruinswick, N.J.: 1995, pp. 121-137.

2. Jairazbhoy, R.A. African Presence in Early Asia, edt. Ivan Van Sertima, Transaction Publishers, New Bruinswick: 1995, p. 59.

3. Gernet, J. Ancient China, From the Beginning to the Empire; University of California Press, Berkeley: 1968, pp. 38, 39.

4. Chandler, W. African Presence in Early Asia, edt. I. Van Sertima, Transaction Publishers, New Bruinswick, NJ: 1995

5. Hardlett, H. A History of Art, (1968, p. 12; Brown & Brown pub.)

6. Bronson, J. African Presence in Early Asia, edt. I. Van Sertima Transaction Publishers, New Bruinswick, NJ: 1995,

7. Li, Dun J. The Ageless Chinese, Charles Scribner's Sons, New York: 1968, 377.

8. Snow, P. The Star Raft; China's Encounter With Africa, Widenfeld and Nicholson, New York: 1988,

## CHAPTER SEVENTEEN

1.  July, R.W. A History of the African People; Second Edition, Charles Scribner's Sons, New York, or (Hunter College and Graduate Center, The City Univ. of New York): 1974, p. 97.

2.  Bohannan, P. Africa and Africans, The Natural History Press, Garden City, New York: 1964,

3.  Davidson, B. The African Genius, 1969, p. 213.

4.  Davidson, B.....

5.  Davidson, B.....

6.  Davidson, B.....

7.  Davidson, B....

8.  Davidson, B....

9.  Murphy, J.E. The Bantu Civilization of Southern Africa, Thomas Y. Crowell Company, New York, NY: 1974, pp. 167-176.

10. July, R.W. A History of the African People, Second Edition, Charles Scribner's Son, New York: 1974, p. 97.

11. Davidson, B. The African Genius, 1969 (from James Prior's, Voyage Along the Eastern Coasts of Africa, London, 1819)

## CHAPTER EIGHTEEN

1.  Williams, C. The Destruction of Black Civilization: Third World Press, Chicago, IL.: 1976.

2. Rogers, J.A. Africa's Gift to America, Helga Rogers Publishing Co., Saint Petersburg, Florida: 1967,
3. Murphy, J.E. The Bantu Civilization of Southern Africa, Thomas Y. Crowell Co., Saint Petersburg, Florida: 1976,

4. Murphy, J.E. The Bantu Civilization of Southern Africa, Thomas Y. Crowell Co., Saint Petersburg, Florida: 1976,

## CHAPTER NINETEEN

1. Chu, Daniel and Skinner, Elliott; A Glorious Age in Africa, Zenith Books, Doubleday and Co. Inc., Garden City New York, NY: 1965, pp. 26, 27.

2. Chu, Daniel and Skinner, E.....

3. Chu, Daniel and Skinner, E.....

## CHAPTER TWENTY

1. Chandler, Wayne B. African Presence in Early Asia, edt. Ivan Van Sertima, "The Principle of Polarity,"Transaction Publishers, New Bruinswick, NJ: 1995, p. 376.

2. Van Sertima, I. They Came Before Columbus, Random House, New York: 1976.

3. Grundy, J. Ancient American, May/June, 1997, p. 18.

4. Gladwin, J. Men Out of Asia, McGraw-Hill, New York: 1947.

5. Heyardhal, Thor National Geographic Magazine, National Geographic Society, "The Voyage of Ra II, by Carlo Mauri, George Sorial, National Geographic Society, Washington DC: 1971, pp.46.

6. Mack, B. Fate Magazine, "Ancient Phoenicians Visited America, Vol. #9, Issue 48, Llewellyn Worldwide Ltd., Saint Paul, Mn: pp. 51, 52.

7. Van Sertima, I. They Came Before Columbus, Random House, New York: 1976.

8. July, R. W. A History of the African People, Scribner's Sons, New York: 1970.

9. July, R.W. A History of the African People, Scribner's Sons, New York: 1970.

10. July, R.W. A Histoy of the African People.....

11. Wichendu, G. "Historical Map of Great African Empires and Kingdoms," The Afrikan Magazine, 1994-1995; Chief Ani Dike Egwuonwu, edt., Afrikan Publishers, Jamaica, New York.

# ABOUT THE AUTHOR

Paul Alfred Barton is a direct descendant of Gyorgis, an Ethiopian Lady of royal background who migrated from Gondar, Ethiopia to the Caribbean during the 1830's. Barton is also the descendant of a Black Carib (Garifuna) great grandfather. The Garifunas are the descendants of ancient African merchants and mariners who had established trading relations with the Americas, hundreds of years before Christ.

Paul Barton is a graduate of Fresno Pacific University with a Bachelor degree in business management. Barton is a prolific writer and specializes in ancient African history, World Black history and culture and epic novels dealing with the exploits of ancient African royalty and adventurers with a mixture of fact and fiction.

Printed in the United States
18950LVS00001B/37